# LONDON
## and its environs in the
# NINETEENTH CENTURY

NORTH & WEST FRONT OF THE BANK OF ENGLAND, FROM LOTHBURY

EAST FRONT OF THE BANK OF ENGLAND, AND NEW TOWER OF
ROYAL EXCHANGE, FROM ST. BARTHOLOMEW LANE

# LONDON

*And its Environs in the*

## NINETEENTH CENTURY,

*Illustrated*

## BY A SERIES OF VIEWS

*From Original Drawings,*

## BY THOMAS H. SHEPHERD,

*with Historical, Topographical and Critical Notices.*

### SERIES THE FIRST, COMPRISING THE EARLIER EDIFICES, ANTIQUITIES, &c.

Drawn by Tho. H. Shepherd.

Engraved by W. Wallis.

TEMPLE BAR, FROM THE STRAND.

*London.*

PUBLISHED NOV 1, 1829, BY JONES & Cᵒ TEMPLE OF THE MUSES,

FINSBURY SQUARE.

# Foreword

*Thomas Hosmer Shepherd spent some fifty years of his long life engaged in the production of hundreds of topographical drawings of the City of London, in turn to be faithfully reproduced on steel plates by a veritable army of skilled engravers as represented by the illustrations in this book. Without the industry and great skill of these men, little would be known about the changing face of London before the introduction of photography towards the end of the 19th Century.*

*Prior to 1820 when engraving on steel was first introduced, the use of copper was almost universal for the production of illustrative printing plates. The pressure required in the printing process caused the plates to wear and distort very quickly with the result that an illustrated edition would not run to more than a few hundred copies thus placing them beyond the reach of all but the very wealthy. The introduction of steel plates, whilst making the work of the engraver more difficult, enabled much finer work to be achieved and had the great advantage of allowing many more impressions to be taken with little loss of definition or plate deterioration. The book from which this facsimile has been taken is a good example of early bookwork employing this method.*

*As you read you will often notice the name of the engraver who executed a particular plate, below the print and on the right-hand side. On the left hand appears the name of the artist who made the original drawing from which the engraver copied his plate. Some of the engravers listed, were later to become engravers and publishers in their own right as for example W. Tombleson whose book on the rivers Thames and Medway is now keenly sought by collectors.*

*The writer's extra-Mural work with colleges, the workers' educational association, and similar adult bodies provides ample proof of an increasing interest in things antiquarian on the part of the public. To the student of London in particular, this book will provide a reference work of great accuracy and absorbing interest.*

J. A. BOOTH                                                                      WESTBURY 1971

Facsimile edition reproduced, printed and published
in Great Britain by T. H. Brickell & Son Limited,
Blackmore Press, Gillingham, Dorset.

1971

# LONDON

# NINETEENTH CENTURY.

---

> " From his oozy bed,
> Old father *Thames* advanced his reverend head ;
> His tresses dressed with dews, and o'er the stream,
> His shining horns diffused a golden gleam.
> Graved on his urn appeared the moon, that guides
> His swelling waters and alternate tides ;
> The figured streams in waves of silver rolled,
> And on their banks AUGUSTA* rose in gold."
>
> POPE.

---

BRIEF HISTORY OF LONDON, FROM THE EARLIEST FOUNDATION OF THE CITY TO THE NORMAN INVASION—FROM THE NORMAN INVASION TO THE REFORMATION—FROM THE ACCESSION OF QUEEN ELIZABETH TO THE FIRE OF LONDON—AND FROM THE REBUILDING OF THE CITY BY SIR CHRISTOPHER WREN—SUBSEQUENT PROGRESSIVE IMPROVEMENTS TO THE PRESENT DAY.

LONDON, the most ancient constitutional borough in England,† is a city of very high antiquity. Without going back to the historical romance of Geoffrey of Monmouth, who attributes its foundation to a descendant of Venus and Anchises, and enumerates seventy successive kings before the arrival of Julius Cæsar; it is sufficient for our purpose, that Cæsar gives no description in his well known narrative of his conquests, of any other kind of town in Britain, than a thick wood fortified by a ditch and a mound. Hence it is concluded that London owes its origin to a later period, even than the invasion of Cæsar.

The first Roman historian who mentions our metropolis by name is Tacitus, who bears honorable testimony to the number and opulence of its merchants, and the abundance of its provisions. Strabo also asserts that the country produced corn, cattle, gold, silver and iron; and that skins, slaves and dogs, excellent for the chace, were imported from our island.

* The name given to London by Constantine the Great, in honor of his mother the Empress Helena.
† Norton's Commentaries on the History, Constitution and Chartered Franchises of the City of London.

The conquests of Claudius, and his able general Plautius, were continued in the reign of Nero by Suetonius Paulinus, who was bravely but unsuccessfully opposed by the natives under the command of their illustrious queen Boadicea. This predatory warfare was continued by the Imperial generals till the time of Domitian, whose legions, under the command of Agricola, achieved the conquest of nearly the whole island. This brave and prudent general provided for its security, by establishing that line of military stations, in the north of England, which was afterwards fortified in the reign of Antoninus Pius, and still remains a monument of Roman greatness.

Thus was the greater part of Britain subjugated: " a conquest," says Gibbon, " that was undertaken by the most stupid" (Claudius), " maintained by the most despotic" (Nero), " and terminated by the most timid" (Domitian) " of all the emperors;" and the successors of Caractacus, Boadicea and their bands of heroes, were compelled to submit to the Roman yoke.

Agricola being appointed governor of Britain exhorted the natives, says Tacitus,* to cultivate the arts of peace, to build temples and houses, and to imitate their enlightened conquerors. This caused London to revive, after the severe defeat of Boadicea, to such an extent, that Herodian in his life of the Emperor Lucius Septimius Severus, who reigned from the year 193 to 211, calls it a great and wealthy city. It extended from Ludgate to Tower Hill in length, and from the causeway above Cheapside to the Thames in breadth.

It is not probable, from the silence of the Roman historians, that London was either a place of great strength, or fortified by a wall, till after those periods wherein they wrote, and the time when it was so protected is a matter of great uncertainty. Maitland attributes the erection of a wall to Theodosius, who was governor of Britain in 369. Dr. Woodward and Mr. Pennant with more probability ascribe it to Constantine the Great, which appears to be confirmed by the number of coins found of his mother Helena. Pennant says, in further support of this conjecture, that in honour of this Empress the city about that time received from her the title of *Augusta*, which superseded its more ancient and clearly British appellation *Londinium*, for only a short period.

London, at this period of its history, had a mint, and was adorned with temples and other public buildings of great magnificence, as the numerous remains of ancient Roman architecture and sculpture that have been discovered in various excavations, within the walls of the city, incontestably prove. The substantial and extensive wall that surrounded it was strengthened and adorned by the Romans with many towers, of so firm a structure that two were in existence in Maitland's time; and Dr. Woodward doubts not, that nearly the whole circuit of the city wall as it stood in 1707 was erected upon the old Roman foundation, which comprehended an area of more than three miles in circumference.

While the mighty empire of Rome was crumbling to pieces, by slow but certain steps, the British island separated itself from its great protector. Roman forces being withdrawn, the natives were left to the ravages of the Saxon pirates, and their neighbouring enemies of Ireland and Caledonia.

* Life of Agricola.

After the departure of the Romans from Britain, about the year 448, the independance of the country was established by the Emperor Honorius, who raised the City of London among other cities to the dignity of a Colony. The supreme command devolved on Vortigern an unfortunate prince, who bears the stigma of having invited the Saxons to protect him against his northern enemies, the Scots and Picts. Whether the Saxons were invited as some authors relate, or whether according to others they invaded a country well known to them, which offered a lure to their cupidity, is of little importance in this brief narration; but that they succeeded and established their dominion under the name of the Saxon heptarchy, from their seven kingdoms is a truth, the effects of which are apparent to the present day.

Hengist, the first of these crafty chieftains, established his government over Kent, Essex and Middlesex, and raised Canterbury to the dignity of his metropolis in preference to London, which remained in possession of the Britons, and afterwards became the chief city of the Saxon kingdom of Essex. London was at this time governed by a chief magistrate under the title of Portgrave, or Portreve.

Towards the latter end of the reign of Ethelbert, about the year 600, a considerable number of the Saxons were converted to Christianity, and Augustine, a monk sent over by Pope Gregory the Great, was ordained archbishop of England. He ordained Mellitus bishop of the East Saxons, who in 610 erected at the expense of Ethelbert a cathedral church in London, and dedicated it to St. Paul, and another in the island of Thorney, which he dedicated to St. Peter. At this time, says Bede, London was a mart town of many nations, yet it was far from that high estate in which it was left by the Romans, for no buildings in brick or stone were attempted by the Saxons till the year 680, and even the churches and monasteries were principally of wood, till the reign of Edgar in 974.

In the year 764 London suffered very considerably by fire, and in 798 it was entirely destroyed by a similar calamity. The city was scarcely rebuilt, when it was again destroyed by a third conflagration, in 801. During the civil wars between the various kingdoms of the Saxons, the Londoners wisely kept neuter, and when their seven kingdoms were united under the sole dominion of the victorious Edgar, in 827, he fixed upon London as his capital, and in 833 with Ethelwolf his son, Withlaf king of Mercia, and the leading men of the realm assembled in London and held a Witena-gemot or parliament; and may thus be considered as the second founder of London, by raising it to that rank among the cities of the kingdom, which it has ever since maintained.

Notwithstanding the success of Egbert, it was not long before London was again the scene of war and devastation, from the invasion of the Danes; which in three subsequent reigns, nearly overwhelmed the whole kingdom in ruin. After sacking and burning the unfortunate city, they found themselves under the necessity of occupying and fortifying it against the successes of the Britons.

The conquests of Alfred restored London to its former greatness, and freed the kingdom from the Danish yoke. This great monarch repaired the walls, and rebuilt the city. He also established that regular system of law and government, and accomplished those great improvements which are enjoyed to the present day.

About a century after the death of Alfred, the Danes and Norwegians sailed up the Thames and besieged the city, which being unable to reduce, they raised the siege, but harassed other parts of the kingdom. London, being abandoned by its pusilanimous monarch Ethelred, who abdicated his throne, and retired into Normandy, was compelled to submit with the rest of England to the yoke of Sweyne king of Denmark. The Londoners however in the reign of Canute his son, joined in the general effort of the whole kingdom, under the brave Edmond Ironsides, the son of Ethelred. The enterprize was so successful, that Canute was compelled to abandon London to his rival, who was there crowned king of England; but being afterwards assassinated, Canute became sole sovereign of the kingdom.

Edward the Confessor is said to be the first monarch, who formally recognised the privileges of London, which had previously subsisted only by custom and tradition, and the city at this period, according to William of Malmsbury, became the resort of merchants from all parts of the world.

On the invasion by William the Conqueror, the citizens of London received him with arms in their hands, and willingly acknowledged him as king, who in return took up his residence in their city, built the tower, and granted them their first written charter, which is still preserved in the archives of the city. In 1077 the greater part of the city was consumed by a casual fire, and in 1086 another dreadful fire began at Ludgate, and consumed the greatest and best part of the city, together with the cathedral of St. Paul, which however was soon rebuilt more magnificently than before. It was in this reign that the church of St. Mary-le-bow in Cheapside was first erected. In the succeeding reign William Rufus erected Westminster Hall, as it now stands, and encompassed the Tower of London with a strong wall. Henry the First confirmed the grants and charter of his father, gave the citizens privilege to elect their own sheriffs and magistrates, and of being amenable to courts only held within their walls. This king, in consideration of an annual payment of £300, gave them also the privilege of electing the sheriff of Middlesex in perpetuity, a right which they enjoy to this day. Matilda the consort of Henry contributed also very largely to the increase of the public buildings of London. In the following reign of Stephen, the city was again devastated by a similar calamity.

During the captivity of the chivalrous Richard Cœur-de-Lion, the citizens of London contributed largely to the sum required for his ransom, and received him with such truly civic magnificence, that a German nobleman, who accompanied the captive monarch to his ancient capital, observed, that had his master the Emperor been aware of the wealth of the king of England's subjects, he would have demanded a much larger sum for his release. The grateful monarch confirmed the citizens in all their privileges, and conferred upon them the conservatorship of the river Thames, made their chief magistrate chief butler to the king, and gave them the power of fixing a standard of weights and measures for the whole realm.

The buildings of London at this period, if we may believe the splendid fictions of Fitzstephen, were grand in the extreme, for he describes the king's palace as an incomparable edifice, and connected with the city by suburbs reaching two miles in length, that the bishops, abbots and noblemen of the kingdom resorted thither, lived in beautiful houses, and maintained very magnificent establishments. As at present, the citizens were well initiated in the luxuries of good living, for they had an immense public cooking establishment on the Thames side, at which dainties of every kind, of very expensive quality, could be had at any time of day or night. They had also public and private schools of philosophy and polite literature; the drama was well understood and cultivated, and Fitzstephen, who was a monk, commends in very high terms the holy exhibition of the miracles and martyrdom of the saints.

In this reign, we have the first appearance of an approach towards a building act; for in the first year of king Richard's reign, in consequence of the frequent fires, it was ordained by the court of aldermen that no houses should after that period be allowed to be built of wood or thatched; but that all of them should have an outside wall of stone raised sixteen feet from the ground,—an ordinance which seems to have been at that time successfully carried into effect.

From the authority quoted by Mr. Norton, one of the late common pleaders of the city, in his able commentaries on the history, constitution and chartered franchises of the city of London, preserved in the liber constitut. Lib. Horne, Lib. Clerkenwell, twelve aldermen were subsequently at a full husting to superintend all city works, and settle disputes about enclosures, party wall, &c. This stability in the structure of houses did not last long; for, according to contemporary accounts, all houses in London were built of wood down to the reign of James I., at which time they began to build with brick.

During the absence of Cœur-de-Lion, his brother and successor JOHN, then called Earl of Moreton, cultivated by all possible means the love of the citizens, with the intention of gaining their interests to procure him the crown, in the stead of Prince Arthur, son of Geoffrey his elder brother. This was attended with such success, that king Richard was succeeded by his brother John, who gave the citizens the privilege of electing their chief officer out of their own body. King John also gave the city three charters, reciting and confirming all the rights and privileges of his predecessors, with many very important additions.

During the disputes that arose between John and the papal see, the citizens, in common with the rest of the kingdom, were excommunicated; still however they would have supported him, had not his tyranny alienated their affection, and drove them to join the Barons in defence of the general national interest. The king resented this, and the citizens retorted by strengthening their walls with a deep ditch, and other defences, which were somewhat retarded by an extraordinary fire on London Bridge, on the 10th of July 1212, whereby upwards of 3000 persons perished either by the flames or in being drowned by overloading the boats that went to their assistance. The bridge was greatly damaged, and a great part of the city consumed.

In 1213 when the articles composing *the great charter* were proposed, resolved on and sworn to, the citizens of London joined their fellow countrymen, and received with joy the means offered them to assist in this glorious achievement, which has become to the present time, the palladium and standard of our liberties.

Almost as soon as the gratifying intelligence of this event could be known over the kingdom, John applied to the pope for an absolution from his solemn oath, and to other foreign potentates for military aid. With this assistance he commenced a civil war against the Barons, who sought and found protection within the walls of the city. He then fulminated against all concerned a thundering anathema from Rome, which was received with indifference. The citizens, although exempted by their charter from going to war, raised, it is said, an army of 20,000 horse, and 40,000 foot, besides fitting out a powerful fleet to protect their commerce.

On Henry III. succeeding to the throne, his first public act was to confirm the great charter. The citizens of London received their young king with every possible demonstration of attachment, but between them and the courtiers who had been the supporters of John there was any feeling but that of cordiality to each other.

On the death of his wise and liberal minister, the Earl of Pembroke, Henry threw himself into the entire guidance of Hubert-de-Burgh, who, as chief minister and justiciary of the kingdom, acted with cruel and arbitrary measures. He suspended the operations of the great charter, and hanged Fitz-Arnulp, a citizen who had been engaged in a tumult against the abbot of Westminster, and two other citizens, without any trial. He also usurped the city authorities into his own hands, caused the king to amerce them in a large sum, and appointed a custos over it instead of their own chief magistrate. When the citizens remonstrated against this infraction of a solemn charter, he demanded a fifteenth of all their moveables for granting a restoration of it. He also prohibited all schools of law to be held in London, where the articles of the great and the forest charters were taken as subjects for discussion.

On the king's coming of age, De Burgh incurred his displeasure, and with a fickleness natural to him, the discarded minister was first given up to the mayor and citizens to be dealt with as he deserved; but on the remonstrance of Ranulph, Earl of Chester, the order was recalled to the great disappointment of the ill-treated citizens.

Great as was the displeasure of the citizens, against the king's measures, they would not omit their usual splendour and liberality at the coronation of queen Eleanor at Westminster; for the mayor, aldermen and chief citizens went out with great splendour to welcome the royal consort. The king's extravagance and misrule brought him into such distress that he was compelled to pawn the crown jewels to relieve his necessities. These national pledges were accepted by the citizens, to prevent their deposit with the Burghers of Antwerp, or the Jews of Amsterdam, the usual money lenders of that day. But, when the king heard who were the lenders of the money, he expressed great contempt for and displeasure at the party.

The king therefore bore no great good will towards his good citizens of London, and proved his regard by most exorbitant exactions, and the various schemes of pillaging he resorted to so disgusted the citizens, that they joined cordially in the league made by the Barons against him.

In this king's reign is the first recorded instance of supplying the city with water, by means of pipes; which was brought from six fountains in the village of Tyburn.

The enmity between the king and the city daily increased, and he exhibited his wrath by fines and curtailment of their ancient privileges; which however they recovered by their wonted energy and perseverance. Henry, on the birth of his son Edward, affected to be reconciled to the city, that he might induce the corporation to take oaths of fealty to the new-born prince; and at the same time he made additional and expensive fortifications to the Tower of London, that he might overawe the rebellious citizens.

In the twenty-fifth year of this king's reign, according to the chronicles of Sir Richard Baker, aldermen were first chosen to rule the wards of the city, but they were changed annually in the manner of the sheriffs; the houses were mostly covered, or thatched with straw, and a former edict that all future buildings should be of stone, with party walls, and covered with slates or tiles, was renewed. In the same year, the king granted a considerable sum towards building the new abbey church at Westminster. A common seal, which in fact, if not in name, now first incorporated the city as a body, was likewise granted in this reign.

Notwithstanding the readiness of the citizens to comply with all the king's reasonable demands, he still continued to oppress them under various pretences; in consideration however of receiving a large sum of money, he granted them a new charter which confirmed all they had hitherto enjoyed. Yet his craving for money and enmity to the city continued unabated, and after numerous acts of tyranny, and conferences, he violated and granted in succession no less than nine different charters. So much had he drained the city by his continual extortions, that the most eminent citizens found difficulty in procuring provisions for their families, and the poor were reduced to a dreadful state of famine.

In consequence of prince Edward breaking open the treasury of the knight's Templars, in 1263, and robbing it of a large sum deposited there by the citizens, the inhabitants commenced retaliation upon the court by assaulting and plundering the houses of Lord Gray and others of the nobility. The barons being engaged in hostilities with the king demanded aid of the Londoners, but Henry, who came and resided in the Tower, endeavoured to cajole them with fair words and promises; finding however they could no longer submit to the arbitrary will of so faithless a monarch, they marched to give him battle; when it was agreed to refer all their differences to the king of France: the latter deciding in favour of Henry, the citizens headed by the constable of the Tower marched to Isleworth, where they destroyed the palace of the king of the Romans, and on their return pulled down the king's summer residence near Westminster. After this they returned in triumph, and further hostilities continued with various fortunes. The king, having routed the barons, called a parliament at Westminster, which enacted " that the City of London, for its late rebellion, should be divested of its liberties, should have its posts and chains taken away, and its principal citizens imprisoned and left to the mercy of the king." In consequence of this act, he imprisoned several of the leading citizens, who went to Windsor to implore his clemency, and dismissed the whole of their magistracy. The corporation at length obtained pardon and a new charter, on payment of 20,000 marks.

It was in this reign the city watching and warding were first established. Westminster Abbey was completed, and many privileges were conferred on the city by prince

Edward the king's son, who, being appointed governor by his father, obtained for the citizens a recognition of their right to choose their own chief magistrate and other immunities, according to ancient charter.

On the death of Henry, his son, then engaged in the Crusades, succeeded to the throne as Edward I., and testified his regard for the citizens of London, by transmitting to them a letter, wherein he ordered the expulsion of the Flemings. This mark of the king's personal regard for a city whose chief magistrate he had been whilst prince, was accepted with such gratitude by the citizens, that they received him on his arrival from Palestine with unbounded joy and magnificence. In return the king acted as moderator, in a violent dissension which broke out as to the choice of a mayor; and in the third year of his reign he honoured the city by appointing its mayor his ambassador beyond seas, and directed four citizens chosen by their fellows to supply the place of mayor during his absence.

In this year the convent of the Black-friars was founded and built by a license from the crown, and also a wall and tower at the head of it for his Majesty's reception. This wall reached from Ludgate westward, behind the houses to Fleet ditch, and thence southward to the river Thames; for the completion of which the king granted the citizens a duty on certain merchandizes for three years.

At this period of Edward's reign, the city first began to be governed by wards as at present, and elected a select body from among themselves called the lord mayor's common council, and were first summoned to parliament by the king's writ. In 1281 London bridge had become so dangerous from decay that the citizens applied to the king for aid, which he granted by authorizing a toll to be collected for its repair, and shortly after gave them certain other duties for the reparation of the public buildings and enclosure of the city. Five of the arches of London bridge having been carried away, a subsidy was granted to the corporation for its repair.

In the twelfth year of this reign, the mayor, aldermen and sheriffs, having been summoned to appear before the justices in Eyre at the Tower, the former refused to appear in his magisterial capacity, but attended as a private citizen: the king was so incensed at this conduct that he immediately deprived the city of all its franchises, and appointed a custos, who held the authority of the mayor for above twelve years; but which was afterwards restored to the citizens in consideration of a moderate fine.

The city, says Mr. Norton, was never after in this reign molested in its rights; and so firmly does the supreme authority of the law appear to have been established, that upon a mandate coming from the king, directed to the mayor and sheriffs, which appeared to infringe the privileges of the citizens, they did not hesitate to return for answer—that they could not be charged to obey it; and they actually refused so to do, with impunity.

In the twenty-eighth year of this reign, the Goldsmith's company of London was invested with the privilege of assay; and in 1304, we first read of a recorder of London, when Geoffrey de Hartlepole, alderman, was chosen to that dignity.

On the death of Edward I. the sceptre was transferred to the feeble hands of his son, Edward II., who began his reign by acts of severity against the city. Part of the fine due from the city to his father being unpaid, he issued a writ of *fieri facias*, from the exchequer, and distrained the goods of the citizens. He was guilty of many other similar acts of tyranny, yet the citizens received him on his first solemn entry, in 1308, with a degree of magnificence that sufficiently testified their loyalty. In this reign, we find the first authentic mention of the *mercantile* constitution of the civic corporation, and of the mercantile qualifications requisite in candidates for the freedom of the city. A number of articles of regulation were drawn by the citizens, approved by the king, and afterwards confirmed to them by a deed known by the title of the first charter of Edward II.

In 1310 the order of knight's Templars in London was subverted, their persons having been arrested in England as well as all over the continent. They were however allowed trifling pensions by the king, during their imprisonment in the four city gates.

The citizens, in resentment of some indignity received from the king, levelled to the ground, a mud wall that had been erected by Henry III. to enclose the Tower, and which encroached within the city walls. The king in punishment for this act of indiscretion fined them in 1000 marks, but renewed to them their former privileges of recovering their rents by *gavelot*. In 1317 the king summoned a parliament at York, and directed the sheriffs to return *two* of their fellow citizens, but in the return to the court, the mayor, aldermen, sheriffs and commonalty returned *three*.

The king having resigned the government entirely into the hands of his tyrannical favorites, the two Spencers, the barons resented this conduct, and summoned a parliament to meet in the city, where the nobility repaired with such a train of attendants, that they equalled in number a considerable army. The conduct of the barons and the citizens was so prudent that the king was compelled to assent to their terms, and gave them many additional privileges, and another charter. The rest of this reign was spent in continual squabbles between the court and the city; both the Spencers were hanged, and the head of the younger one stuck upon London bridge. The king, who had taken refuge in Wales, was sent to London, and confined in the Tower. The parliament voted his deposition in 1327, and his son Edward, then only fourteen years of age, was chosen to succeed him.

The young king Edward III. was received by the Londoners with great enthusiasm, and with the constitutional consent of his parliament granted them an ample charter, comprising the power of trying prisoners within their own jurisdiction, and of trying citizens convicted of crimes in other parts within the city, called the rights of *infang-theft* and *outfang-theft*. He also added by a second charter the village of Southwark to the jurisdiction of the city.

In 1329, several ambassadors from foreign kingdoms having arrived, the king ordered a grand tournament to be performed in Cheapside, in honour of his illustrious visitors, which is a proof of the estimation in which he held the citizens, whose foreign trade had increased to such an extent, that in 1331 the customs of the port of London, at the very low rate of duty at that period, amounted to above £8000 a year.

In 1338 an expedition was formed against France, and the prince of Wales, afterwards known by the title of the Black Prince, who was regent during his father's absence, issued a precept to the mayor, aldermen and sheriffs of London, commanding them to shut up and fortify their city next the Thames, against a French fleet, that had already invaded the realm in several places. In the following year the citizens advanced to the king the sum of 20,000 marks, raised by a general assessment on each ward. In this king's reign another dispute arose between him and the Londoners, concerning an encroachment on their liberties, by the judges holding an inquisition in the Tower, which ended in a general enquiry, and a new charter.

The king, wanting money to carry on the war with France, endeavoured to raise some, by compelling every citizen possessed of £40 a year to take upon himself the order of knighthood, and a writ was accordingly issued to the sheriffs; but the citizens, not being so fond of honours as in later times, availed themselves of certain exceptions, and directed the sheriffs to return a refusal.

In the year 1346 David, king of Scotland, who had been taken prisoner at the battle of Nevil's cross, was lodged in the Tower. About this time, a bridge at Westminster was first proposed, though it was not erected till within the last century. In the twenty-eighth year of this reign, such amity existed between the king and the citizens, that he granted them another most liberal charter, giving them the privilege of bearing maces of gold or silver before their chief magistrate, the same as before himself.

In 1357 the city was honoured with the grandest triumphal procession that its records can boast of. This was the entry of Edward the Black Prince, accompanied by his royal prisoner John king of France, who were met in Southwark by upwards of 5000 citizens on horseback, and richly accoutred. This enlarged procession was met by the mayor, aldermen, sheriffs and the chief companies in their formalities with stately pageants, at the foot of London Bridge. The streets of the city were adorned with the richest tapestries, and with plate, silks and other furniture, exhibiting their wealth. This cavalcade lasted from three in the morning till noon.

Henry Picard, a past lord mayor of London, had the honour in 1363 of entertaining, at his mansion in the city, the kings of France, Scotland, and Cyprus, together with his own sovereign and his gallant son the Black prince. In furtherance of the war against France, the corporation of London lent the king a considerable sum, and at the same time petitioned the king and parliament against several encroachments on their privileges. In 1374 our great poet Chaucer was appointed comptroller of the customs in the port of London; and in the fifteenth year of the king's reign, he granted the citizens two other charters, one explanatory of the right of choosing aldermen, and the other relative to the encouragement of foreign artificers, a wise policy, to which however the citizens objected as tending to impoverish them, and to diminish their privileges.

Although this conduct of the king did not ingratiate him much with the citizens, yet it did not lessen their respect for the royal family; for in the same year that the king gave these privileges to foreigners, they entertained the princess of Wales, widow of the Black prince, her son prince Richard and their suite at Kennington, with a grand masquerade performed by 130 citizens on horseback, who set out from Newgate and proceeded over the bridge through Southwark to Kennington.

About this time Wickliffe being cited before the spiritual court in St. Paul's cathedral, and a warm altercation having ensued between John duke of Lancaster the king's son, and the bishop of London, the citizens took part with the latter. This conduct so highly incensed the prince, that he moved in the king's name in parliament, of which he was president, that from that day there should be no more mayor of London, and many other things subversive of its rights and privileges. Great riots ensued in consequence, and the mob attacked the Savoy, then the palace of the duke of Lancaster, murdered a priest and committed various other acts of atrocity. The mayor and commonalty waited on the king, who gave them a favourable reception and answer, but shortly after, the king's infirmities and the duke's ill will increasing, the mayor, sheriffs and aldermen were summoned to attend his majesty at Kew near Richmond. On this occasion they were less successful; for the mayor and several of the aldermen were dismissed from their offices, and others appointed by virtue of the king's writ. Shortly after this the king died and was succeeded by his grandson Richard II.

The reign of Richard II. is one of the most remarkable in the annals of the city; for, as Mr. Norton observes, we must refer to this period the present establishment of the civic government. At the coronation of this king, he being then only eleven years of age, the citizens claimed their right of acting as chief butler, which being allowed, the lord mayor officiated in that capacity. On this occasion, also, we find the first mention of a champion, although the present family of the Dymokes claim a more ancient date. The young king, in testimony of his regard for the citizens, gave them a confirmatory charter and a mandate for maintaining their widows. He also proposed to reside within the city and offered his mediation between them and his uncle, the duke of Lancaster. After this the young king made his grand entry into the city, for which the most magnificent preparations were made.

The credit of the citizens was so high at this period, that in the assessment for that poll tax, the indecent collection of which caused the insurrection headed by Wat Tyler, the aldermen were entitled and rated as *barons*, and the lord mayor as a *right honourable earl*. This insurrection occurred in 1380, when Sir William Walworth was mayor. After many successes in their way from Maidstone to Blackheath, destroying the Temple and other public buildings in the city, they sent a message to the king and demanded a parley. The insurgents possessed themselves of the Tower, seized and beheaded the archbishop of Canterbury and Sir Robert Hales, under circumstances of peculiar cruelty. They murdered many ancient citizens and foreign merchants, and committed other atrocities; and at last agreed to a conference in Smithfield. One of the conditions proposed by their leader was that he should have a commission to behead all lawyers, escheators and others learned in the law. At this conference Tyler behaved with such insolence to the king, that Sir William Walworth as chief magistrate felled him to the ground. The presence of mind displayed by the king, and the successful issue of his address to the insurgents, are too well known to need repetition. The king knighted the lord mayor and several of the aldermen, and in the opinion of many writers granted the augmentation of the dagger to the city arms in commemoration of this event. He also granted the corporation a new seal, and other honours and privileges.

In this reign the regalia and crown jewels, pledged to the citizens, were redeemed, but the king imposed so many exactions upon them, and made so many attempts to abridge them of their privileges, that on the landing of the duke of Hereford (afterwards Henry IV.), in Yorkshire, he was instantly invited to take up his residence in the city. This conduct materially tended towards the resignation of Richard. In this reign the wards were first represented in common council as at the present day.

The new king Henry IV. was crowned at Westminster on the 13th October 1399, at which the lord mayor and aldermen of London were admitted to their ancient rights of chief butler of England. In 1400 Emanuel Palæologus, emperor of the Greeks, arrived in England, and was met by the king and nobility at Blackheath, and received by the lord mayor, aldermen, and citizens in a splendid manner. In this year also, says Fabian, Guildhall was built, instead of an old little cottage in Aldermanbury. The walls of the city in this reign were in a regular and complete state of repair, and a clear ditch was kept around them. The streets were now for the first time lighted with public lanterns, whence Mr. Norton justly infers, that the internal police of the city was under tolerably good regulation. The conservancy of the Thames was also confirmed to the citizens, who at this period were so wealthy that on a public loan the celebrated Richard Whittington advanced £1000, while the opulent bishop of Durham could only advance 100 marks. Whittington also rebuilt Newgate, the library of the Grey Friars, part of Bartholomew's Hospital and the college of priests on College Hill, recently pulled down and rebuilt on a new site, near the Highgate archway.

On the death of Henry IV., whose body is supposed to have been thrown into the Thames, the throne was filled by the gay and gallant Henry V., who confirmed the citizens in their ancient privileges. The festivities of lord mayor's day 1415, were joyfully heightened by the arrival of the news of the king's great victory at Agincourt, which was communicated to Nicholas Wotton, when proceeding to Westminster to be sworn. Moorgate was built in the same year for the convenience of the citizens to frequent the fields of Finsbury and the neighbouring villages. On the return of the triumphant king the citizens received him with every possible demonstration of joy. Tapestry illustrative of his victory, and other showy embellishments, were displayed in the streets, and the city conduits ran with wine. The lord mayor, aldermen and citizens, went in grand cavalcade to the king at Westminster, and presented him with the (then) large sum of £1000 in gold, in two rich basins of the same metal and value.

The citizens, also, in honour of their king, received the emperor Sigismund in the most splendid manner, and advanced large sums to the king in aid of his war in France. Holborn was first paved in 1417; and in 1419, a year celebrated as the third mayoralty of the famous Sir Richard Whittington, Sir Thomas Eyre, a past lord mayor, built Leadenhall as a public granary. This warlike monarch died in France on the 31st of August, 1422, and was buried, with much ceremony, in the cathedral of St. Paul, James, king of Scotland, officiating as chief mourner, attended by the princes of the blood, the leading nobility and gentry of the kingdom, with the lord mayor, aldermen and principal citizens.

Henry VI. succeeded his father, being only eight months and a few days old. He was carried in his mother's lap in an open chair through the city to the parliament, then sitting at

Westminster. In 1423 Newgate was rebuilt at the expense of funds left by Sir Richard Whittington, and many other improvements were made to the city. After the young king's coronation in France, in 1431, he was received by the mayor and citizens of London at Blackheath and conducted to the city, with great splendour; and two days after the mayor and aldermen attended the king at Westminster, and presented him with a golden hamper, containing £1000 in golden nobles.

In the year 1438 Sir William Eastfield, knight of the Bath and lord mayor of London, brought, at his own expense, water into the city from Tyburn and Highbury-Barn, and erected public conduits in Fleet Street, Aldermanbury and Cripplegate. In the following year, the abbot of Westminster granted to the mayor and citizens of London and their successors a head of water, at Paddington, which contributed much to the service of the city. The king granted a sum of money for repairing the cross in Cheapside, and in 1443 the common council granted also 1000 marks towards erecting a new conduit at the western end. In 1448 the king pawned his plate to two London goldsmiths, and in 1450 the well known Jack Cade headed a rebellion, and took possession of the city, striking his sword upon London stone and proclaiming himself "Lord of London." He exercised sovereignty within the city, and put the lords Say and Cromer to death without trial. The citizens incensed at the conduct of some of his followers, who had plundered two wealthy aldermen, united with the king's troops in the Tower, and cut off the rebel party. Three of the aldermen and many citizens however lost their lives in the conflict.

The putting down of this rebellion, chiefly by the bravery of the citizens, gave such satisfaction to the king, that he made the lord mayor, Geoffrey Fielding, a privy counsellor, which is the first instance of a lord mayor of London being raised to so important a rank. The custom of the new lord mayor being rowed up to Westminster first occurred in this reign in 1454, when John Norman, the lord mayor elect, built an elegant barge at his own expense. This example was followed by several of the chief companies, who attended him in their respective barges splendidly decorated.

The citizens distinguished themselves at this period by several revolts against the vacillating government of the duke of York, who had been appointed protector. One of these, as related by Fabian, was in the monastery of St. Martin's-le-grand, where a number of the inhabitants who had grossly insulted the citizens had taken refuge. The lord mayor and aldermen on learning the scandalous treatment of their fellow-citizens, by the retainers of the court, forced the sanctuary and brought off the assailants. The dean complained to the king, who summoned the recorder and a deputation of aldermen to attend him in Herefordshire, where on hearing the case, he commanded the citizens to keep the aggressors in custody till his return. Another riot was occasioned by that jealousy of their liberties that always distinguished the Londoners; for in May 1456 a young mercer, who had been denied the privilege of wearing his dagger in some city in Italy, meeting an Italian in Cheapside with a dagger by his side, reproached him with his countrymen's conduct, snatched his dagger from his side and broke his head with it. This led to a general commotion and a destruction of the houses and properties of most of the Italian merchants in London. Several other commotions, which were said to have been promoted by the king's enemies, occurred in the city. In consequence of one, that occurred in Fleet Street, between the students of the inns of court and the inhabitants, in which the queen's attorney was killed, the principal of Furnival's, Clifford's and Barnard's inns were committed prisoners to Hertford castle, and William Taylor the alderman of the ward, with some other eminent citizens, was committed to the castle at Windsor.

In the beginning of the year 1458, a reconciliation having been proposed between the king and the duke of York, the king and queen, with the dukes of York, Exeter and Somerset, the earls of Warwick, Northumberland and Salisbury, with many others of the principal nobility, attended by their respective retinues, arrived in the city for that purpose. The lord mayor caused a guard of 5000 trust-worthy citizens to keep guard every day under his own immediate command, and 2000 to relieve them by night, under the command of three aldermen. By which prudent measure the peace of the city was preserved.

A compromise having taken place, the results were made known to the public, and a grand procession to St. Paul's followed on the 5th of May 1458, in which the nobility walked in pairs, one of each party hand in hand, and the duke of York leading the queen with every external appearance of cordiality.

This hollow truce lasted however but a short time; the king's party became successful and the duke of York was compelled to flee to Ireland. Lord Scales was commanded by the king to take possession of the city, but the citizens favouring the Yorkists, the lord mayor refused to permit an armed force to enter within its walls. Lord Scales, however, suspecting that the citizens intended to admit the earl of March, took possession of the Tower, and threatened to lay the city in ashes, in case the rebels were admitted. His threats were disregarded and lord March was received by the citizens with loud acclamations of joy. Scales kept his word and bombarded the city from the Tower, with such effect as to destroy a number of buildings, but the earl of Salisbury blocked up the Tower on every side and saved the city from further destruction.

By the death of the duke of York, in a dreadful battle between the partisans of the rival houses of York and Lancaster, his son Edward Plantagenet, who is above mentioned as earl of March, succeeded to his father's title, and prosecuted the unholy war with the most implacable resentment. The earl of Warwick distrusting the citizens and not choosing to be cooped up within their walls, marched out against the queen's army, where he was defeated in a desperate battle at Barnard's Heath, near St. Alban's.

The young duke of York entered London on the 21st of February 1461, and was received by the citizens, who had previously cut off the queen's supplies, with the greatest rapture, and he was proclaimed king by a large body of them in Clerkenwell Fields on the proposal of the earl of Warwick. A council was immediately held at Baynard's Castle; the new king rode in procession to St. Paul's, and, after being crowned at Westminster, returned to the city by water, where, taking up his residence at the bishop of London's palace, he was proclaimed king by the name of Edward IV. In truth, says Mr. Norton, the good will of the citizens was thought by Edward to be so main a bulwark of his throne, that he never failed during the course of his reign to use every means of preserving it. Besides securing to them in the most ample manner their ancient privileges, he increased them by the grant of several very beneficial charters; and even condescended to live among them on terms of the most convivial familiarity.

Edward, though only in the twentieth year of his age, had scarcely ascended the throne, when he exhibited symptoms of a sanguinary disposition. He beheaded an opulent citizen, a grocer in Cheapside, for saying he would make his son heir to the crown, meaning his own shop, of which it was the sign. On the same day he marched his army through the city out at Bishopsgate, in search of his rival the unfortunate Henry, to whom he gave victorious battle at Towton, in Yorkshire. On his return he went from his palace at Sheen to London, and was met at Lambeth by the lord mayor and aldermen, with all their formalities, dressed in scarlet, attended by 400 citizens in green, and mounted on horseback. By this splendid escort he was conducted to the Tower, whence two days after he was similarly escorted to Westminster, and crowned with great splendour.

The city of London never before stood in such great estimation as in this reign, nor had its citizens ever before possessed so great an influence in settling the government. Its fortifications were so complete, and so well guarded, as often to defy, in this stormy period of its history, the most powerful armies. Edward, in gratitude for such signal services, granted the citizens many immunities, and four several charters. He also gave the first charter to the German merchants of the steel yard.

At this period the citizens were so tenacious of their privileges, that upon a grand entertainment being given by the judges at Ely House, to which the mayor, aldermen, sheriffs and many of the principal citizens were invited; the most honourable place being assumed by the lord treasurer Baron Ruthen, the lord mayor claimed precedency as having pre-eminence of all persons, after the king, within the liberties of the city. The treasurer remained inflexible, and the lord mayor retired with his fellow citizens, and entertained them himself with great hospitality.

On May day 1465, the king married the beautiful and accomplished Elizabeth Woodville, and she was crowned at Westminster a few days afterwards, when he showed his esteem for the citizens by installing their lord mayor, Sir Thomas Cook, a knight of the Bath. In this year the king enlarged and strengthened the fortifications of the Tower of London, and erected a scaffold and gallows on Tower Hill, but, on the remonstrance of the mayor and citizens, he declared by proclamation that it was not to be considered in derogation of their rights.

In the year 1466 the before-mentioned Sir Thomas Cook was impeached of high treason and committed to the Tower; and notwithstanding his acquittal, he was obliged to purchase his liberty by paying to the king the exorbitant sum of £8000. At this period, the court of Edward was graced with ambassadors from almost every power in Europe; but none shone so resplendently as Anthony, Bastard of Burgundy, who was sent over by his brother the count de Charolois, duke of Burgundy, to conclude a marriage between that prince and the Lady Margaret, sister to the king. The bastard, who was greatly celebrated for his chivalrous prowess, challenged the lord Scales, brother to the queen, to contend with him in various feats of arms. The challenge being accepted, the king commanded lists to be prepared in Smithfield, and magnificent galleries to be erected for the reception of the illustrious spectators.  The tournament lasted three days, and the English knight was declared the victor.   In June 1468 the princess Margaret set out for Burgundy, to celebrate her nuptials with the duke, and was met in Cheapside by the lord mayor and aldermen, who in the name of themselves and their fellow citizens presented her with two rich basins, containing 100 lbs. of gold in each.

The next year of Edward's reign was distinguished by many popular commotions, which were principally excited by the earl of Warwick, who felt himself neglected.  When this nobleman, who is distinguished in our history by the name of the king-maker, took up arms openly against Edward, the earl of Rivers, father to the queen, was made prisoner and beheaded.  The king was also placed in confinement at Middleham Castle, from which he escaped to Holland, leaving his queen in the Tower of London; who fearing her life fled to the sanctuary at Westminster.   On the queen's departure, the custody of the Tower was entrusted to the lord mayor, Sir Richard Lee and the aldermen, who removed the deposed king Henry from the place of his imprisonment to the royal apartments.

After many conflicts in which the neighbouring villages of Limehouse, Ratcliffe, and St. Katherine's, were plundered and burned, the parliament that was summoned by Warwick and the duke of Clarence, in the name of king Henry, was adjourned to St. Paul's, where it sat from November till Christmas.   To avoid committing his fellow citizens by taking part in these violent proceedings, the lord mayor, John Stockton, feigned sickness. Edward did not remain idle; for on the 12th of March 1471 he landed in England, assisted by his brother-in-law the duke of Burgundy, and proceeded with all possible expedition to London.   On his arrival, the lord mayor and aldermen demanded and obtained possession of the Tower in Edward's name, and on the 11th of April following he again entered his capital in triumph, and was received by the citizens with the highest demonstrations of joy.   Edward put himself immediately at the head of his forces, and left the city, to which Warwick was hastening by forced marches, and on the 14th of April, being Easter Sunday, the two armies met near Barnet, and a desperate battle was fought, in which no quarter was given on Edward's side, Warwick was slain, and Edward confirmed on his throne.   Edward hastened to London, immediately after this sanguinary conflict, and proceeded to St. Paul's, where he deposited his own and his enemies' standards.   The citizens indulged as usual in splendid festivities in commemoration of the event.

An adventurer, known by the name of the Bastard Falconbridge, who, after having been vice-admiral of the channel, commenced pirate, entered the suburbs of Southwark with an army of 17,000 men.   On the 14th of May, 1471, he attempted to enter the city by the way of the bridge; which however he found to be so well fortified and defended that he could not succeed, although he proceeded to storm it.   A party of his army crossed the river elsewhere, and made their way into the city by the way of Aldgate, but were driven out by the valour of the citizens, headed by one of their Aldermen, Robert Bassett. Being thus defeated, Falconbridge embarked at Blackwall, and sailed round to Sandwich, where, after a battle with Edward, he was taken prisoner, and, with several of his companions, was executed, and their heads fixed upon London Bridge.   The king was so gratified with the gallant defence of the citizens, that he knighted the lord mayor, John Stockton, twelve of the aldermen and the recorder. On the 21st of May, Edward entered the city in triumph, and the next morning king Henry VI. was found dead in the Tower.

The following year, 1472, will be ever memorable in the history of London, by the introduction of the art of printing into England, by William Caxton, citizen and mercer of London. The first book printed in London by this eminent citizen was a treatise on chess, translated by himself from the French, and dated 1474. This noble art soon got into great repute, for previous to Caxton's death, which occurred in 1491, we find Theodore Rood, John Lettou, William Macheline and Wynkin de Worde, foreigners, and Thomas Hunt, an Englishman, all printers within the city.

In the year 1475 an act of common council was passed, by which the election of the lord mayor and sheriffs, which had till then been in the whole body of the citizens, was vested in the masters, wardens and liverymen of the several city companies, as at the present day.

The gates, walls and other fortifications of the city, being in a very decayed state, the lord mayor and aldermen resolved to repair them, with bricks made and burned in Moorfields; and that the expense of such repairs should be defrayed by a collection raised among the inhabitants at large. But the sum not being sufficient, the draper's, skinner's and goldsmith's companies repaired various parts, and the town ditch was also cleansed.

The king, who long wanted to get rid of the Duke of Clarence, summoned the lord mayor and aldermen to attend the privy council, to witness the accusations that were trumped up against him. With their consent, he was committed to the Tower, where he was tried, condemned and executed, in so private a manner, that the mode of it is a secret to this day. In June, 1479, the citizens purchased a third and fourth charter from the king at a large expense, and in the September following a dreadful pestilence raged in London till the November in the following year.

To evince his great regard for the citizens of London, the king invited the lord mayor, aldermen and chief citizens in 1480 to a grand hunt in Waltham Forest, in which several deer were killed and the entertainment concluded with a sumptuous feast. Shortly after this, to show his regard for the city ladies, his majesty, whose gallantry towards them, is broadly hinted at by Philip de Commines, sent a present of two harts, six bucks and a ton of wine to the lady mayoress, who entertained the aldermen's wives and other ladies with this royal donation at Draper's Hall.

This monarch, after an eventful reign of twenty-three years, died at Westminster on the 9th of April, 1483, and was succeeded by his son Edward V., who was then in the thirteenth year of his age. The reins of government were assumed by his uncle Richard, Duke of Gloucester, as protector during the king's minority, and he was immediately proclaimed in London. The queen mother on hearing of this appointment, and of Gloucester's imprisoning the lords Rivers and Gray, Sir Thomas Vaughan and other friends of the young king, in Pomfret Castle, immediately left London and fled for refuge to the sanctuary at Westminster. The citizens also caught the general alarm, took up arms in great number and joined the nobility, who had done the same, until they could learn the motives for thus making a captive of their young king.

The Duke of Gloucester, unwilling to incense the Londoners, sent Lord Hastings, who was much esteemed by them, into the city, to assure them of the uprightness of his intentions. This pacified them in some degree, and, on the 4th of May, he and the young king were met at Hornsey Park by the lord mayor, aldermen and five hundred of the principal citizens, richly dressed and mounted on horseback. This splendid retinue of Londoners escorted the king and his attendants with great pomp to the city, where he was received with great joy, and the same night took up his residence in the palace of the Bishop of London. Gloucester performed his part so well on this occasion, that he rode before the king barehead, exclaiming to the people " behold your king;" and on his arrival at the bishop's palace renewed his oath of allegiance, in which he was followed by all the prelates and nobles present, together with the lord mayor and aldermen of London.

The young king was splendidly lodged in the palace of the Tower of London, where he was speedily joined by his younger brother the Duke of York; and great preparations were made for the proposed coronation. But on the 13th of June one part of the privy council met at Westminster, for the purpose of notifying to the city magistrates in due form the day of the coronation, and the other part, with the protector, met in the Tower. Here that extraordinary scene was performed, where emissaries of the protector proclaimed treason, wounded Lord Stanley on the head with a pole axe, and seized him with the Archbishop of York, the Bishop of Ely and Lord Hastings. The latter of these noblemen, whom Gloucester had inveigled by his dissembling into his grasp, was immediately executed on a log of wood which lay accidentally in a court of the Tower.

As an apology for this summary outrage, the protector sent for the mayor, aldermen and leading citizens of London, on whose concurrence he founded his chief hopes of success, and, besides a hypocritical speech, he issued a proclamation which was read throughout the city. This proclamation, says Sir Thomas More, in his life of Edward V., was, although got up in such haste, in such good style of composition, at so great length and so beautifully engrossed on parchment, that, as was sarcastically observed by a citizen, it seemed certainly penned in the spirit of prophecy. This apology failing in its intended effect, Gloucester tried other measures to engage the aid of the citizens, and made their lord mayor Sir Edmund Shaw a privy councillor; by which means he obtained the interest of Dr. Ralph Shaw, his brother, a very eloquent and popular preacher, who abused his faculties and his calling by preaching to the citizens at St. Paul's Cross in favour of the usurper.

The impression intended to have been made on the citizens, by this sermon, having failed in its object, a new expedient was resorted to. Orders were sent to the lord mayor, Sir Richard Shaw, who had become a complete tool of the protector's, to convene a common hall. This meeting was accordingly held, but Mr. Norton has rescued the citizens from a part of the obliquy that has been attached to them for this act, by the discovery* that it

---

* Norton's Com. p. 170, n.

was a meeting out of the common course, and not regularly convened according to the statute. No entry of it is therefore to be found in any of the city books, although every other in Richard's protectorate and reign are duly entered. The plausible speech of the Duke of Buckingham and the conduct of the citizens on this memorable occasion are well known and need not be repeated in this brief abstract of civic history. The result was, that Richard was proclaimed king, and his first act of sovereignty was the murder of his two nephews, one of them being his king to whom he had twice sworn fealty.

The great body of the citizens returned to their homes in grief, but the members of the corporation attended the usurper's coronation, with the lord mayor as cup bearer, in great pomp. Their claim in this particular, says Mr. Norton, was formally allowed and still remains on record in the town clerk's office. The new king, Richard III., to testify his gratitude for this honour, took up his residence among the citizens at Baynard Castle.

The death of Richard III., in the memorable battle of Bosworth Field, placed his successful rival, the Earl of Richmond, on the throne of England, with the title of Henry VII. The first act of the new king was to enter his capital, and he was met on his way by the lord mayor, aldermen and chief citizens at Highgate, and received in Shoreditch by the principal corporate companies in their formalities. Henry, however, entered the city in a close litter, and did not condescend to court the suffrages of the corporation, whose conduct to his predecessor could not much have gratified him; but proceeded direct to St. Paul's, where he returned public thanks for his great and auspicious victory, and deposited the standards taken in the battle. He took up his residence at the bishop's palace, where on the following day he assembled a council and solemnly renewed the oath he had previously taken before the battle of Bosworth.

In the session of parliament held in 1487-8, the jurisdiction of the lord mayor of London, and his successors, over the river Thames was confirmed, and although the citizens were liberal in their loans, benevolences and other contributions to the king's necessities, less cordiality subsisted between the monarch and his good citizens of London in this reign than in almost any other in our history. Yet upon one occasion the king gave the citizens a grand entertainment in Westminster Hall, and conferred the honour of knighthood on the lord mayor.

On the 4th of October, 1501, Katherine of Arragon, infanta of Spain, landed at Plymouth, and made a grand public entry into the city on the 12th of November. The corporation received the princess with due honours and splendour, and on the 14th of the same month, she was married in St. Paul's Cathedral to Arthur, Prince of Wales, in the presence of the lord mayor and chief citizens, who were subsequently entertained in the great hall of the Bishop of London's palace. The newly married couple resided for a few days in the city, and were then escorted by the lord mayor, aldermen and the corporate companies of the city in their splendid barges to Westminster.

In the year 1502 king Henry took down the old and decayed lady chapel at the east end of Westminster Abbey and a tavern that adjoined it, and erected on their sites the splendid mausoleum that bears his name. The river Fleet was also this year cleansed out, widened and made navigable to Holborn Bridge; and about five years afterwards dean Collet founded that excellent institution St. Paul's School, which has been recently augmented, and the school house rebuilt by the Mercers' Company, his trustees.

On the 22nd of April, 1509, the king died at his palace of Richmond, leaving an unexampled treasure in money, jewels and plate locked up in its vaults, and was immediately succeeded by his eldest surviving son, who was proclaimed the next day with the usual solemnities, and with the style and title of king Henry VIII. The new king, shortly after his proclamation, married the widow of his deceased brother Arthur, and proceeded with his queen from the Tower to Westminster through the city, the streets, houses and public buildings being splendidly decorated.

The new king, imitating the conduct of some of the eastern monarchs, in 1510 went into the city in the garb of a yeoman of the guard, to witness the grand cavalcade of the city watch on the eve of St. John. He was so pleased with the ceremony, which, twice in every year, was accompanied by the lord mayor and city officers in state, that he returned on St. Peter's eve, with his queen and the principal nobility. The procession, which was very grand, was illuminated by nearly a thousand large lanterns fixed on the ends of long poles. The whole formed a grand sight and gave the highest satisfaction to the royal pair.

In this reign may be dated the commencement of what may be called an English royal navy, of ships of war, established by the government for the national defence. The fraternity of the Trinity House was instituted in 1512, and the dock yards of Woolwich and Deptford established. In the following year the batteries or forts at Gravesend and Tilbury were first constructed as a defence for the upper part of the Thames. In 1523 the city ditch was again cleansed, the fortifications looked to and other public improvements effected.

In 1522 the Emperor Charles V. arrived in England on a visit to king Henry, who met him at Dover, and accompanied him to Greenwich. On their arrival in the city, the lord mayor, aldermen and sheriffs, in all their formalities, attended by the principal citizens on horseback, received them with a magnificence that would be almost incredible, did we not know from incontestible authority the pompous habits of the age of Henry VIII. The emperor was conducted to Blackfriar's, and the princes and nobility of his retinue to the new palace at Bridewell. The king and queen of Denmark also paid the king a visit in this year, and were as splendidly received and lodged by the citizens. St. Peter's eve occurring during their stay, their majesties went to the King's Head in Cheapside, to witness the splendid ceremony of mustering the city watch.

Shortly after this period, Henry, by the advice of his minister Wolsey, ordered a survey of the kingdom, in order to take a tenth of the property of the laity, and a fourth of that of the clergy, but the opposition raised to this measure by the citizens rendered it necessary to avoid a rigid exaction. The sum thus raised being insufficient, a parliament was summoned and met at Blackfriars on the 15th of April, 1523, but the supplies demanded were granted so unwillingly, and with such restrictions, that no parliament was called for seven years after.

By an act of parliament of the fourteenth and fifteenth of Henry VIII., c. 2, the jurisdiction of the city corporations was to extend two miles beyond the city, namely, the town of Westminster, the parishes of St. Martin in the Fields, and our Lady in the Strand, St. Clements Danes without Temple Bar, St. Giles's in the Fields, St. Andrews in Holborn, the town and borough of Southwark, the parishes of Shoreditch, Whitechapel, St. John's Street, Clerkenwell, and Clerkenwell, St. Botolph without Aldgate, St. Katherines near the Tower, and Bermondsey.

Such were the suburbs of our great metropolis in 1524. They were greatly detached, and the intervals were principally public fields. The Strand was then occupied by mansions and dwellings of the nobility, which were surrounded by large and splendid gardens; and a considerable portion of the parishes of St. Martin and St. Giles were literally, as they are still called, in the fields, as were also a great portion of the city of Westminster, and the parishes or villages of Clerkenwell, Shoreditch, and Whitechapel, and the borough of Southwark.

The plague raged so fiercely in London, towards the latter part of this year, that the King and his court removed to Eltham; Michaelmas term was adjourned, and the city was so deserted by its inhabitants, that the ensuing Christmas was denominated, from its lack of usual mirth and festivity, "the still Christmas."

Wolsey being appointed ambassador extraordinary to the French court, in 1527, made a pompous departure from the city, attended by a numerous train of the chief nobility, gentry, and clergy, to the amount of twelve hundred horsemen; and in the same year two embassadors extraordinary arrived from the court of France, and made a grand public entry into the city. They were lodged in the bishop of London's palace, and liberally entertained by the lord mayor and corporation.

The rumour of the king's intended divorce from queen Katherine was so ill received by the citizens of London, on the arrival of cardinal Campeijus as joint commissioner with Wolsey for that purpose, that insurrections were apprehended. To allay this feeling, the king addressed a numerous assemblage of nobles, prelates, the lord mayor, aldermen, and principal commoners of the city, in the hall of his palace of Bridewell.

The behaviour of the citizens, in the measure of Henry's attempt to throw off the power of the papal yoke, so pleased the king, that he granted them extended powers, by his last charter dated the 13th of April in the 22nd year of his reign, which is preserved in the im-peximus charter of Charles II.; and commanded a general muster of the defensible men of the city, whom he reviewed in the fields between Whitechapel church and Stepney. The lord mayor, aldermen, recorder, and sheriffs, attended the muster, accoutred in white armour, and black velvet coats embroidered with the city arms, with gold chains about their necks, velvet caps on their heads, and gilt battle axes in their hands, attended by pages, servants, and a great number of the citizens on horseback superbly dressed. They passed in review before the king and his splendid court, who expressed themselves abundantly satisfied with their martial appearance.

On the public declaration of the marriage of the king with Anne Boleyn, Henry ordered the lord mayor and citizens to make preparations for conducting her from Greenwich by water to the Tower; and that the city might be decorated on her proceeding the following day to Westminster, to be crowned. This was performed with all the corporation's wonted magnificence and splendour, aided by all the city companies and principal citizens. The queen was highly pleased with the magnificence of the procession, and, on her arrival, returned the mayor and citizens her sincere thanks for their pompous attendance.

An act of parliament was passed, in 1534, for paving the west-end of the high street in London, between Holborn and Holborn bridge, and also the streets in Southwark; and in the following year the common council granted two-fifteenths towards defraying the expenses of bringing water from Hackney to Aldgate, where a conduit was erected for the use of the eastern part of the city.

In the same year, Henry assumed the title of supreme head of the church; and, in order to show his title thereto, beheaded Fisher, bishop of Rochester, and Sir Thomas More for denying his supremacy. In May 1536 he imprisoned and beheaded his second queen Anne Boleyn, at which horrible murder, the lord mayor, aldermen, and sheriffs were compelled to attend; and married on the next day Jane Seymour, who died in the October following, twelve days after the birth of Prince Edward.

In the year 1538 the common council passed an act for the better regulation and preservation of the navigation of the Thames; and other regulations were made by the citizens for the improvement of the city and its liberties. In the following year, the king, fearing that some of his continental neighbours, stirred up by the pope, might attack his dominions, put himself in a state to receive them:—and, among other means of defence, ordered all his subjects from the age of sixteen to sixty to be mustered. He also issued a similar commission to the lord mayor of London, Sir William Foreman, who immediately mustered the citizens of those ages at Mile-end. This was the greatest muster ever made by the citizens of London previous to those of the volunteers during the French revolutionary war, consisting of three divisions of five thousand men each, exclusive of pioneers and other attendants. They marched in martial order through the city to Westminster, where they were reviewed by the king and the nobility, who expressed great satisfaction at their splendid and soldier-like appearance.

On the public entry of the Princess Anne of Cleves, Henry's new bride, she was met on Blackheath on the 3rd of January, 1540, by the king, accompanied by the lord mayor, aldermen, and citizens of London, with all the foreign merchants resident in the city, and escorted in grand state to the royal palace at Greenwich. The royal pair were conveyed in the grand city barges, with the lord mayor and chief citizens, to Westminster, where they were married, and in a few months after divorced. On the 8th of August, of the same year, Katherine Howard, to whom the king had been some time privately married, was publicly declared queen of England.

About this time Robert Brocke, one of the king's chaplains, invented the method of making leaden pipes for conveying water under ground, without the use of solder, and Robert Coope, a goldsmith of the city, was the first who made them, and put the invention in practice. In 1541 an act of parliament was passed for paving the street leading from Aldgate to Whitechapel church, the upper part of Chancery Lane, the way leading from Holborn Bars to St. Giles's in the Fields, as far, says the statute, as any habitation is on both sides of the street, Gray's-Inn Lane, Shoe Lane, and Feuters (now Fetter) Lane. At this period, says Hakluyt, the merchants of London had extended their foreign trades to the Brazils. On the 12th of February 1542 Henry beheaded another of his queens, Catherine Howard, and her confident lady Jane Rochfort, on Tower Hill.

In consequence of a scarcity this year, the common council of London passed an act restraining the lord mayor from having more than seven dishes at dinner or supper, the aldermen and sheriffs being limited to six, the sword-bearer to four, and the mayor's and sheriff's attendants to three, with other laws against luxurious feasting.

The parliament of this year passed two acts relative to the city, one for the better paving of such parts of the city and suburbs as were omitted in the former act, and the other for the embanking and dividing Wapping Marsh. In 1541 Tilbury Fort was built of stone, being previously only a mud fort, and a battery opposite to it at Gravesend, and the city was this year visited with a violent attack of the plague, that carried off many of its inhabitants. In 1545 the twelve chief companies of the city advanced the king a large sum on a mortgage of certain of the crown lands, and alderman Read, who had refused a benevolence, was sent as a common soldier into Scotland. In the same year the citizens raised and completely fitted out a regiment of 1000 foot soldiers, as a reinforcement to the army in France.

On the conclusion of a peace between England and France, it was proclaimed and commemorated in the city with great splendour on Whitsunday 1546; and on the arrival of the French ambassador in the August following, who landed at the Tower wharf, he was met by the lord mayor, aldermen and citizens, and conducted to the Bishop's palace, where he was presented by the city with four large silver flagons richly gilt, besides wine and other costly gifts.

The king having dissolved, among many others, the priory and old hospital of St. Bartholomew in Smithfield, he founded it anew shortly before his death, and endowed it with a handsome revenue, on condition that the city should contribute an equal sum. This proposal being accepted, the new foundation was incorporated by the name of " The hospital of the mayor, commonalty and citizens of London, governors for the poor, called Little St. Bartholomews, near West Smithfield."

Shortly after this act of charity, king, Henry VIII. died, on the 28th of January 1547, and was succeeded by his son Edward VI., then in the ninth year of his age. His maternal uncle, whom he created duke of Somerset, was chosen protector of the kingdom, and guardian of the youthful king. The lord protector commenced his office by knighting the king, who being qualified took the sword of state, and conferred a similar honour upon the lord mayor, Sir Henry Hoblethorn.

The reformation in religion now assumed a more steady aspect than in his turbulent father's reign. The rood, and other emblems of popery, were formally removed from St. Paul's. The gathering of the city watch, that had been put down by Henry, was revived in all its ancient splendour by Sir John Gresham, then lord mayor.

The city, together with the nation at large, disliking the administration of Somerset, after many bickerings, deputed alderman Sir Philip Hobby to remonstrate with the king, who in consequence committed the lord protector to the Tower, to which place he was conducted by the citizens with marks of exultation.   In the year 1550 the king granted a charter which conveyed to the city, in the most ample terms, a very extensive property in Southwark, the manor and all manorial rights over it, together with a large jurisdiction, both civil and criminal.   This valuable estate, says Edward Tyrrell, Esq.*, deputy remembrancer of the city, has been considered as applicable to the maintenance of London Bridge, and is now charged with the payment of a large sum for rebuilding the present bridge.   No trust of this nature, continues this eminent legal authority, is mentioned in the charter; and, after payment of the existing charges, the estate ought to revert back to the corporation.

The citizens in 1551 joined in security to the bank of Antwerp for money advanced to the king; and having purchased, with the manor of Southwark, the hospital of St. Thomas the Apostle, they repaired and enlarged it at a considerable expense.   The king, in return, incorporated the lord mayor, commonalty and citizens of London, governors of the hospital, together with those of Christ and Bridewell: the former for the relief and education of young and helpless children, and the latter for the lodging of poor wayfaring people, the correction of vagabonds and disorderly persons, and for providing them with work.

On the 6th of July, 1553, the young king died, leaving a will, which set aside his sisters, Mary and Elizabeth, and left the crown to the lady Jane Grey.   Some preparations were made to carry this into effect; but, as the sense of the nation was against disturbing the succession, the council met at Baynard's Castle, when, after consulting the lord mayor, aldermen, and recorder, they all proceeded to Cheapside, where they proclaimed the princess Mary, daughter of king Henry VIII., queen of England.   After which ceremony they proceeded to St. Paul's, where the Te Deum was sung in commemoration.   On the 3d of August the new queen made her public entry into the city, preceded by the lord mayor in a crimson velvet gown, bearing a golden sceptre.

Although the queen promised liberty of conscience in religion to all her subjects, she restored the papist Bonner to the see of London, whose chaplain in a sermon at St. Paul's took leave to cast reflections upon the memory of the deceased king Edward.   This so incensed the Londoners, that they hissed the preacher, pelted him with brick-bats and stones, and one of them threw a dagger at him with so good an aim that it stuck in the pulpit.

In the first year of her reign, Mary demanded a loan of £20,000 from the city, which was levied upon the aldermen and 120 of the chief commoners.   On the last day of September in the same year the queen rode in great state from the Tower, through the city, to Westminster.   The citizens received her with such respect, that on her alighting at the palace at Whitehall she publicly thanked the lord mayor.   On the following day she was crowned with the greatest magnificence, the lord mayor and twelve of the chief citizens officiating as chief butler; for which service the mayor received a gold cup and cover, weighing seventeen ounces, as his fee.

* In his notes to Norton's Com. p. 500.

The proposed marriage between the queen and Philip of Spain was first publicly announced by the lord chancellor, to the lord mayor, aldermen, and forty of the principal commoners, who were summoned to attend the privy council for this purpose. This announcement occasioned the commotion called Wyat's rebellion, in which queen Mary had great reason to apprehend the entire defection of the city, whose power and influence she so much dreaded, that she suddenly repaired in person to the Guildhall, where she was met by the lord mayor, aldermen, sheriffs, and the chief of the city companies. She harangued them in a long and soothing speech, which had a good effect, and she left the city in the care of the lord mayor and the lord Howard.

The termination of this rebellion, which, however, was not accomplished without much bloodshed, was followed by dreadful scenes of persecution. The city jury, who acquitted Sir Nicholas Throckmorton at Guildhall, were commanded to appear before the council, and fined £500 each.

The marriage, however, took place, and the royal couple made a public entry into the city, which was sumptuously adorned, and they were received with great testimonials of attachment.

At this period of the civic history, the expenses of serving the public offices had become so great that many of the principal citizens retired from the city rather than incur them. The common council therefore restrained them by a sumptuary act, which regulated the economy of every festival, and added for the first time an allowance out of the city chamber to the lord mayor, in alleviation of his charges in entertaining his fellow citizens on lord mayor's day. The allowance thus granted in consideration, as the act expresses it, of the great annual expense of the mayor and sheriffs, in providing a sumptuous entertainment at Guildhall on lord mayors' days, and for the honour of the city, was the sum of £100 a year.

Such a raging fever occurred in London towards the end of the year 1555, that great numbers of the citizens were carried off, and, among others of the higher classes, seven aldermen fell victims to its ravages within ten months. In the year 1557, says the author of The Present State of England, a work printed in 1683, drinking glasses were first manufactured in England. The finer sort were made in Crutched Friars, and fine flint glass, nearly equal to that of Venice, was first made about the same period in the Savoy near the Strand.

In March 1558 the queen borrowed of the chief city companies the sum of £20,000 on the security of certain lands, and allowed them twelve per cent. annual interest thereon. In the November of the same year queen Mary departed this life, and was succeeded by her sister the princess Elizabeth, who was proclaimed queen in London with the usual formalities and with great demonstrations of joy. The lord mayor, aldermen, sheriffs, and commonalty of the city met their new sovereign at Highgate, in her way from Hatfield, and conducted her with great pomp to the tower of London. On the 14th of January following the queen rode through the city to Westminster, and was addressed by the recorder in the name of his fellow citizens.

On the 4th of June, 1561, the spire of St. Paul's cathedral was struck by lightning and consumed ; and in 1563 the plague again broke out in London with great violence. The first manufacture of knives in England, says the before quoted author of The Present State of England, was established in the same year by Thomas Matthews, a cutler on Fleet Bridge. The English company of merchant adventurers, obtained a charter in the year 1564 from queen Elizabeth, which constituted them a body politic, and gave them many important privileges.

In 1566 Sir Thomas Gresham, an opulent city merchant, built his celebrated exchange, which was subsequently named royal by the queen. At his death he bequeathed it to the mayor and citizens of London for ever. The advantages which the city offered to foreigners were such, that in 1580 the numbers of Dutch, French, and Italians, had so increased that the lord mayor and aldermen remonstrated to the queen against the vast increase of new buildings and number of inhabitants within the city and its suburbs. Her majesty therefore issued a proclamation, by which it was forbidden to erect any new building within three miles from the city gates, where no former house could be remembered to have been by any one living.

The tide machinery at London Bridge, for raising water for the supply of the inhabitants, was erected in 1582 by an ingenious German of the name of Peter Maurice, who received great encouragement from the corporation.

During the period of the threatened Spanish invasion, the citizens of London aided the public cause by supplies of soldiers, money, and other services of war. Sir Thomas Sutton, the founder of the charter house, an eminent London merchant, frustrated it for one year, by securing all the money in the bank of Genoa, at a considerable loss to himself. In 1589 the corporation lent the queen £15,000, and supplied her with 1000 men; and in 1594 the lord mayor and common council fitted out six ships of war and two frigates, stored for six months, and added 450 soldiers. In the year 1599 the Spaniards threatened a second invasion, notwithstanding the dispersion of their celebrated armada in 1588, and the citizens not only aided the queen as before, but formed an honorary body guard from the most eminent of their body.

Owing to the exorbitant price of pepper and other spices, as charged by the Dutch East India Company, the queen granted a charter in the year 1600 to a company of London merchants, under the denomination of " the Governor and Company of Merchants of London trading to the East Indies," which has since risen to such great eminence both in the commercial and political world.

In Rymer's Fœdera (vol. xvi. p. 448) is another proclamation of Elizabeth for restraining the increase of buildings in the metropolis, by which she commands all persons to desist from any new buildings of any house or tenement within three miles of any of the gates of London, unfinished buildings on new foundations to be pulled down, and other restrictive clauses. It is a remarkable circumstance, that, notwithstanding the readiness with which the citizens of London always answered the demands of the queen, she granted them no charter or immunities, nor even confirmed those of her predecessors, during her long reign. In fact, as appears from Norton's Commentaries, the citizens had no charters granted them from the fourth year of Edward VI. to the third of James I.; and yet as appears from the custom house lists, published in Anderson's History of Commerce (vol. ii. p. 960), London exported at the latter end of Elizabeth's reign three times as much as all the rest of England together.

This great queen died on the 23rd of March, 1603, and was succeeded by king James VI. of Scotland, who was proclaimed in Cheapside by the lord mayor and citizens with the usual pomp and ceremony. Owing to the plague, which raged in this year with great violence, the public reception of the new king was deferred till the following spring, when he was received and entertained by the citizens in a most sumptuous manner.

James also, in imitation of his predecessor, issued a proclamation against the extension of buildings in London, and granted his first charter, which gave the corporation many valuable privileges. In 1607 his majesty granted them a second and more extended charter, wherein, among other immunities, he enlarged the limits of the civic jurisdiction by comprising within it the districts of Duke's place, Great and Little St. Bartholomews, Blackfriars', Whitefriars', and Cold Harbour, with a proviso (which they still claim) that the inhabitants of Blackfriars' and Whitefriars' shall be exempt from particular contributions of scot, and watch, and ward, and from the particular offices of constable and scavenger.

In the year 1609 the king assigned the whole province of Ulster in Ireland to the citizens of London, on condition of their establishing an English colony in that country, under the government of a committee of aldermen and common councilmen, which is still continued under the title of the Irish Society of London.

In this reign Sir Hugh Middleton formed that useful undertaking called the New River, which was began in 1608 and completed in 1613; and in 1611 Sir Thomas Sutton founded the establishment called the Charter-house, in the ancient convent of Carthusian monks, called the Chartreuse. In the twelfth year of his reign James granted the citizens his third and last charter, which confirmed the admeasurement of coals in the port of London from Yantlet Creek to Staines Bridge. In 1616 the citizens colonized the town of Derry, to which they gave the name of Londonderry, and built the town of Coleraine. In the same year they sent the first civic deputation to Ireland, and presented each of the above named corporations with a rich sword of State.

The lord mayor and citizens took such umbrage at the king's "Book of Sports," which tolerated certain sports on the Sabbath day, that, to show their contempt for his majesty's orders, they stopped one of the royal carriages as it was driving through the city in the time of divine service. This gave great offence to the king, but after some concessions it was passed over.

A resolution having been made of repairing the cathedral of St. Paul, the king, the prince of Wales, and many of the chief nobility went in great state from Whitehall to the city, on Sunday March 26th, 1620. The royal party was met at Temple Bar by the lord mayor, the aldermen, the sheriffs, and the rest of the corporation, and attended the cathedral, where divine service was performed, and measures concerted for the execution of this great work, which was afterwards so splendidly executed by his able architect, the celebrated Inigo Jones.

In the year 1624, an act of parliament was passed to make the river Thames navigable for barges, lighters and boats from London to Oxford; and on the 27th of March 1625 king James died at his favourite residence at Theobalds, near Cheshunt in Hertfordshire. This circumstance being known, the lord mayor, aldermen, sheriffs and common council repaired to Ludgate, where they met the privy council and the young king, whom they proclaimed with the usual ceremonies.

The coronation and public entry of the king and his bride, to whom he had been married but a few days, was postponed as in the former reign on account of the plague, which again ravaged the metropolis.   Charles had scarcely began to reign, when dissensions arose between him and the citizens, twenty of the principal of whom he imprisoned for refusing a loan of money.   The disputes between the king and the citizens continued during the whole of his unhappy reign, and the levying of ship-money was a fruitful source of continual warfare between his ministers and the citizens.   In 1636 an order was sent from the privy council commanding the lord mayor and aldermen to shut up all the shops in Goldsmith's Row, namely, the south side of Cheapside and Lombard Street, that were not occupied by goldsmiths.   This order not being complied with, it was backed by a decree of the court of star-chamber.   The citizens paid no regard to either of these orders, and the king sent farther orders and farther threats, which were equally disregarded.

Notwithstanding these disputes, the corporation received a charter from the king, for which they paid a large sum.   It recites and confirms all the preceding charters from William the Conqueror to his own time, and grants the citizens farther immunities.   This charter was not long respected; for in 1639 the ministry commenced a suit in the court of star-chamber against the lord mayor and citizens, which took from them all their dearly purchased possessions in Ulster, and they also amerced them in a fine of £50,000.   The parliament however interfered, and obliged the king to annul the decree and to confirm the grant of his father to the citizens.   The city being called on in the year following to raise a large body of men, to serve against the Scots, a rising of the city apprentices took place, who marched to Lambeth in order to murder the archbishop of Canterbury, and, being afterwards joined by above 2000 of the populace, they rushed into St. Paul's, drove out the high court of commissioners, tore up all the benches, exclaiming no bishops ! no high commission.

Such like turbulent scenes, between the king and the citizens, were of constant recurrence.   The court amerced the corporation and imprisoned some of its aldermen for refusing compliance to its arbitrary commands.   At last the differences between them arose to such a height that the king forbade the citizens from presenting any petition to him concerning redress of grievances.

On the king's return from Scotland, he was received by the lord mayor and corporation, with great distinction.   After dining with them at Guildhall, the king embraced the lord mayor at parting, and invited him and the rest of the aldermen to his palace at Whitehall the ensuing day ; where he made the lord mayor a baronet, and knighted all the aldermen who attended.

Notwithstanding this apparent cordiality, the king almost immediately afterwards deprived the citizens of their command over the Tower, and appointed one of his own officers to govern it.   On the dispute between the king and the house of commons, when he attempted to seize five of its members in person, they fled to the city for protection. The citizens armed themselves in their defence. The king came into the city and demanded the impeached members of the common council, who with great firmness refused to deliver them up. The citizens delivered this refusal by way of remonstrance, directed to the king, from the lord mayor, aldermen, and common council.

The grand committee appointed by the house of commons, to deliberate on the state of the nation, assembled for safety in Guildhall, and afterwards accompanied the five accused members in great state to Westminster, where they were received by the city trained bands, who were publicly thanked for their services, and ordered to attend the house daily. After Charles's departure from the metropolis, the parliament demanded large supplies of men and money from the corporation, and on its refusal they committed the lord mayor, Sir Richard Gurney, to the Tower.

Shortly after the battle of Edgehill, the common council passed an act for fortifying the city, which was done with such despatch, that a rampart, with bastions, redoubts and other bulwarks, was shortly erected round the cities of London and Westminster, and the borough of Southwark. The citizens took such a decided part in the civil war between Charles and his parliament, that, on hearing of a proposed reconciliation, the lord mayor convened a court of common council, who presented a petition to the house of commons against any accommodation. They also in 1644 sent two well provided regiments to the assistance of Sir William Waller, the parliamentary general.

After the decisive battle of Navesby had secured the triumph of the parliamentary army, both houses of parliament attended a thanksgiving sermon at Christ Church, Newgate Street, and were afterwards entertained by the corporation. The victorious party kept up the best possible terms with the citizens, who aided them by loans and contributions. When the house of commons had become openly a tool of Cromwell, and threw off the mask, violent quarrels took place between the leaders of the parliamentary faction and the corporation. At the trial of the king, several of the leading citizens were appointed among the number of the king's judges, but, after his condemnation and death, many of the aldermen absolutely refused to proclaim a commonwealth.

On this overthrow of our ancient monarchy, the house of commons usurped the supreme power, and commanded the lord mayor to proclaim an act for the abolition of monarchy. This was peremptorily refused, and the house immediately committed the refractory mayor to the Tower, fined him £2000, and degraded him from his office. Cromwell however, finding it to his interest, became reconciled with the citizens, and borrowed a large sum of money from them to defray the expenses of his expedition to Ireland. On the installation of the usurper, at Whitehall, the lord mayor and entire corporation attended the ceremony, and invited the protector to a grand entertainment, who in gratitude returned thanks to his faithful citizens, and conferred the kingly honour of knighthood on the lord mayor.

Cromwell and the citizens remained on fair terms till the protector's death, on the 3rd of September, 1658, when the lord mayor and the privy council proclaimed his son Richard lord protector of the kingdom. Disputes between the new protector and the citizens soon began, and the city was forthwith put into a posture of defence. The council of state ordered general Monk to take possession of the city with his army, who, however, after a slight attempt at destroying the gates, endeavoured to keep on good terms with the citizens, who, in return, elected him major general of their forces.

Monk and his party, finding all things ripe for the restoration of the exiled monarch, sent him an invitation to return to his dominions. The king sent grateful answers to the parliament and his friends, and a letter to the lord mayor, aldermen, and common council, who immediately sent fourteen of their body, with a present of £10,000, and an order that Richmond Park, which had been given to them by Cromwell, should be presented to his majesty. The day following he was proclaimed in the city by the lord mayor and corporation amidst the universal and joyful acclamations of the citizens. The king received the civic deputies with unfeigned joy and conferred upon them the honours of knighthood. He also confirmed to the city their estates in Ireland, of which they had been illegally deprived by his father, by which tenure the corporation and the twelve chief livery companies still hold them; and conferred upon them that which Mr. Norton emphatically calls a grand inspeximus charter. This charter is usually appealed to as the text of the city charters, and is generally called by pre-eminence *the inspeximus charter*. In the same year the Royal Society was established, which has ever since retained its original high rank in science.

In the beginning of May, 1665, London was again visited by the most dreadful of those periodical maladies called the plague, which had so often ravaged this city. This mortality, which swept away upwards of 90,000 persons, has been admirably narrated by Daniel Defoe, to whose interesting pages our readers are referred for the particulars of its melancholy details.

In the following year occurred that dreadful visitation the great fire of London, which, although it was at the time a great calamity and public loss, may be truly considered as a benefit to all who have succeeded that calamitous period. By its means the city was purified from its narrow and incommodious streets and infectious timber houses, and it occasioned a more noble city to rise upon its ruins. The city of Charles II. and of Wren, however it may be surpassed in point of private buildings, and magnificent streets, by the improvements of George IV. and the able architects of our day, as the pages and illustrations of this work show, yet exhibits in its beautiful cathedral, and other works of that great architect, buildings of admirable beauty and proportion.

Charles immediately assembled both houses of parliament, who passed an act for erecting a court of judicature to settle all the differences between landlords and tenants; and shortly after another for rebuilding the city, which contained rules and directions for all persons concerned therein. The court of common council also passed an act for regulating the widths and other details of the proposed new streets and thoroughfares, which was so approved, by the king and privy council, that it was confirmed and directed to be enforced by an order of council on the 8th of May. Many of these orders of council, printed for the only time from a manuscript book of orders, in the life of Sir Christopher Wren by the author of this work, and formerly in his possession, but now the property of professor Soane of the Royal Academy, prove the great zeal of the king and all his court to rebuild the city with splendour; but it was counteracted by private interests and cabals. Many other public acts and edicts, both of parliament and of the common council, were passed for accomplishing this great undertaking, and on the 29th of October 1675, when Sir Robert Viner commenced his mayoralty, the king dined with the corporation at Guildhall, and accepted the freedom of the city from the hands of Sir Thomas Player the chamberlain.

In 1676 a great part of the borough of Southwark was destroyed by fire, but was rebuilt under the direction of commissioners in a similar style of improvement with those going on in the city of London; which was attempted to be burned a second time in 1679.

After Charles II. found himself secure upon his throne, he began like his predecessors to fleece and punish the citizens, who in return opposed his oppressive measures with great firmness. Party dissensions ran high, particularly against the Duke of York on account of his religion. The king, disliking the proceedings of the corporation, proceeded to still more arbitrary measures, and issued a writ of *Quo Warranto* against the city to try the validity of its charter, asserting that its liberties and privileges were usurped. In the Trinity term following (1683), chief justice Jones pronounced the charter to be forfeited. Eight of the aldermen were degraded, and also the lord mayor, a new one being appointed by the king, to continue during his pleasure. The recorder was displaced by one of the king's partizans, and in fact the city was arbitrarily deprived of all its rights and privileges. Among the public improvements of this period must be mentioned that about the year 1683 the delivery of letters by the penny post was first established in London, by an upholsterer of the name of Murray.

In 1685 an event occurred which has been of more importance to the population and manufactures of the city, than almost any other during these turbulent times; namely the revocation of the edict of Nantes by Louis XIV. This religious persecution drove eight hundred thousand industrious artizans and manufacturers from France into England. The greater part of these refugees, who were principally silk weavers and dyers, and ingenious manufacturers, settled themselves in the neighbourhood of Spitalfields, St. Giles, and Soho. That faithless and arbitrary monarch Charles II. died on the 6th of February 1685; but his successor James II., who remembered the city's attacks upon him and his religion, did not prove much better. Charles satisfied himself with seizing only the city charters; but James attempted to infringe those of all the corporate companies, whom he conceived to be the most effectual barriers against his premeditated introduction of popery. He imprisoned alderman Cornish, and afterwards hanged him opposite his house at the end of King Street, Cheapside.

Finding himself deserted by almost all his subjects, James began to conciliate the citizens, and on the 6th of October, 1688, restored the city charter by the hands of his chancellor Jeffries, and, at a subsequent court of common council, an order was made to restore the liverymen of the several companies who had been deprived of their privileges.

On the flight of James, and the landing of the Prince of Orange, the lords spiritual and temporal assembled in Guildhall, where they signed and published their celebrated declaration, which sealed the liberties of their country. The Prince of Orange was invited to assist in forming a free government, and in settling the administration of public affairs. This public act was immediately followed by an address from the lord mayor, aldermen, and common council, and another from the court of lieutenancy of the city, expressing similar sentiments. Many tumults took place in the city during this state of interregnum; and in one of them the infamous judge Jeffries was discovered in the disguise of a sailor at Wapping, waiting for an opportunity to escape from a country whose justice he had so abused, where he was seized by the populace, and beaten to such a degree, that he shortly after died of his bruises.

On the abdication of James, the Prince of Orange called a council of such persons as had been members of any of Charles the second's parliaments, together with the lord mayor, the aldermen, and fifty of the court of common council, to consult on the settlement of the government; and raised a loan from the city of two hundred thousand pounds to pay the soldiers. The government being finally settled in the persons of William Prince of Orange and the princess Mary his consort, daughter of the dethroned monarch, as king and queen of England, they were proclaimed in the city with the usual honours, and many acts of courtesy passed between the king and the citizens. He restored the charter of Charles II., under the authority of an act of parliament, and granted them another, which constituted certain of the aldermen justices of the peace within the city, and restored the citizens to all their ancient rights and privileges.

In the year 1694 the establishment of the Orphan's fund took place, and that now great commercial and political corporation the Bank of England was instituted. This year is remarkable also for the death of queen Mary, on which occasion the lord mayor and corporation presented an address of condolence to the king. In 1697 the king visited the corporation on his return from Holland after the treaty of Rhyswick, and was received with cordial and sincere regard.

On the death of James II., in France, the French king caused his son to be proclaimed king in his stead, notwithstanding the late treaty of peace with William. This conduct was so highly resented by the citizens, that they presented a very spirited address to the lords justices who governed in the king's absence.

King William dying at Hampton Court on the 21st of February, 1702, the princess Anne, daughter of James, was proclaimed queen, to the universal satisfaction of the nation. On the great victory over the French, her majesty attended a public thanksgiving at St. Paul's, accompanied by both houses of parliament, when the citizens rendered the ceremony more than usually splendid.

In 1703 the city was doomed to another great calamity; for in the night of the 16th of November there happened the most dreadful storm of wind that had occurred in the memory of man. It began about ten at night, and raged with unabated violence till seven in the morning. The damage done to the buildings of the metropolis was prodigious. The newly built and the then building churches were variously injured, and the damage done in the city alone has been estimated at two millions of money. It was on this occasion, when Sir Christopher Wren was informed that all his new steeples had been damaged, replied with the rapidity of thought " not St. Dunstan's I am sure :" and the mathematical architect was right, for it was almost the only one that was perfectly undamaged.

The standards, colours and other military trophies taken by the duke of Marlborough at Blenheim, having been deposited in the Tower, were escorted in grand procession through the city, and put up in Westminster Hall.

The year 1710 is celebrated in civic history, as that wherein fifty new churches were ordered by act of parliament to be erected within the cities of London and Westminster, and two shillings a chaldron laid on coals to defray the expenses; and 1713 for the peace with France, when both houses of parliament came in procession into the city and joined the lord mayor and citizens in a public act of thanksgiving in St. Paul's cathedral.

Queen Anne died on the 1st of August 1714, when the elector of Hanover was proclaimed king, with the usual solemnities, as George I., and was attended by the corporation. He knighted the leading members and dined in public with them on the following lord mayor's day at Guildhall, when he conferred a patent of baronetcy on the lord mayor, and gave £1000 to the poor debtors.

On the threatened invasion, the city displayed its usual loyalty whenever their king behaved with even tolerable propriety, and the rebellion in Scotland under the earl of Mar was but of short duration. The year 1720 will always be memorable in our history for the celebrated scheme of plunder known by the name of the South-sea bubble, which reduced nobles, merchants, bankers, clergymen, lawyers and tradesmen to utter ruin.

In consequence of the great increase of the western suburb of London in 1722, the society called the Chelsea water-works company was established by the authority of parliament to supply them with water; and another useful act for the regulation of party-walls, and water-spouts overhanging public streets, was also enacted. In 1724 Guy's hospital, of which an account will be found in our further pages, was built and endowed by a bookseller whose name it bears, and the city increased in wealth and importance.

On the 11th of June 1727 the king died at Osnaburgh in Germany, and was succeeded by his son George II., who was immediately proclaimed by the lord mayor and corporation in the ancient and usual manner, and publicly congratulated by them on his accession to the throne. The king and queen afterwards dined at Guildhall, where they were entertained with great splendour and hospitality. On the 26th of February 1733 the corporation petitioned the house of commons and obtained leave by act of parliament to stop up and arch over Fleet ditch, and subsequently erected Fleet market on its summit, which has been very recently taken down and converted into Farringdon Street. Fleet market was opened on the 30th of September 1737, and was taken down about the same month of the year 1829.

In 1738 the citizens rendered themselves unpopular with the court party by their strenuous and successful opposition to the general excise laws. The miscarriage of this odious measure was celebrated by public rejoicings all over the metropolis, and the effigy of Sir Robert Walpole, the minister who projected it, was burnt amidst great acclamations. Sir Robert retaliated by calling the citizens *a set of sturdy beggars*, and circulated printed lists of the members of the corporation with the addition of their several trades and companies, in order to bring them into contempt by showing the low nature of the callings of many of them. The citizens again testified their dislike of the premier, by rejecting the senio alderman from the office of lord mayor for voting in favour of the minister.

Until about this period no particular building had been provided for the use of the lord mayor for the time being. Each chief magistrate held his mayoralty either at the hall of his company, or in a private mansion of his own, erected or enlarged for the purpose; of which private mansions there are yet many remaining in the city. This method being found inconvenient, and deficient in appropriate grandeur for the growing importance of the office, the corporation resolved to build a mansion for the use of the lord mayor. After much deliberation the site of Stocks market, which had recently been removed to Fleet market, was fixed upon, and the first stone was laid by the lord mayor (alderman Perry) on the 25th of October, 1739, with great ceremony. It was finished in 1753, Sir Crisp Gascoigne being the first lord mayor who inhabited it. The year 1739 is also celebrated in our history for the establishment and erection of the Foundling Hospital. On the 15th of August, 1741, the king granted the city a new charter, which after reciting the charter of Charles II., and also that of William and Mary (which only appointed certain of the aldermen to be justices, and required either the mayor or recorder to be of the quorum), constitutes* *all* the aldermen for the time being justices of the peace, and makes the mayor, the recorder, and all those aldermen who have passed the chair, of the quorum. This charter is the last which has been granted to the city.

On the erection of the rebel standard in Scotland by one of the Pretender's sons, a message was sent by the king to the lord mayor and corporation, who waited on his majesty with a loyal address. This was followed on the succeeding day by one from the merchants of the city. The principal inhabitants formed themselves into volunteer corps for the national defence, and the members of the inns of court formed themselves into a regiment under the command of the lord chief justice Welles. The corporation subscribed a voluntary contribution of money, in which they were joined by the quakers, who transmitted warm woollen clothing to the army. The close of this rebellion by the battle of Culloden is well known, and the corporation sincerely congratulated their constitutional king on the happy event. The surplus of the money raised by the corporation, and not required for the public service, was distributed to various useful charities.

On the 18th of December, 1755, the court of common council resolved to petition parliament for leave to build a new bridge over the Thames at Blackfriars, which was presented on the 13th of January following, and an act of parliament shortly after obtained for that purpose. This period is also celebrated for the establishment of that useful charity, the Marine Society, by the benevolent exertions of Jonas Hanway.

The city experienced another calamity from the ravages of fire, by the total destruction of the timber bridge that was erected over the Thames, while the last important additions, repairs, and improvements were going on. The colours taken from the French at Louisburgh, were escorted in grand procession on the 6th of September, 1758, from Ken-

* Norton's Commentaries, p. 530.

sington Palace to St. Paul's Cathedral, where they were deposited as national trophies; and on the 16th a number of pieces of artillery and mortars taken at Cherburgh were similarly conducted through the city to the Tower.

The first step towards the many recent improvements in the city may be said to have been taken about this time; for at a court of common council held on the 17th of June, 1760 (the same month wherein the first pile was driven for the building of Blackfriars' Bridge), the committee of city lands were empowered to put in execution an act of parliament passed in the ensuing sessions for widening and improving the several streets in the city. Their first work was to open the east end of Crutched Friars into the Minories. The city gates were also sold and pulled down; and the statue of queen Elizabeth, which stood on the western side of Ludgate, was purchased by alderman Gosling, and set up against the east end of St. Dunstan's church in Fleet Street, from which place it will shortly be removed when that ancient edifice is pulled down.

A few days after the king had been waited on with a congratulatory address by the lord mayor and corporation on the completion of the conquest of Canada by the capture of Montreal, he expired suddenly on the 25th of October, 1760, and was succeeded by his grandson George III.

The new king was proclaimed on the following day in the front of Saville House in Leicester Square, his then residence, in presence of the leading nobility and gentry, and the lord mayor, aldermen, and common council, who afterwards proclaimed the youthful monarch with the customary formalities in the usual places within the city.

No reign has ever been of more importance in our history than that of George III. Whether it be considered for its duration, its military and political struggles, or the great improvements in the public and private buildings that have taken place in the metropolis: improvements, however, that are honourably rivalled by those of our present king.

The mayor and corporation attended the coronation of the king and queen, and their majesties honoured them by dining with them in public at Guildhall. The court of common council erected a statue of the king in the Royal Exchange, and voted portraits of their majesties to be put up in Guildhall; other civilities and courtesies passed between the new king and the citizens, which were not of longer duration than those of their predecessors. On the 12th of August, 1762, the queen gave birth to a prince, his present majesty, and on the 14th the lord mayor, aldermen, and common council, waited on the king with a congratulatory address.

Shortly after this event, the first disputes between the king and the citizens began by the arrest of John Wilkes, under the authority of the now exploded system of general warrants. These disputes continued for a length of time, with little credit and less profit to either party.

Among events of more peaceful and lasting interest, the common council voted £500 to the Society of Arts in the Adelphi, and the king established the Royal Academy of Arts. On the 14th of May, 1770, the lord mayor (Beckford) laid the first stone of the new prison of Newgate, which was the last public act of that eminent person's life, whose merits were acknowledged by his fellow citizens in erecting a bad statue in Guildhall to his memory.

About this period the corporation got into a dispute with the house of commons, whose authority in the city they denied by refusing to execute their warrants, and even by discharging the prisoners that were arrested by them. The house resented this contempt by committing the lord mayor (Crosby) and alderman Oliver to the Tower. The conduct of these two magistrates was so much approved by the common council that a vote of thanks was given them, and a committee appointed to conduct their defence at the expense of the city. At the prorogation of the parliament they were liberated as a matter of course, and the procession from the Tower to the Mansion House partook of the nature of a triumph.

In the year 1777 the angry feelings which had been playing about the political horizon, between the British colonies in America and the mother country, began to assume a more decided feature, and the citizens of London took an active part in the discussions. Warm disputes also arose relative to the right of impressing seamen within the city, which was strenuously opposed by the corporation. The civil war which now raged between England and her American colonies was opposed by the citizens in every possible way, and the opponents of government were flatteringly received in all their public meetings. John Wilkes was elected chamberlain of the city on the 22nd of November, 1779, by a very large majority.

In the following year the city was disgraced by those memorable riots which had religion for their pretended basis. Its principal leader, lord George Gordon, was at length committed to Newgate, and the peace of the city re-established. The lord mayor, alderman Kennett, was tried for his misconduct during these disgraceful scenes and found guilty.

Owing to reasons which have never been publicly acknowledged, the health of the king suffered extremely, and his majesty's mental powers sank under their exertions. This occasioned great and real public grief; for the private virtues of George III. were acknowledged by all classes of his subjects. The corporation and members of the city took part with the ministry in the memorable regency question, which was suddenly put an end to by the king's recovery. On the 10th of March, 1789, the day on which his majesty's recovery was officially announced to the public, the whole metropolis was splendidly illuminated, and all ranks joined in congratulations. On the 19th the corporation presented a loyal and sincere address, and on the 23rd of April his majesty, accompanied by the queen, the royal family, both houses of parliament, and the whole corporation of London, attended a public service at St. Paul's cathedral, to return thanks for his recovery. The procession from Westminster, and the reception in the city, were equally grand and suitable to the occasion.

The next occurrences that are memorable in the city history are the long revolutionary war with France, the peace, the popular regency and peaceful reign of our present king, during which period the metropolis has received those splendid improvements that are the subjects of our other volume. " But it is true," says Mr. Norton in his commentaries, " that many events, exciting intense temporary interest of a political nature, have from time to time agitated the city; but as none of them produced a lasting, if any, effect on its genuine corporate privileges or constitution, it is conceived the history of them may be properly left to those volumes which have treated of them at large."

## St. Paul's Cathedral.

The cathedral church of St. Paul is not only the master-piece of its illustrious architect, Sir Christopher Wren, but is at the same time one of the purest specimens of Italian architecture, and altogether the finest modern Protestant cathedral in Europe.

With the ancient cathedral that stood on this spot, previous to the fire of London, this work has nothing to do; yet the fine Corinthian portico, that was most inappropriately added to its west end by Inigo Jones, must not be passed by without recording the opinion of the celebrated earl of Burlington in its favour, who, when viewing the smaller columns of the present building, exclaimed " when the Jews saw the second temple they wept."

After many accidents by tempests and fire, the ancient cathedral became so dilapidated that the dean and chapter, in 1662, fitted up a portion of the choir for divine service; and in the following year a royal commission was issued under the great seal appointing Wren to be the architect to the proposed repairs, and ordering a survey and report of its condition to be made: for which purpose he commenced taking a series of plans and sections of every part of the structure, and laid down his intended improvements. Among these he proposed adding an Italian cupola to Jones' Corinthian portico, which, with the Gothic spire and pointed arches of the rest of the ancient edifice, would but have increased the jumble of its discordant parts.

To the credit of Charles II., who had improved his taste and knowledge of the fine arts during his exile from his kingdom and his throne, one of the principal objects which occupied his mind on his return was the reparation of that cathedral which had engaged the talents of his father, and grandfather, and their tasteful architect Inigo Jones. During the government of the commonwealth the revenues of the cathedral had been confiscated, its clergy expelled, its ancient monuments profaned, saw-pits dug in various parts of its sacred inclosure, and its venerable choir converted into horse-barracks for the Oliverian troopers.

Charles, on his restoration, expelled the rabble from their quarters in the cathedral, restored the clergy, and commenced the work of reparation with zeal and honesty. John Evelyn was also employed with Wren on this survey, and agreed with him that the expansion of the walls was the effect of decay and stress of the roof, and not a purposed design for increasing an optical effect! as some of the other surveyors reported.

During the discussion of this and other points relating to the cathedral, the deliberations of the commissioners were closed by the awful burning of the greater part of the city, which struck terror into the minds of the whole nation.

After this dreadful conflagration, which has however conferred important benefits on succeeding generations, Wren was appointed one of the commissioners, as well as architect, for rebuilding the ruined city and the cathedral. His first operation was to fit up a portion of the dilapidated cathedral, by way of a temporary choir, in which the dean and prebends might perform divine service until the old cathedral should be repaired, or a new one be built.

The fruitless endeavours to repair the old cathedral continued till the year 1668, when the question was nearly brought to an issue by the falling of part of the western end, which had been fitted up for a temporary choir.    After various deliberations, letters, reports and meetings, Wren's judgment and science prevailed over the narrow-mindedness and self-suffi-ciency of his opponents.    An order was therefore issued by the king in council to take down the walls, clear the ground, and to adopt other proceedings, exactly as recommended in the architect's report.    A portion of the duty on coals, which was levied for the rebuilding of the city and parochial churches, was set apart exclusively to the cathedral.

In the year 1671, and during the progress of the works, Wren found the site so encum-bered with the old materials and rubbish, that it was impossible to proceed with the neces-sary investigation of the ruins, which, contrary to his opinion, the commissioners were still anxious to repair.    He therefore obtained proper authority, sold the old materials, and had the money paid into the chamber of the city in aid of the new building.

It was not till the year 1673 that the futile idea of repairing the old cathedral was aban-doned, when the architect was desired to make designs for an entire new edifice, worthy the honour of the country, and calculated to rival every edifice of its kind in Europe.    Wren, therefore, prepared various designs for the new cathedral, and submitted them to the king and the commissioners.    Finally, one was adopted and the works were began, under a royal commission bearing date November 12, 1673.

Sir Christopher, having appointed his officers, and began clearing the ruins, preparatory to laying the new foundation, the great work of rebuilding, instead of repairing the cathedral, commenced.    The various annoyances that he sustained during its progress are satisfactorily detailed in works which relate to this subject.    Suffice it to say, in this more brief account, that in the beginning of the year 1675 the first contract was made for a portion of the works between the commissioners and the architect on the one part, and Thomas Strong, who also built the church of St. Stephen's, Walbrook, and other public buildings under Sir Christopher, on the other.    Shortly afterward, the king and the privy council approved the designs, and issued a warrant dated the 14th of March, 1675, directed to the commissioners, empowering the architect to proceed and complete his great work.    The first stone was laid the 21st of June following; and in the beginning of April, 1685, the walls of the choir and the stupendous arched vaults below the pavement were completed, as well as the two beautiful semicircular porticoes of the north and south transepts. In 1687 the commissioners contracted for roofing the nave and aisles of the choir, and in 1694 it was finished as far as the stonework, and the scaffolds of this part were struck both from within and without.    Evelyn in his diary records it as being a piece of construction without reproach.    On the 2nd of December, 1696, the choir was opened for divine service on the day of the public thanksgiving for the peace of Rhyswick; and on the 1st of February, 1699, that beautiful portion of the building, the morning prayer chapel, was also opened for divine service with appropriate cere-monies.

In 1708 the works of the cathedral approached so near to completion that on the 23rd of February Sir Herbert Mackworth, in the house of commons, brought up from the commis-sioners a report that the cupola was ready for covering, and it was ordered to be done in the manner now seen. The statue of Queen Anne in the fore court of the cathedral, carved by Bird, was erected during the course of this year.

In the year 1710, when Sir Christopher had attained the seventy-eighth year of his age, the highest stone of the lantern on the summit of the cupola was laid by his eldest son Christopher, assisted by the architect, Mr. Strong the master mason, and the lodge of free-masons, of which Sir Christopher had been for many years the active as well as acting master. In the following year the well known persecution, so fully related in the various pamphlets of the day, was began against the architect, who appealed to Queen Anne without much success.

Thus was this noblest of Protestant cathedrals began and completed, as far as building goes, in the space of thirty-five years, by one architect, one principal master mason, and under one bishop of London; while the Catholic cathedral of St. Peter's, at Rome, occupied a space of 150 years in building, was the work of more than twenty architects, supported by the treasure of the whole christian community, under the protection and pontificates of nineteen successive popes, attended by the best artists of the world in sculpture, painting and musaic, and facilitated by the ready acquisition of marble from the neighbouring quarries of Tivoli.

In the year 1714 the commission for building the cathedral expired, and in May 1715 a new commission was issued, dated the 1st of George I., for the carrying on, finishing and adorning the cathedral of St. Paul. In 1717 the commissioners erected the balustrade round the whole building on the summit of the upper cornice, in direct opposition to the wishes and declared opinions of its architect.

The plan of St. Paul's cathedral is a long, or, as it is architecturally termed, a Latin cross, widened at the west end by projections that form the morning prayer chapel and the court of consistory. In the angles of junction, where the north and south transept cross the naves, are similar projections that form buttresses to the cupola, and serve for vestries and staircases. Each end of the transept is terminated by a beautiful semicircular portico, which for originality of design, beauty of execution, justness of proportion and appropriateness of character, are not surpassed in any modern building.

The intersection of the body of the cathedral by the transepts is formed into a grand and spacious area. The four great piers that support the cupola are boldly perforated, which gives surprising lightness and elegance to the design. The end of the choir is terminated by a semicircular recess in which is the altar.

We will first take a view of this cathedral from the river, where, overtopping the lofty warehouses that crowd upon its base, it looks like a palace of the Cæsars rising from a dunghill. The contrast, however, in a picturesque point of view, is in favour of the cathedral, and serves to enhance its beauties, while it conceals one of its greatest defects, the double tier of stories without, to only one story within. The lower of these stories is of the Corinthian order, after that of the Pantheon at Rome, and the upper of the composite, in which the architect has used his own invention in its composition, without deviating from ancient rules of harmony and proportion.

In this view of the cathedral, the before-mentioned projections in the angles of the inter-section of the transepts and body come beautifully into play, as wings to the elevation of the transept, and correspond harmoniously with the projections of the consistorial court that adjoins the south-western tower.   See plate of the *view of St. Paul's Cathedral from the river*.   The variety of light and shade occasioned by this arrangement of the parts, and the reflection of how necessary these beautiful additions are to the stability of the work, are, when thus considered, doubly pleasing and satisfactory, and raise our opinions of the talent and ingenuity of its eminent architect.

Of the towers I will speak when we consider the western elevation, but in no view does the majestic cupola appear to more advantage than from this situation.   First, the plain *tambour* or base of the peristyle rises above the roof, with plain simplicity, and forms a lofty base to its superstructure, which is sufficiently beautiful at a distance, and absolutely necessary in a nearer point of view to elevate the columns above the entablature of the main building.   This circular stylobate is crowned by an efficient cornice, which supports a cir-cular peristyle of thirty-two Corinthian columns of singular beauty and originality of style. Eight pairs of these columns are connected by walls which contain staircases, and moreover serve as buttresses and points of support to the cupola and its interior cone which rise above them.   The other columns are detached; and the depth of shade produced by the retroces-sion of the interior sloping wall, that forms the back of the portico of the peristyle, forms a contrast of exquisite beauty.

The columns are somewhat loftier or more slender in their proportions than the Vitruvian canons allot to the Corinthian order.   The bases are higher than authorities allow, and the capitals are also similarly elongated, and have but one row of leaves round the bell of the capital under the volutes instead of two.   Such variations from standard authorities can only be ventured upon by a consummate master of the art, who knows the requisites for producing a satisfactory effect.   The lofty situation of these columns diminish the apparent number of their modules in height, by the angle in which they are mostly seen, and columns of a more just proportion would have appeared shortened of their fair proportions at such an height.   So also of the capitals, as to height, and as to the single row of water leaves in-stead of the two rows of raffled leaves as the order requires, the variation is an improvement in effect, at the distance from which they are mostly viewed.   A true Corinthian, at that height would not have produced half so fine an effect as this artist-like composition of Wren.

The entablature of this majestic peristyle is unbroken, and encircles it, as the belt of Saturn does its mighty planet in the heavens.   Above this rises a necessary, and therefore beautiful, balustrade.   Not such a one as the great architect complained of having forced upon his work, like an edging of Mechlin lace, upon the broad cloth habit of an English yeoman; but as a necessary appendage and protection to the circular terrace walk behind it: in fact it is a gallery.

Over and within this gallery rises a circular attic, divided by as many pilasters as there are columns in the peristyle below.   Between them are square sunk panels, some of which

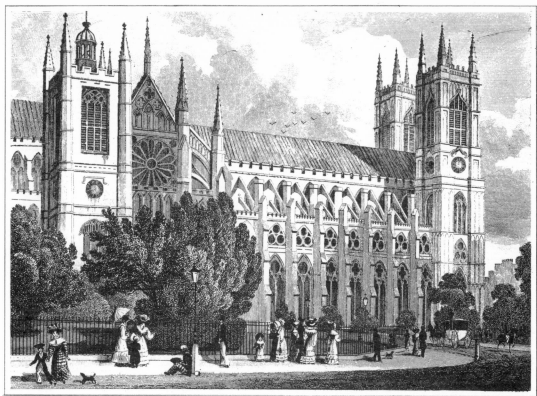

WESTMINSTER ABBEY, AND ST. MARGARET'S CHURCH.

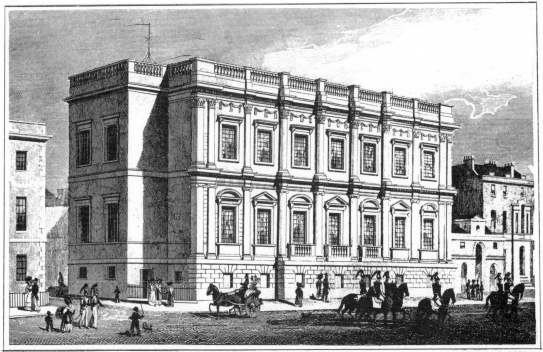

BANQUETING HOUSE, WHITEHALL.

have perforated angles for light and air, and from the cornice of this supplementary order the outer and upper cupola arises of a semi-elliptic form, beautifully ribbed and fluted in massive lead. Alternately the ribs are shortened and give light to the windows within, in a manner much more beautiful, scientific, and effective than the lantern windows that disfigure its majestic prototype in modern Rome.

The summit of the cupola is surmounted by a circular iron gallery, called by the vergers and showmen of the cathedral " the golden," though it does not appear that it was ever gilt. Inside of this is elevated the lofty lantern, which is composed of a stylobate, a kind of quadrangular temple of the Corinthian order, which is surmounted by a well-proportioned attic, covered by a quadrangular cupola and a magnificent ball and cross, which from having been recently renewed by Mr. Cockerell, the present architectural surveyor of the cathedral, and splendidly gilt, shines in the evening sun like a meteor in the distant sky.

The coarsely carved figures of the apostles, which crown the pediment and acroteria of the south transept, are softened by the distance from which they are here seen into more beauty than their clumsy hewing, for it can scarcely be called carving, would seem to warrant. They may indeed be eminently called *architectural statues*, for they are built and constructed with masonic skill.

## WESTMINSTER ABBEY,

the collegiate church of St. Peter, presents a most imposing and splendid specimen of the Gothic style. Sebert, king of the East Saxons, is supposed to have founded it about the year 610, but having been destroyed by the Danes, it was rebuilt by Edward the Confessor, in 1066. Henry III. pulled down the Saxon pile, and in 1245 commenced building the present magnificent structure, which was slowly, but progressively continued by succeeding monarchs. The final completion of this stupendous architectural pile was reserved for Sir Christopher Wren, by whom the two stately towers at the west front were built. The length of the church, within the walls, is 660 feet; at the nave it is 72 feet broad, and at the cross, 195. The Gothic arches and side aisles are supported by forty-eight pillars of grey marble, each composed of slender clusters covered with ornaments. On entering the west door, the whole body of the church presents itself at one view, the pillars dividing the nave from the side aisles being so contrived as not to obstruct the side-openings ; nor is the sight terminated to the east but by the fine painted windows over Edward the Confessor's chapel; and the pillars terminate towards the east by a sweep, enclosing this chapel in a kind of semi-circle. These pillars, as far as the gates of the choir, are filleted with brass, but all beyond with stone. In conformity to the middle range of pillars, there are others in the wall, which as they rise, spring into semi-arches, and meet in acute angles with their opposites, which, in the roof, are adorned with a variety of carvings. At the bottom of the walls, between the pillars, are shallow niches, arched about eight or ten feet high, wherein the arms of the original benefactors are depicted ; round these are their titles, &c., but they are mostly concealed by the monuments. On the arches of the pillars are galleries of double columns, fifteen feet wide, covering the side aisles, and enlightened by a middle range of windows, over which is an upper range, still larger: these, with the four capital windows facing the north, east, south, and west, enlighten the whole fabric in an admirable manner. The choir is a late improvement, and made more commodious for the celebration of divine worship, performed every day at ten in the morning, and at three in the afternoon. Round the choir are eleven chapels.

This structure contains a great number of monuments of kings, statesmen, heroes, poets, and persons distinguished by fortune, genius, learning, and science. Nothing, indeed, can be more solemn than a solitary walk in this mansion of the illustrious dead; nor can any thing be more just and beautiful than Addison's reflections on this subject in the *Spectator*, see page 37, *Jones's Edition*.

## The Banqueting-House, Whitehall.

This building, considered the most correct and elegant in England, was begun in 1619, from a design by Inigo Jones. It is only a small part of the plan of a vast palace, intended to be worthy the residence of the British monarchs, but left incomplete, on account of the unhappy times that followed. The ceiling of this noble room was painted by Rubens, who had £3000 for his work. The subject is the apotheosis of James I. It forms nine compartments. The middle one represents our pacific monarch on his earthly throne, turning with horror from Mars and other discordant deities, and giving himself up, as it were, to the amiable goddess he had always adored, and to her attendants, Commerce and the Fine Arts. A few years ago this ceiling underwent a repair by the masterly hand of Cipriani. The Banqueting-House has long been converted into a chapel; and George I. granted a salary of £30 a year to twelve clergymen (six from Oxford, and six from Cambridge), who officiate a month each.

In the court behind the Banqueting-House is a statue, in brass, of James II., by Grinlin Gibbons. It is a fine performance, possessing grace and dignity in a superior degree. In front of the Banqueting-House, on a scaffold, Charles I. was beheaded, on the 30th of January, 1648—9. His majesty passed from the Banqueting-House to the scaffold through one of the windows.

In Whitehall Chapel have been deposited the eagles, colours, and other trophies obtained from the French during the late revolutionary war. This took place, with great ceremony, on the 18th of May, 1811; and in January, 1816, the eagles taken at the battle of Waterloo were placed here.

## Somerset House.

The original extensive palace of Somerset House, built about the year 1549, by Edward Seymour, duke of Somerset, uncle to Edward VI., and protector of England, formerly stood on this site. It was built in a style of architecture composed of the Grecian and the Gothic: but in 1775 the whole of the structure was demolished, in consequence of an act of parliament; and the present extensive edifice, from a design of Sir William Chambers, has been erected, for the accommodation of all the public offices—those of the Treasury, the Secretary of State, the Admiralty, the War, and the Excise, excepted. The front of

SOMERSET HOUSE, STRAND.

EAST INDIA HOUSE, LEADENHALL STREET

D

this edifice, next to the Strand, consists of a rustic basement, supporting a range of columns in the Corinthian order, crowned in the centre with an attic story, and adorned at the extremities with a balustrade. The grand entrance, by three lofty arches, opens to a spacious and elegant vestibule, ornamented with Doric columns.

The southern front, towards the Thames, is erected on a terrace fifty-three feet wide; and the building, when finished, will extend about 1100 feet. The terrace is supported on a rustic basement, erected upon an arcade, consisting of thirty-two arches, each twelve feet wide, and twenty-four high. The grand central arch is intended for the reception of the royal barges. The length of this arcade is relieved by projections, ornamented by rusticated Ionic columns; and the effect of the whole of the terrace, viewed from the water, is very noble. The public are excluded from this terrace; but it would form one of the most delightful promenades in the world, as it commands a view of a very beautiful part of the river, with Blackfriars, Waterloo, and Westminster bridges. In the court of this structure is a statue of the present king, and at his feet is the figure of the river Thames pouring wealth and plenty from a cornucopia. The rooms of the Royal Society, the Antiquarian Society, and the Royal Academy, occupy a part of the main building towards the Strand. The entrance to these rooms is by the vestibule. Over the door of the Royal and Antiquarian Societies is the bust of Sir Isaac Newton; and over that of the Royal Academy is the bust of Michael Angelo Buonarotti. Somerset Place also contains the following public offices:—the Auditor of Imprests, Clerk of the Estreats, Duchy Courts of Lancaster and Cornwall, Hackney Coach, Hawkers and Pedlars, Horse Duty, Lord Treasurer's, Remembrancer's, Lottery, Navy, Navy Pay, Pipe and Comptroller of the Pipe, Salt, Sick and Hurt, Signet, Stage-coach Duty, Stamp, Surveyor of Crown Lands, Tax, Victualling, and Wine Licence.

## The East India House,

in Leadenhall Street, is distinguished by a stately entrance, beneath a portico of six fluted Ionic columns, supporting a frieze, and two wings surmounted by a balustrade. The tympanum in the centre contains several figures, the principal of them representing his Majesty George the Third, leaning on his sword in his left hand, and extending the shield of protection over Britannia, who embraces Liberty. On one side Mercury, attended by Navigation, and followed by tritons and sea-horses, as emblems of commerce, introduces Asia to Britannia, before whom she spreads her productions. Order, accompanied by Religion and Justice, appears on the other side, and behind them the city barge, with other attributes of the metropolis; near which are Integrity and Industry. In the western angle is a representation of the Thames, and in the eastern, that of the Ganges. Above the pediment is a fine statue of Britannia, with a spear in her left hand, and the cap of Liberty upon it: Asia sits upon a camel in the east corner, and Europe upon a horse in the west.

The interior of this vast edifice, which extends nearly the length of Lime Street, contains the grand court room, the principal ornament of which is the fine design, in bas-relief, of Britannia seated on a globe, on a rock by the sea-shore, looking towards the east; her right hand leaning on a union shield, her left holding a trident, and her head decorated by a naval crown. Behind her are two boys, one leaning on a cornucopia, the other diverting himself among flowing riches.  Female figures, emblematic of India, Asia, and Africa, presenting the different productions of their climes: Thames, with his head crowned with rushes fills up the groupe.   The pictures in this room are Fort St. George, Bombay, St. Helena, Cape of Good Hope, Fort William, and Tellicherry.—Committee room.   An excellent painting of General Lawrence.—Old sale room.   Marble statues of Lord Clive, Sir George Pococke, and Major-General Lawrence, in Roman habits, dated 1764; Sir Eyre Coote, in regimentals.—Committee of correspondence room.   Portraits of Marquiss Cornwallis, Warren Hastings, Esq., the famous Nabob of Arcot, and another Nabob; Views by Ward, of various specimens of Indian architecture, vine of Trichinopoly, Viri.   Malli rock, Bramins' bath at Chillimbrum, east view of Madura, Tippy Colum, Tanks, and the Mausoleum of the Seer Shaw, Choultry of Seringham, south entrance of the pagoda at that place, and various views of Choultries.—New sale room contains several paintings illustrative of India, and other commercial attributes.—Library.   A very considerable collection of interesting and curious Indian literature.   In circular recesses, at the east end of this Library, are busts of Warren Hastings, and Mr. Orme, the historian.   Every book known to have been published in any language whatever, relative to the history, laws, or jurisprudence of Asia is to be found here, besides an unparalleled collection of manuscripts in all oriental languages, and among them Tippoo Saib's copy of the Koran.   Here are also several volumes of Indian plants, and other representations of the arts, manners, and costume of the Orientals, besides the printed books of the Chinese.—The Museum contains the Babylonians' inscriptions, written in what is called the nail-headed character, upon bricks supposed to have been the facings of a wall, strongly cemented together by bitumen.   A fragment of jasper, upwards of two feet in length, is also to be seen here, entirely covered with inscribed characters.  Here are likewise the trophies and the mantle of Tippoo Saib: and, in fact, such a diversity of rare and curious articles, as to render this Museum inferior to none in the display of oriental rarities.   The whole is to be seen for a small gratuity to some of the officers, court days, &c., excepted.

## St. James's Palace

was originally an hospital founded by some devout citizens of London, before the Conquest, and, after being augmented, was rebuilt in the reign of Henry III.   When this hospital was surrendered, with many others, during the rapacious reign of Henry VIII., its revenues amounted to £100 per annum.   Henry demolished most of the old fabric, and on its site founded the present palace, called by Stow, "a goodly manor."   Though the exterior of St. James's is inconsiderable, it certainly is not mean.   It is a brick building, and the entrance to the rooms of state is by a staircase that opens into the principal court next to Pall Mall; at the top of this are two guard rooms, one on the left, called the queen's, and the other the king's guard room.   Immediately beyond the latter, is the Presence Chamber, now used only as a passage to the principal rooms.   The Presence Chamber opens into the centre room, called the Privy Chamber, where there is a canopy, under which his majesty used to receive private addresses.   On the right are two drawing-rooms, one within the other, and at the upper end of the further one, a throne with its canopy; here the king receives cor-

Drawn by Tho. H. Shepherd.

ST. JAMES'S PALACE, PALL MALL.

Drawn by Tho. H. Shepherd.

Engraved by S. Lacey.

THE OLD WHITE HART TAVERN, BISHOPSGATE STREET.

poration addresses : the nearer room is a kind of anti-chamber, where the nobility are permitted to sit down, whilst their majesties are present in the further room, there being stools and sofas for that purpose.   In the grand drawing-room is a large magnificent chandelier of gilt silver, and in the grand levee-room, a very noble bed, with furniture of crimson velvet, manufactured in Spitalfields.   Among the pictures in this palace are those of Jeffery Hudson the dwarf, of Henry Lord Darnly, consort of Mary, Queen of Scots, and father of James I., his hand resting on his brother, Charles Stuart, earl of Lenox, in a black gown; the famous picture of Mabuse, of Adam and Eve, with the curious anachronisms of navels, a fountain richly carved, &c.

On the west side of the court-yard is the Chapel Royal, a plain contracted room, supposed to have been the same used as when belonging to the hospital; the ceiling is divided into small painted squares.   The service is performed here in the same manner as at cathedrals; its establishment is a dean (usually the bishop of London), a lord-almoner, a sub-dean, and forty-eight chaplains, who preach in their turns before the Royal family.   There are also twelve gentlemen of the chapel, two organists, ten choristers, a sergeant, a yeoman, a groom of the vestry, &c.

The other parts of this palace are very irregular in their form, consisting of several courts. Some of these have been appropriated to the use of the branches of the Royal family; others are occupied by the king's servants, or granted as a benefit to their occupiers.

## The Old White Hart Tavern, Bishopsgate Street.

This ancient tavern, now pulled down, bore the date of 1480 upon its front; but it is by no means probable that this was the original building, although the extreme length of windows, and other appearances about it, were indications of its being very ancient.   There is great probability of its having been the hostellary, or inn, belonging to the Old Priory of Bethlem, for the entertainment of strangers, as was customary in those times.   The Old Priory, which was on the east, or Bishopsgate Street side of Moorfields, was given to the citizens of London, for the use of lunatics, by Henry VIII.

## The British Museum

is in Great Russell Street, and was built on a French model, by the first duke of Montague, being originally called Montague House.   This building has, for many years past, been appropriated to the reception of *The British Museum*.   The entrance to the vestibule, on the west side, is under tall arches, and leads to the various rooms for studying and copying.   The staircase and ceilings were painted by Baptiste, Rousseau and La Fosse; those of the former representing Cæsar and his military retinue, attended by chiefs of provinces which he had conquered.   In a compartment are the feasts and sacrifices of Bacchus; in another, the rivers Nile and Tiber are emblematically represented.   The ceiling exhibits the story of Phæton, who, with all the ardour of youth, is driving the sun's chariot, accompanied by the hours, represented as females.   In the first room, this story is completed on the ceiling.   Over the north door, leading to the saloon, is a fine portrait of Sir William

Hamilton, by Sir Joshua Reynolds. The adjoining room, proceeding northward, was the reading-room till the winter of 1803, when, not being deemed sufficiently light, the appendages for study and research were transferred to the next room north, which is surrounded by shelves of books, secured by wire; it has a vaulted ceiling, a handsome cornice, and a large marble chimney-piece, four windows, and several portraits on the walls. The first room on the first floor is ornamented with real fluted composite pillars, in pairs, which have an elegant carved entablature and festoons between the capitals. Over the doors are medallions, surrounded by sphinxes and cherubim dropping flowers. The ceiling is semi-oval, and richly painted, with Jupiter hurling his lightning at Phæton. In the room for the Cottonian and king's manuscripts is an original copy of *Magna Charta*, enclosed in a glass frame, with a fragment of the seal, totally defaced. In consequence of the paleness of the ink, and the increasing illegibility of the manuscript, the trustees permitted Mr. J. Pine to engrave a fac simile of the perfect charter, surrounded by the arms of the twenty-five barons who witnessed the king's act.

It is impossible to give a detail of the various articles with which this museum is so amply supplied. Among those in the hall are to be found enormous skulls and tusks of elephants, a prodigious ram, warlike trophies taken from the French army in Egypt, a Roman tomb, about three feet long and eighteen inches deep, a curious wooden chest, an Indian canoe, many Roman pigs of lead with inscriptions, a fine specimen of petrified wood, a model (in wood) of Blackfriar's Bridge, and another of an Indian carriage. Against the side of the staircase are many Grecian and Roman inscriptions, and upon the stairs, antique fountains, a model of a first rate man-of-war ready to launch, her tender, a large marble foot, &c. Sir William Hamilton's collection is rich in ancient armour, jars, vessels of stone and wood, urns, asbestos, &c., &c. In the second room are some curious mummies, pictures, medallions, specimens of cut paper, vases of flowers, &c., &c.

The Otaheite and South Sea rooms abound in curiosities, natural and artificial, from those parts of the world. Other rooms contain cases of minerals, fossils, shells, petrifactions, reptiles, &c.; the spoils of the Egyptian campaign; baths, coffins, fragments of columns, and Roman statuary. But a volume would not contain a description of every article, of curiosity, utility, and interest, in this vast collection, which has lately received the addition of the Elgin marbles.

In the bird-room are some curious nests; and among the birds, the Egyptian Ibis, and several varieties of the bird of Paradise, the American humming-bird, &c.

In the great hall, the most curious articles are the Egyptian tombs, &c., covered with hieroglyphics.

Formerly, persons wishing to view this national depository of curiosities, were required to leave their names, and attend at a fixed hour on some other day appointed, when they were hurried through the rooms without respect to their taste, object, or curiosity; but now, any decently dressed person may, every Monday, Wednesday, and Friday (Christmas, Easter, and Whitsun weeks, with the months of August and September excepted), between the hours of ten and four, obtain free admission, without fee or delay, on simply writing his or her name and address in a book, and may pass away as many hours as is agreeable, in viewing

BRITISH MUSEUM, GREAT RUSSEL STREET.

CARPENTER'S HALL, LONDON WALL

and studying this immense and valuable collection. An elegant synopsis of the contents of the entire museum, consisting of 150 pages, is sold at the door at two shillings, for those who may choose to purchase, and this serves as a guide to the inspection of every thing there.

The Slonian and Cottonian collections deposited there, have often been described; but the Museum has, within these few years, been enriched by various novelties of matchless interest, and, above all, by the Egyptian antiquities acquired by the capitulation of Alexandria, 1801 ; among which is the famous rosetta stone, containing the triple inscription, the supposed sarcophagus of Alexander, and many fragments of sculpture, coeval with the earliest periods of Egyptian history. Here are also arranged, with the most elegant taste, the large collection of Greek and Roman statues, and other sculptured marbles, formed by the late Charles Townley, Esq., and purchased by parliament for £20,000 ; in number, 313. Another recent addition is the splendid and perfect collection of minerals formed by the late Charles Greville, purchased by parliament for £13,727 : the whole are disposed in cabinets, containing 550 drawers, while specimens of the drawers are exhibited in glazed compartments over them. Besides these natural objects, the literary additions made within these few years are very considerable : thus the Hargrave library, of valuable law books, which cost £4925 ; the Landsdowne MSS.; Halhed's Persian and Sanscrit MSS ; 500 volumes of curious tracts, collected by the late Dr. Lettsom ; Tyssen's Saxon coins ; eighty-four volumes of scarce classics, belonging to Dr. Bentley, with Robert's series of the coins of the realm, from the Conquest to the present time; and for which many of the best patrons of literature, nearly connected with this national establishment, have considerable claims upon the gratitude of the country.

For the *Elgin marbles,* or the *Athenian sculptures,* two spacious rooms were built, in 1816, on the ground floor, adjoining the Townley and Egyptian galleries. The smaller room contains the spirited sculptures recently dug up at Phygalia, together with correct casts of statuary, the originals of which still adorn Athens. On the ground floor of the other room are displayed the Athenian marbles or sculptures, consisting of several statues, as the *Theseus,* &c., &c. : at the height of six feet from the floor, the *Friezes ;* and a few feet higher, the *Metopes :* many of these, being the work of *Phidias,* are exceedingly interesting. United to the Townley and other collections, the suite of rooms here exhibit the finest display of the art of sculpture in the world. The trustees of the Museum recently purchased colonel Montague's complete collection of *Zoology,* as formed by him in Devonshire, and which has been arranged and opened to public inspection. A splendid room has lately been erected for the reception of the valuable collection of books, presented by his late majesty, George IV.

## CARPENTERS' HALL,

at present occupied by Messrs. Kent, Luck, & Co., the most extensive concern of any in the Metropolis in the carpet trade, stands on the south side of London Wall. The entrance to the premises is under a large arch, with four Corinthian pillars at the sides ; and over the centre is a bust of Inigo Jones, and the arms of the Company. Within a pleasant area, intersected by gravel walks and grass-plots, is the part used as the Hall, consisting of a Doric basement, and porticoes at each end, supporting a rustic story, ornamented with cornices and pediments. The original roof was of oak, which has long given place to a stuccoed ceiling, handsomely decorated.

## The Tower of London

stands in a spacious but very irregular area on the banks of the river, to the east of Tower-street-ward. It is inclosed by a high brick wall, having battlements above, and port-holes at the angles below, for the admission of cannon. This wall is surrounded by a broad deep ditch; and what is called Tower-hill, without this ditch, is indeed a rude uneven ground of different heights, which does not appear to have been ever formed to any regular level, since the earth was injudiciously laid round at the first digging of the ditch. Tower-hill is bounded by buildings all around, and some good houses are to be found on the north and west sides.

The Tower at first consisted of no more than what is at present called the White Tower; which, on doubtful authority, has been said to have been built by Julius Cæsar; though other authorities assert it to have been marked out, and a part of it first erected, by William the Conqueror in the year 1076, with a view to secure himself and followers a safe retreat, in case the English should ever have recourse to arms to recover their liberties. That this was the builder's design, evidently appears from its situation on the east side of London, and its communication with the river, whence it might be supplied with men, provisions and military stores, and it still seems a place rather calculated for defence than offence. After the death of the Conqueror in 1087, his son William Rufus in 1098 surrounded it with walls and a broad and deep ditch, which was in some places 120 feet wide; several of the succeeding princes added additional works, and Edward III. built the church. Since the restoration, it has been thoroughly repaired: in 1663 the ditch was scoured; all the wharfing about it was rebuilt with brick and stone, and sluices made for letting in and retaining the Thames water as occasion may require; the walls of the White Tower have been repaired; and a great number of additional buildings have been added. At present, beside the White Tower, are the offices of ordnance, of the Mint, of the keepers of the records, the jewel office, the Spanish armoury, the horse armoury, the new or small armoury, barracks for the soldiers, handsome houses for the chief officers residing in the Tower, and other persons: so that the Tower now seems rather a town than a fortress. New barracks having been erected on the Tower wharf, the ditch was in the year 1758 railed round to prevent for the future all those melancholy accidents which had frequently happened to people passing over Tower-hill in the dark.

The Tower is in the best situation that could have been chosen for a fortress, it lying only 800 yards to the eastward of London bridge; and consequently near enough to cover this opulent city from invasion by water. It is to the north of the river Thames, from which it is parted by a convenient wharf and narrow ditch, over which is a drawbridge, for the readier taking

Drawn by Tho. H. Shepherd.

OLD LONDON BRIDGE, FROM SOUTHWARK.

Drawn by Tho. H. Shepherd.

TOWER OF LONDON, FROM THE THAMES.

HORSE GUARDS, PARLIAMENT STREET.

THE MINT, TOWER HILL

in or sending out ammunition and naval or military stores. Upon this wharf is a line of about sixty pieces of iron cannon, which are fired upon public occasions.

The wharf is inclosed from Tower-hill at each end, by gates opened every morning for the convenience of a free intercourse between the respective inhabitants of the tower, the city, and its suburbs. Under this wharf is a water gate through the Tower-wall, commonly called Traitor's Gate, by which it had been customary, in former and more arbitrary times, to convey state prisoners privately by water, to and from the Tower: but the lords committed to the Tower for the last rebellion were publicly admitted at the main entrance. Over this water-gate is a regular building terminated at each end by a round tower, on which are embrasures for cannon, but at present none are mounted there. In this building are an infirmary, a mill, and the water-works that supply the Tower with water.

The principal entrance into the Tower is by three gates to the west, one within the other. The first of these opens to a court, on the right hand of which is the lion's tower, where a number of curious wild animals are kept. The second gate opens to a stone bridge built over the ditch; at the inner end of which is the third gate, much stronger than the two former; having a portcullis to let down upon occasion, and being guarded not only by soldiers, but by the warders of the Tower. Under this gate, on the right hand, is the drawbridge for foot passengers to and from the Tower wharf.

## THE HORSE GUARDS.

A little to the north of the Treasury, and opposite to the Banqueting-house at Whitehall, is the grand entrance into St. James's-park, through the building called the Horse-guards. This building consists of a centre and two wings, and has an air of solidity perfectly agreeable to the use for which it was constructed. It receives its name from the horse-guards, who, while the king is at St. James's, are here on duty, two at a time being constantly mounted and completely armed, under two handsome porches detached from the building toward the street, and erected to shelter them from the weather. This structure is equally calculated for the use of the foot as well as the horse on duty.

In the centre of this edifice is an arched passage into St. James's-park, and the building over this has a pediment, in which are the king's arms in bass relief. But this arch, as it is the passage of his majesty to and from the house of Peers, should have been more lofty and noble. At each extreme of this centre is a pavilion. The middle face of the cupola presents a dial; and the aperture in the lower part of this, and on the several stages of the other, are well calculated to break the plainness, without weakening the building, either in reality or appearance. The wings are plainer than the centre. They each consist of a fore front projecting a little, with ornamented windows in the principal story, and a plain one in the sides. Each has its pediment, with a circular window in the centre; and the whole has a proper air of strength and plainness.

E

## The Mint, Tower Hill,

is from a design of Mr. Smirke, jun., for the various purposes of coinage, and is upon an extensive plan, as it contains every department necessary for the different operations in coining, and residences for the principal officers. The building is composed of a long stone front, consisting of three stories, surmounted by a handsome balustrade. The wings are decorated with pilasters; the centre with demi-columns, and a pediment ornamented with the arms of the United Kingdom. Over the porch is a gallery, balustrades, &c., of the Doric order. A fire which broke out here in the summer of 1815 did considerable damage in the interior, but happily did not injure the appearance of this beautiful edifice.

On this spot formerly stood *East Minster*, or the abbey of St. Mary of the Graces, founded by Edward the III., in 1349, in consequence of a fright at sea, on his return from France, when he vowed if he got safe on shore he would found a monastery to the honour of God and the Lady of Grace. This foundation, had the intention been effected, was to rival Westminster, but it did not succeed, although continued till the dissolution by Henry VIII. Previously to the building of the New Mint, the old Victualling office here had been converted into warehouses for tobacco.

## The King's Mews, Charing Cross.

This place is of great antiquity, and is thus denominated from the word *mew*, a term used among falconers, signifying to moult or cast feathers. It was used for the accommodation of the king's falconers and hawks, so early as the year 1377; but the king's stables at Lomesbury (now called Bloomsbury) being destroyed by fire in the year 1537, King Henry VIII. caused the hawks to be removed, and the mews enlarged and fitted up for the reception of his Majesty's horses; and the royal stables have till lately been since kept in this place.

The old building being greatly decayed, the north side was erected in the present magnificent manner in the year 1732. This side of the Mews is exceedingly noble, particularly the centre, which is enriched with columns of the Doric order, and a pediment. The smaller pediments and rustic arches under the cupolas or lanterns, are properly subordinate to the principle one, but set so close to the balustrade, that its intention as a gallery is destroyed.—A fine view is presented, both of this building and of St. Martin's Church, by the spacious new opening from Pall Mall east. The buildings of the Mews, originally used as stables, are now appropriated to the exhibition of useful mechanical arts, and manufactures.

## The Admiralty, Parliament Street.

A little to the south of Charing-cross, on the west side of the street leading thence to Westminster-abbey, and nearly opposite to Scotland-yard, is situated the Admiralty-office, a massy building of brick and stone. It has two deep wings, and is entered by a lofty por-

THE KING'S MEWS, CHARING CROSS.

THE ADMIRALTY, PARLIAMENT ST.

tico, supported by four very tall stone columns, with Ionic capitals, to which there is an ascent by a few steps; but this portico, which was intended as an ornament to the building, rather disgusts than pleases, in consequence of the immoderate height of the columns. It is said that the architect who built this portico had made the shafts of a just length, when it was observed that the pediment interrupted the light of some of the apartments, in consequence of which he was compelled to violate every rule of architectural proportion, and carry his columns to the roof of the building. Happily, however, this clumsy pile is concealed from view by a very handsome screen, built by Messrs. Adams, in the centre of which is an arched gateway, over which runs a balustrade. On each side of the gate is a niche, surmounted by a pedestal, on which is the figure of a winged sea-horse. In front of the screen is a colonnade of the Doric order, and at each extremity are three niches, above which are triangular pediments; in one of these pediments is a basso-relievo of the prow of a Roman galley, and in the other the bow of a British three-decked man of war.

Besides a hall and other commodious apartments for transacting business, in the main building, the wings are formed into six spacious houses, and are adapted for the residence of the lords commissioners of the admiralty.

This office was originally held in the large house at the south end of Duke-street, Westminster, which overlooks St. James's Park; but in the reign of King William it was removed to Wallingford House, on the same spot as the present building.

## SMITHFIELD,

as it is generally called, or West Smithfield as it is sometimes termed to distinguish it from East Smithfield on Little Tower Hill, is the greatest market for black cattle, sheep, and horses in Europe; it was celebrated as a horse market by Fitz Stephen, towards the close of the twelfth century. It is also a market for hay and straw. The name is thought to be derived from its being a smooth or level field; but this is mere conjecture. Anciently it was much larger than it now appears, its area having been greatly contracted by the surrounding buildings: the whole west side extended as far as the sheep market does at present, and was called the Elms, from the number of those trees that grew there. This appears to have been the place of execution for offenders in the year 1219. Henry II. granted to the priory of St. Bartholomew the privilege of a fair to be kept annually at Bartholomew tide, on the eve, the day, and the morrow, to which the clothiers of England and the drapers of London repaired, and had their booths and standings in the church-yard within the priory, which was separated from Smithfield only by walls and gates. The gates were locked every night, and watched, for the safety of the goods deposited there; and the narrow street or lane, afterwards built where the cloth was sold, still retains the name of Cloth Fair. This fair, which was at first instituted for the conveniency of trade, was at length prolonged to a fortnight, and became of little other use but for idle youth and loose people to resort to: upon which it was again reduced to the original term of three days, and the booths for drolls and plays in the middle of Smithfield, by the falling of which many people had lost their lives, were ordered to be no longer erected.

In the days of chivalry, tournaments used to be held in Smithfield before our kings and their courts, of which several instances are upon record; and, during the memorable struggle between gloomy superstition and the common sense of mankind, numbers of sincerely pious Christians were here consigned to the flames by the Romish clergy, for daring to dispute the dogmas of the Catholic church.

Spacious as Smithfield is, and although recently enlarged, it is now so surrounded with streets, that the keeping a beast market there is highly improper on account of the dangers the neighbouring inhabitants, and indeed those in all parts of the town, are exposed to from the fury of exasperated oxen. The fellows employed to drive these creatures from the market to the slaughter-houses are much more destitute of rational powers than the harmless animals they treat with a wanton inhumanity that calls for legal restraint; for, however necessary such employments may be, it is far from being necessary that the animals, by an unhappy necessity devoted to death for our support, should be more injuriously treated than the case requires : a consideration that, if we have not sympathy enough to attend to on the real merits of the case, ought at least to be rectified for public safety.

When London had a regular wall and gates, this market was without the wall, though near enough to render it convenient, as slaughter houses were situate in and about Butcher-hall Lane, between Newgate and Aldersgate. It is therefore much to be lamented, that under the great alteration of circumstances, this market is not removed, as contemplated, to some convenient spot about Islington; where it might be formed into a regular spacious square, surrounded by slaughter-houses and other convenient buildings, so contrived as not to be offensive even in appearance. If any material objection occurred to this removal, it may be worth considering whether it is not practicable to erect slaughter-houses in the neighbourhood, somewhere about Chick Lane, or other ruinous parts; and to stop all the avenues into Smithfield during the market hours, except such as led to the slaughter-houses, or to places built for the reception of cattle, till it was convenient to kill them.

Beside the market at Islington, above hinted, another might be established somewhere near the borough of Southwark, to prevent the driving of cattle through the metropolis; and, if these could be carried into execution, Smithfield might be converted into a noble regular square, either for the purpose of trade, or as private dwellings. It is, however, much to be doubted, after all, whether this market, if removed, could be kept detached from other buildings; and that, disagreeable as the neighbourhood to such a place is, let it be placed wherever it may, whether a town would not quickly be collected round it.

### HUNGERFORD MARKET

is situated between the Strand and the Thames. In this place was anciently a large house and garden belonging to the Hungerfords of Fairleigh in Wiltshire. In the reign of Charles II. Sir Edward pulled down the family mansion, and converted it into several buildings, and among them this market, which from its proximity to the Thames, and the convenience of the stairs for gardeners to land their goods at, was principally designed as a market for

Drawn by Tho. H. Shepherd.                    Engraved by T. Barber.

SMITHFIELD MARKET, FROM THE BARRS.

Drawn by Tho. H. Shepherd.                    Engraved by T. Barber.

HUNGERFORD MARKET, STRAND.

vegetables; the plan however failed, and the market never flourished. Here is a good market-house, on the north side of which is a bust of one of the Hungerfords, and over it a French church; but the market house is turned to little account, and the whole is intended to be removed to make way for modern improvements, now become the order of the day.

## The Old College of Physicians, Warwick Lane.

This is a very noble structure of brick and stone, the entrance to which is through a grand octangular porch, crowned with a dome that finishes in a cone. The inside was designed by Sir Christopher Wren, and is very elegant and well enlightened. The central building, which contained the library and other rooms of state and convenience, was the design of Inigo Jones. The ascent to the door is by a flight of steps, and in the under part is a basement story.

The whole front is decorated with pilasters of the Ionic and Corinthian orders. In the centre over the door-case was the statue of king Charles II. placed in a niche; and directly opposite, on the inner front of the octangular porch, that of Sir John Cutler. The buildings that compose the two sides of the court are uniform, and have the window cases handsomely ornamented. The orders are well executed, and the whole edifice is both beautiful and commodious.

The different apartments belonging to this college consist of a committee room, a library, furnished with books by Sir Theodore Mayern and the marquis of Dorchester, a great hall for the quarterly meetings of the doctors, a theatre for anatomical dissections, a preparing room, with thirteen tables, containing all the muscles in the human body; and over all there are garrets to dry the herbs for the use of the dispensary. In the hall were the portraits of several of the most eminent of the faculty; among which were those of Sir Theodore Mayern, physician to James I. and Charles I.; Harvey, who discovered the circulation of the blood; Sir Edmund King, the transfuser of blood from one animal to another; Sydenham, who first introduced the cool regimen in the small-pox; and the celebrated anatomist, Vesalius. The latter was a very good portrait on wood by Calkar. Here were also busts of Hervey, Sydenham, and Mead.

This society's first college, which was given them by Dr. Linacre, physician to king Henry VIII., was in Knightrider Street. They afterwards removed to a house which they purchased in Amen-corner, where Dr. Harvey built a library and a public hall, which he granted for ever to the college and endowed it with his estate, which he resigned to them in his life-time. Part of this estate is assigned for an annual oration in commemoration of their benefactor, and to provide a good dinner for the society. This building perished in the flames in 1666; after which the present edifice was erected on a piece of ground purchased by the fellows.

The faculty having recently removed their college to the splendid new building, Pall Mall East (see *Jones' Metropolitan Improvements*, forming a companion volume to this work), the present structure has been purchased and is occupied by Mr. Tyler the brass founder.

## WHITTINGTON COLLEGE, COLLEGE HILL.

On the east side of College-hill is the parish church of St. Michael Royal, so denominated from its dedication to St. Michael, and its vicinity to the Tower Royal.   It is a rectory, the patronage of which appears to have been in the prior and canons of Canterbury as early as the year 1285, when Hugh de Derby was collated thereto.

The church was rebuilt, and, by licence from Henry IV. in the year 1410, made a college of the Holy Spirit and St. Mary, by Sir Richard Whittington, four times mayor, for a master, four fellows, clerks, choristers, &c., contiguous to which was erected an alms-house, denominated God's house, or hospital, for the accommodation of thirteen persons, one of whom to be chief, with the appellation of tutor.

To encourage so laudable an undertaking, the lord mayor and commonalty of London, in the year 1411, granted a spot of ground whereon to erect the intended college and hospital. But, Sir Richard dying before the accomplishment of the work, it was soon after finished by his executors; who made laws for the good government thereof, by which the master of the college (besides the accustomed rights and profits of the church) was to have an annual salary of ten marks; the chaplains eleven marks each; the first clerk eight marks; the second seven and a half; the choristers each five marks a-year; the tutor of the alms-house sixteen-pence a week; and each of the brethren fourteen-pence.

The extensive charity and numerous acts of benevolence of this worthy citizen could not, however, secure an undisturbed repose to his ashes; for in the reign of Edward VI. the incumbent of the parish, a wicked and rapacious priest, imagining that Whittington's beautiful monument was a repository of something more valuable than his terrestrial remains, caused it to be broken open; but, being disappointed of his expected prey, robbed the body of its leaden covering, and re-committed it to the tomb.  In the following reign the body was again disinterred, and inclosed in lead, and for the third time deposited in its sepulchre, where it remained unmolested till the great fire of London involved its resting place in the common ruin.

While this college remained, the master and wardens of the Mercer's company, who were trustees of it, nominated the rector for the approbation of the monks of Canterbury, being one of the thirteen peculiars belonging to that see.

The old church was destroyed by the fire in 1666, after which the present structure was erected in its stead, and made parochial, for this and the adjoining parish of St. Martin, Vintry, the church of which was not rebuilt.  It is a plain, substantial, stone building, enlightened by a single series of large arched windows, placed so high that the doors open under them.  The tower is divided into three stages, and is surrounded at top with carved open work, instead of a balustrade: from hence rises a light and elegant turret, adorned with Ionic columns, which ends in a regular diminution, and supports the vane.

Drawn by Thos. H. Shepard.

PHYSICIAN'S COLLEGE, WARWICK LANE.

Engraved by W. Watkins

WHITTINGTON'S COLLEGE, COLLEGE HILL.

Drawn by Thos. H. Shepard.

HERALD'S COLLEGE, BENNET'S HILL.

## HERALDS' COLLEGE, BENNET'S HILL.

On the east side of Bennet's Hill stands the Herald's College or office. The old building where this office was kept was destroyed by the fire in 1666; and, by the act for rebuilding the city, the present edifice was to have been begun in three years after. The estimate of the expense for building it amounted to £5000, but the corporation, not being able to discharge that sum, petitioned his majesty for a commission to receive the subscriptions of the nobility and gentry. This petition was referred to the commissioners for executing the office of earl marshal; and upon their report was granted on the 6th of December, 1672. But the commission directing the money collected to be paid to such persons, and laid out in such a manner, as the earl-marshal should appoint, so disgusted the officers that it caused a coolness in them to promote the subscription; in consequence of which, though they had reason to hope for large contributions, little more than £500 were raised. What sums were farther necessary were made up out of the general fees and profits of the office, or by the contribution of particular members.

The north-west corner of this building was erected at the sole charge of Sir William Dugdale; and Sir Henry St. George, Clarencieux, gave the profits of some visitations made by deputies appointed by him for that purpose, amounting to £530. The houses on the east side, and south-east corner, were erected upon a building lease, agreeable to the original plan, by which means the whole was made one uniform quadrangular building, as it now appears. It is a very handsome and well designed edifice; and the hollow arch of the gateway is esteemed a great curiosity.

The college being finished in the month of November, 1683, the rooms were divided amongst the officers according to their degrees, by mutual agreement, which was afterwards confirmed by the earl-marshal; and these apartments have been ever since annexed to the respective offices. The insides of the apartments were finished at different times by the officers to whom they belonged.

The front of this building is ornamented with rustic, on which are placed four Ionic pilasters that support an angular pediment. The sides, which are conformable to this, have arched pediments, which are also supported by Ionic pilasters. Within is a large room for keeping the court of honour; as also a library, with houses and apartments for the king's heralds and pursuivants.

This corporation consists of thirteen members; viz. three kings at arms, six heralds at arms, and four pursuivants at arms. They are nominated by the earl-marshal of England, as ministers subordinate to him in the execution of their offices, and hold their places by patent.

Though these offices are of great antiquity, little mention is made of their titles or names before the time of Edward III. In his reign heraldry was in high esteem, as appears by the patents of the kings of arms which refer to that period. Edward III. created the two provincials by the titles of Clarencieux and Norroy; he also instituted Windsor and Chester heralds, and bluemantle pursuivant, besides several others by foreign titles. From this time we find the officers of arms employed abroad and at home, both as military and civil officers; as military officers, with our kings and generals in the army, carrying defiances and making truces, or attending at tilts, tournaments, or duels; as civil officers employed in negociations, and attending our ambassadors in foreign courts; at home, waiting on the king at court and parliament, and directing all public ceremonies.

In the fifth year of the reign of Henry V. arms were regulated, soon after which that prince instituted the office of garter king of arms; and at a chapter of the kings and heralds, held at the siege of Rouen, in Normandy, on the 5th of January, 1420, they formed themselves into a regular society, with a common seal, receiving garter as their chief.

The first charter of incorporation was granted by king Richard III., who assigned them a proper office and residence. This charter was afterwards confirmed by Edward VI. and queen Mary, the latter of whom not only incorporated them again, but also granted them the messuage or house called Derby-place, which formerly belonged to the earl of Derby, and which was destroyed by the fire of London.

The kings at arms are distinguished by the following titles:—*Garter, Clarencieux, Norroy.*

The office of garter king of arms was instituted by king Henry V. for the service of the most noble order of the garter; and for the dignity of that order he was made sovereign within the office of arms, over all the other officers subject to the crown of England, by the name of garter king of arms of England. By the constitution of his office he must be a native of England, and a gentleman bearing arms. To him belongs the correction of arms, and all ensigns of arms usurped or borne unjustly; and the power of granting arms to deserving persons, and supporters to the nobility and knights of the bath. It is also his office to go next before the sword in solemn processions, no one interposing except the marshal; to administer the oath to all the officers of arms; to have a habit like the register of the order, baron's service in the court, and lodgings in Windsor-castle: he bears his white rod, with a banner of the ensigns of the order thereon, before the sovereign. When any lord enters the parliament chamber, it is his post to assign him his place, according to his dignity and degree; to carry the ensign of the order to foreign princes, and to do, or procure to be done, what the sovereign shall enjoin relating to the order; with other duties incident to his office of principal king of arms.

The other two kings are called provincial kings, who have particular provinces assigned them, which together comprise the whole kingdom of England; that of Clarencieux comprehending all from the river Trent southward, and that of Norroy all from the river Trent northward.

These kings at arms are distinguished from each other by their respective badges, which they may wear at all times, either in a gold chain or a ribbon, garter's being blue, and the provincial's purple.

The kings of arms were originally created by the sovereign with great solemnity on some high festival; but, for a considerable time past, they have been created by the earl-marshal, by virtue of the sovereign's warrant. When one of these officers is created, he takes his oath; wine is poured upon his head out of a gilt cup; his title is pronounced; and he is invested with a tabard of the royal arms richly embroidered upon velvet; a collar of SS. with two portcullises of silver gilt; a gold chain, with a badge of his office; and the earl-marshal places on his head the crown of a king of arms, which formerly resembled a ducal coronet; but since the restoration it has been adorned with leaves resembling those of the oak, and circumscribed with these words, MISERERE MEI DEUS SECUNDUM MAGNUM MISERICORDIAM TUAM. Garter has also a mantle of crimson satin, as an officer of the order, with a white rod or sceptre, with the sovereign's arms on the top, which he bears in the presence of the sovereign; and he is sworn in a chapter of the garter, the sovereign investing him with the ensigns of his office.

The heralds at arms are distinguished by the following titles:—*Somerset, Richmond, Lancaster, Windsor, Chester, York.*

These six heralds take place according to seniority. They are created with the same ceremony as the kings, taking the oath of a herald, and are invested with a tabard of the royal arms embroidered upon satin, not so rich as the kings', but better than the pursuivants', and a silver collar of SS.

The kings and heralds are sworn upon a sword as well as a book, to show that they are military as well as civil officers.

The pursuivants are *Rouge Dragon, Blue Mantle, Portcullis, Rouge Croix.*

These are also created by the earl-marshal, and when they take their oath of pursuivant are invested with a tabard of the royal arms upon damask. It is the duty of the heralds and pursuivants to attend in the public office, one of each class together, in monthly rotation.

It is the general duty of the kings, heralds, and pursuivants, to attend his majesty at the house of peers, and upon certain festivals at the chapel royal; to make proclamations; to marshal the proceedings at all public processions; to attend the installation of the knights of the garter, &c.

These heralds are all the king's servants in ordinary; and therefore, whenever it happens that the earl-marshal is absent, they are sworn into their offices by the lord-chamberlain.

Their meetings are termed chapters, which they hold once a month, or oftener if necessary, wherein all matters are determined by a majority of voices of the kings and heralds, each king having two voices.

These officers, as before observed, have apartments in the college annexed to their respective offices. They have also a public hall, in which the earl-marshal occasionally holds courts of chivalry. Their library contains a large and valuable collection of original records of the pedigrees and arms of families, funeral certificates of the nobility and gentry, public ceremonials, and other branches of heraldry and antiquities.

The arms of the college and corporation are argent, St. George's cross between four doves azure, one wing open to fly, the other close, with this motto, DILIGENT AND SECRET. Crest, a dove rising on a ducal coronet. Supporters, on either side a lion guardant argent, gorged with a ducal coronet. These arms, crest, and supporters are upon the common seal, thus circumscribed, *Sigillum commune Corporationis Officii Armorum.*

## HABERDASHERS' HALL, MAIDEN LANE.

This very handsome ancient brick building, stands on the north side of Maiden Lane and the corner of Staining Lane. The room called the Hall is very spacious and lofty, is paved with marble and Purbeck stone, and wainscoted above twelve feet high. At the west end, where there are two arched apertures, is a screen beautifully ornamented with pilasters of the Corinthian order. The Company of Haberdashers, which is the eighth in order of precedency, was anciently known by the name of Harriers and Milainers, from their dealing principally in merchandise imported from Milan. They were afterwards incorporated by Henry VI. in the year 1467, by the style of "The fraternity of St. Catherine the Virgin, of the Haberdashery of the city of London." At present, however, they are denominated "The Master and four Wardens of the fraternity of the art or mystery of Haberdasher, in the city of London."

This corporation is governed by a master, four wardens, and a numerous court of assistants. It is a livery company, and has at all times been of such repute that they have been entrusted with the benefactions of many pious persons, pursuant to the wills and directions of whom, they pay annually, for charitable uses several thousand pounds.

## SADLERS' HALL, CHEAPSIDE.

This Hall stands at the south-east angle of Foster Lane, and fronting towards Cheapside. It is a very neat building, the inside of which is adorned with fret-work wainscoting, and, though small, exceeds many others both in beauty and convenience. The Hall itself is situated in a small court, with a handsome gateway entrance to the street.

This Company is of great antiquity, as appears by a convention between them and the dean and chapter of St. Martins'-le-grand, about the reign of Richard I. They were not however legally incorporated till Edward I. granted them a charter by the style of "The Wardens, or keepers and commonalty of the mystery or art of Sadlers of London." It stands as the twenty-fifth livery company in the City List, and is governed by a chief or prime, three other wardens, and a court of assistants.

## MERCHANT TAYLORS' HALL, THREADNEEDLE STREET.

The entrance to this edifice is by a large handsome gateway, adorned with two demy columns, the entablature and pediment of which are of the Composite order. Above the entrance are the arms of the Company finely executed in stone. Formerly, within were tapestry hangings, containing the history of their patron, St. John the Baptist, which, though old, were curious and valuable. The great hall is very extensive and, from its size better adapted for meetings of large public bodies than any other in the city, and is therefore occasionally appropriated to such purposes.

Drawn by Tho. H. Shepherd.

Engraved by W. Watkins.

HABERDASHER'S HALL, MAIDEN LANE.

SADLER'S HALL, CHEAPSIDE.

Drawn by Tho. H. Shepherd.

Engraved by W. Watkins.

MERCHANT TAYLOR'S HALL, THREADNEEDLE STREET.

F

The Company was anciently denominated "Taylors and Linen Armorers," and incorporated by letters patent of the fifth of Henry IV., in the year 1466; but several of the Company being eminent merchants and Henry VII. a member thereof, he by letters patent, in 1503, re-incorporated the same under the title of "The Master and Wardens of the Merchant Taylors of the fraternity of St. John the Baptist." They are governed by a master, four wardens, and a court of assistants. Their livery is numerous, and their estates very considerable: out of which they pay to charitable uses, pursuant to the wills of the respective donors, some thousands per annum. They stand as the seventh of the city companies.

## THE LATE FLEET MARKET

### (now Farringdon Street.)

This market, recently removed, and now called Farringdon Market, was erected on the ancient watercourse of the Fleet Rivulet, or as it was afterwards denominated when it became choked with filth, Fleet Ditch.

This rivulet was increased in its course to the Thames by Turnmill-brook, or the river of Wells, and a stream called the Old Bourn, and was formerly navigable as high as Holbornbridge, or, according to some authors much higher; for Maitland relates that an anchor had been found, a short time before he wrote his history of London, at Black Mary's-hole and that it was commonly reported that one had been found at Pancras. However this may be, it is certain that flood-gates were erected in it in 1606, and that after the fire of London it was cleansed, enlarged, and made capable of bringing barges of considerable burden to Holborn-bridge, where the water was five feet deep in the lowest tides. The side walls of this canal were built of stone and brick, and the wharfs on each side were thirty-five feet in breadth and covered with warehouses for storing provisions, coals, and the various commodities brought here for the supply of that part of the metropolis contiguous to it.

Over this canal were four bridges of Portland stone, viz. at Bridewell, Fleet Street, Fleet Lane and Holborn.

In clearing it from the rubbish of the fire, in 1670, many Roman utensils were found at a depth of fifteen feet; and still lower a great quantity of Roman coins, in silver, copper, brass, and other metals, which were conjectured to have been thrown in by the terrified inhabitants, at the approach of Boadicea, with her army of Britons. The silver coins were the ring money of several sizes, from that of a crown to a silver two-pence, each having a snip in the edge.

Besides these antiquities, a number of others were found, marked with Saxon characters, such as arrow heads, spur-rowels of a hand's breadth, daggers, seals, and keys, and a considerable number of modern medals with crosses, crucifixes, &c.

But the expense of keeping this canal navigable proving extremely burdensome to the citizens, it was at last neglected, and became a great and dangerous nuisance, which occasioned the city to apply to parliament for power to arch it over, and make it level with the street; and, having obtained an act for that purpose, the work was begun in the year 1734, and a market house, with other conveniences, being erected on the place, it was opened on the 30th of September, 1737, by the name of Fleet-market.

This market consisted of two rows of shops, almost the whole length of it, with a passage between, paved with rag-stone. In the centre was a turret, with a clock; and at the north end was a large area for dealers in vegetables.

By the act of parliament to enable the citizens to erect this market, the fee-simple of the ground on which it stood was vested in the mayor, commonalty and citizens of London, for ever, with a proviso that sufficient drains should be kept through the channel, and that no houses or sheds, exceeding fifteen feet in height, were to be erected thereon.

On the east side of this market, between Ludgate Hill and Fleet Lane, is the Fleet-prison, which was a place of confinement for debtors as early as the reign of Richard I.

It is a brick building of considerable length, with galleries in each story, that reach from one end to the other, in which are the rooms for the prisoners. There are about 125 of these rooms, besides a common kitchen, coffee and tap-rooms; and behind the prison is a spacious area, in which the prisoners walk, and exercise themselves at different diversions.

## LUDGATE HILL, FROM FLEET STREET.

The grand and truly picturesque view which this point of the metropolis presents to the pedestrian, has induced our artist to select it as a subject for an engraving; and it would be difficult to find one more imposing, and combining so many beautiful objects within so small a focus, in any part of the metropolis. Looking to the right, as you approach Ludgate Hill from Fleet Street, is Bridge Street—spacious, open, and with regularly built houses of the first class, and terminated by that fine object, Blackfriars' Bridge. On the left, and forming a continuation of the same line of street, but crossed by Ludgate Hill and Fleet Street, with their ever-moving multitudes, is Farringdon Street, late the site of Fleet Market, and now forming, under its new denomination, a very wide and handsome thoroughfare. In the front view, the eye catches to the right the obelisk, and, opposite to it, that splendid specimen of domestic architecture, the Albion Fire and Life Insurance Office. Extending in front, on the left hand, a small distance from the Old Bailey and adjoining the London Coffee House, is the neat and slender little spire of St. Martin, which serves to give increased effect by contrast to its colossal neighbour, St. Paul's, the dome of which, and part of the beautiful portico and pediment forming the grand entrance, thus terminates and crowns the vista; the whole bounded on the right and left, as far as the eye can reach, by some of the most elegant shops to be met with in the metropolis.

FLEET MARKET, FROM HOLBORN BRIDGE.

LUDGATE HILL, FROM FLEET STREET.

## CHURCH OF ST. STEPHEN, WALBROOK.

At a small distance from the south end of the Mansion-house, and on the east side of Walbrook, stands the parish church of St. Stephen, Walbrook, which owes its name to its dedication to St. Stephen, the Protomartyr, and its situation. It appears by ancient records that a church dedicated to the same patron was situated near this spot, but on the opposite side of the stream, prior to the year 1135, when it was given to the monastery of St. John in Colchester, by Eudo, Sewer to Henry I. How long the patronage was possessed by this fraternity, or for what consideration they parted with it, does not appear; but in 1428, it belonged to John duke of Bedford; in which year Robert Chichely, mayor, gave a plot of ground on the east side of the water course, 208½ feet in length, and sixty-six in breadth, to the parish of St. Stephen, to build a new church thereon, and for a church-yard; and in the following year he laid the first stone of the building for himself, and the second for William Stondon, a former mayor, deceased, who left money for the purchase of the ground, and towards the charge of the building; the remainder being supplied by Chichely.

Robert Whittington, draper, afterwards made a knight of the bath, purchased the advowson of this rectory from the duke of Bedford, in 1432. From him it passed into the family of Lee, two of whom of the name of Richard, supposed to be father and son, the former being a knight and the latter an esquire, served the office of mayor in 1460 and 1469. The last of these presented to it in 1474, after which he gave it to the Grocers' Company, in which it still remains.

The old church being destroyed by the fire of London, the present edifice was erected in its stead by Sir Christopher Wren; and is considered by many to be the master-piece of that great architect: it is even asserted that Italy cannot produce any modern structure equal to this in taste, proportion, elegance and beauty.

It is a noble structure of stone, but its external beauties are hid from the sight by the adjacent buildings, except the steeple, which is square to a considerable height, and is then surrounded with a balustrade, within which rises a very light and elegant tower in two stages; the first adorned with Corinthian, and the second with Composite columns; and covered with a dome, from which rises a vane.

The principal beauties of this church are, however, within; where the dome, which is spacious and noble, is finely proportioned to the church, and divided into small compartments, elegantly decorated, and crowned with a lantern; the roof, which is also divided into compartments, is supported by very noble Corinthian columns, raised on their pedestals. It has three aisles, and a cross aisle; is seventy-five feet long, thirty-six feet broad, thirty-four feet high to the roof, and fifty-eight feet to the lantern. On the sides under the lower roof are circular windows, but those which enlighten the upper roof are small arched ones. Over the altar, at the east end, is a large beautiful painting of the stoning of St. Stephen, which was presented by the Rev. Dr. Wilson, and put up in the month of September, 1776. The painting and frame together cost 700 guineas. The christening font is of fine white marble, curiously carved.

After the fire of London, the new church of St. Stephen was made the parochial church of this parish and that of St. Bennet, Sherehog, in Cheap ward, the church of which was not rebuilt.

## CHURCH OF ST. MARY WOOLNOTH, LOMBARD STREET.

At the north-east corner of Sherborne lane, on the south side of Lombard street, stands the parish church of St. Mary Woolnoth, which is so called from its dedication to the Virgin Mary, and its being originally situated near the Woolstaple; the syllable *noth*, corrupted from *neath*, signifying near. The Woolstaple was the place for weighing wool, and stood in the church-yard of St. Mary Woolchurch Haw, to the east of the Stocks-market.

This church is of some antiquity, as appears from John de Norton being rector thereof in the year 1355; and, from various circumstances, it is supposed that a Roman temple, perhaps the Temple of Concord, stood originally on this spot; for in digging the foundation for the present edifice, which is one of the fifty new churches appointed by parliament to be erected within the bills of mortality, in the year 1719, there were found a considerable number of tusks and bones of boars and goats, with several models and pieces of metal, some tesselated work, part of an aqueduct, and a great variety of Roman earthen vessels, both for sacred and profane uses; and at the bottom was found a well, full of dirt, which being removed, a fine spring of salubrious water arose, wherein was fixed a pump.

The old church was not entirely destroyed by the fire of London; the steeple escaped the flames, and the walls were repaired. But these, in length of time, falling greatly to decay, it was thought necessary to pull down the whole; in consequence of which, it was rebuilt of stone, in the year 1719, in the manner it now appears.

This is a very handsome structure, but the ornaments of it were till lately hid from the sight by the neighbouring buildings. The windows are on the south side, where the edifice is entirely surrounded by houses; and the front of it, which is bold and majestic, is still so obscured, that it cannot be seen to advantage. On the north side, which fronts Lombard street, instead of windows there are three very large and lofty niches, adorned with Ionic columns, and surrounded with a bold rustic; and over these is a large cornice, upon which is placed a balustrade. The entrance is at the west end, by a lofty rustic arch, over which rises a broad shallow tower, ornamented with six composite columns in the front, and two on the sides; upon this are raised two small towers in front, crowned with balustrades; from one end of which rises a flag-staff, with a vane.

This church is a rectory, the patronage of which was anciently in the prioress and convent of St. Helen's, in Bishopsgate Street, till at the dissolution it fell to the crown; when king Henry VIII. granted it to Sir Martin Bowes, in whose family the patronage has ever since continued. The living was greatly improved by the parish of St. Mary Woolchurch being annexed to it, the patronage of which is in the crown; and, from the time St. Mary Woolnoth was erected, it has been the parochial church for both parishes.

Drawn by Tho. H. Shepherd.

ST. STEPHEN, WALBROOK.

Engraved by R. Acon.

ST. MARY WOOLNOTH, LOMBARD ST.

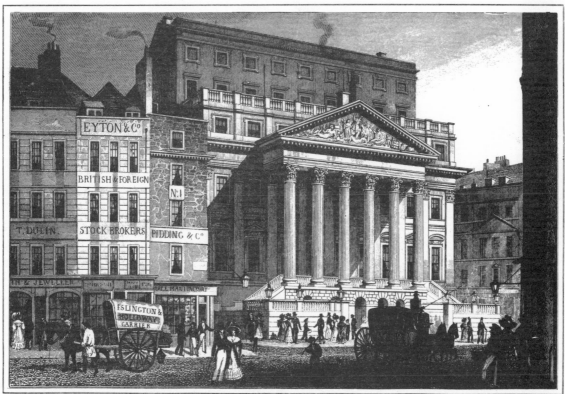

Drawn by Tho. H. Shepherd.

Engraved by W. Wallis.

THE MANSION HOUSE, FROM THE BANK

## The Mansion House.

This is a building of considerable magnificence, though, from its confined and low situation, it has an appearance of heaviness, which, on an elevated spot, in an area proportionate to its magnitude, it would be free from. It is substantially built of Portland stone, and has a portico of six lofty columns of the Corinthian order in the front, the pilasters under the pediment and on each side being of the same order. The basement story is very massy, and built in rustic. In the centre of this story is the entrance to the kitchen, cellars, and other offices; and on each side rises a flight of steps, of very considerable extent, leading up to the portico, in the middle of which is the door that opens to the apartments and offices where business is transacted. The stone balustrade of the stairs is continued along the front of the portico; and the columns, which are wrought in the proportions of Palladio, support a large angular pediment, adorned with a very noble piece of sculpture, representing the dignity and opulence of the city of London, finely designed, and well executed by Mr. Taylor.

The principal figure represents the genius of the city, in the dress of the goddess Cybele, clothed with the imperial robe, alluding to her being the capital of this kingdom, with a crown of turrets on her head, holding the prætorian wand in her right hand, and leaning with her left on the city arms. She is placed between two pillars, or columns, to express the stability of her condition; and on her right hand stands a naked boy, with the fasces and axe in one hand, and the sword with the cap of liberty upon it in the other, to show that authority and justice are the true supports of liberty, and that while the former are exerted with vigour the latter will continue in a state of youth. At her feet lies a figure representing Faction, as it were in agony, with snakes twining round his head; intimating that the exact government of this city, not only preserves herself, but retorts just punishment on such as envy her happy condition. In the group farther to the right, the chief figure represents an ancient river god, his head crowned with flags and rushes, his beard long, a rudder in his right hand, and his left arm leaning on an urn, which pours forth a copious stream; the swan at his feet shows this to be the Thames: the ship behind, and the anchor and cable below him, very emphatically express the mighty tribute of riches paid by the commerce of this river to the city to which it belongs. On the left hand there appears the figure of a beautiful woman, in a humble posture, presenting an ornament of pearls with one hand, and pouring out a mixed variety of riches from a cornucopia, or horn of plenty, with the other; signifying the abundance which flows from the union of domestic industry and foreign trade. Behind her is a stork, and two naked boys, playing with each other, and holding the neck of the stork, to signify that piety, brotherly love, and mutual affection, produce and secure that vast stock of wealth, of various kinds, which appears near them in bales, bags, and hogsheads; so that every thing in this piece is not barely beautiful and ornamental, but at the same time instructively expressive of the happy condition of that great city, for the residence of whose chief magistrate this noble building was erected.

Beneath this portico are two series of windows, which extend along the whole front; and above these is an attic story with square windows, crowned with a balustrade.

The building is much deeper than it is wide; it has an area in the middle, and at the farthest end is an Egyptian Hall, which is the length of the front, very lofty, and designed for public entertainments. Near the ends at each side is a window of extraordinary height placed between coupled Corinthian pilasters, and extending to the top of the attic story.

The inside apartments and offices are exceedingly noble, and elegantly furnished. On the west side of the building is a commodious door for the admittance of private company; and on the east side is the entrance to the justice room. The greatest inconvenience which attends this edifice arises from its being so crowded with houses, especially on the sides, that the rooms are dark; and even in the front there is not a sufficient area to enlighten the building. Notwithstanding this imperfection, it is certainly a very noble structure, and well calculated for the discharge of that business, and the dignity of that magistrate for whom it was erected.

The whole expense of building the Mansion house (including the sum of £3900, paid for purchasing houses to be pulled down) amounted to £42,638. 18s. 8d.

### The Tablet in Pannier Alley.—King Charles's Porter and Dwarf.

Pannier Alley is named from a stone monument erected on the 6th of August, 1688, having the figure of a pannier, on which a naked boy is sitting, with a bunch of grapes held between his hand and foot, and underneath the following couplet:—

> When you have sought the city round,
> Yet still this is the highest ground.

Over the entrance of Bull Head Court, Newgate Street, is a small stone, sculptured with the figures of William Evans, the gigantic porter belonging to Charles I., and his diminutive fellow servant Jeffery Hudson, dwarf to the said monarch, as represented in the engraving.

Jeffery Hudson, when he was about seven or eight years of age, was served up at table in a cold pie at Burleigh on the Hill, the seat of the Duke of Buckingham; and as soon as he made his appearance was presented by the Duchess to the Queen, who retained him in her service: he was then but eighteen inches in height. In a masque at court, the gigantic porter drew him out of his pocket to the surprise of all the courtiers. He is said not to have grown any taller till after thirty, when he shot up to three feet nine inches. Soon after the breaking out of the civil war, he was made a captain in the royal army. In 1664, he attended the queen into France, where he had a quarrel with a gentleman named Crofts, whom he challenged. Mr. Crofts came to the place of appointment, armed only with a squirt. A real duel soon after ensued, in which the antagonists engaged on horseback: Crofts was shot dead the first fire. Jeffery returned to England after the Restoration, and was afterwards confined in the gate-house at Westminster, on suspicion of being concerned in the Popish Plot. He died in confinement, in the sixty-third year of his age. Ashmole's

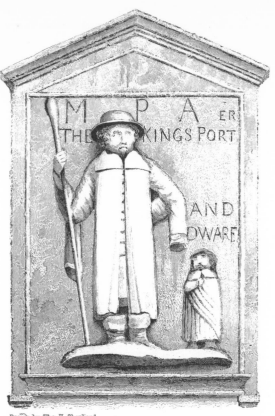

Drawn by Tho. H. Shepherd.

KING CHARLES 1<sup>ST</sup> PORTER & DWARF, NEWGATE STREET.

Engraved by T. Barber.

A FIGURE AND TABLET, IN PANNIER ALLEY, NEWGATE ST.

Drawn by Tho. H. Shepherd.

Engraved by T. Barber

EXETER 'CHANGE, STRAND.

NOW PULLED DOWN

Museum at Oxford contained his waistcoat, breeches, and stockings; the former of blue satin, slashed, and ornamented with blue and white silk; the two latter were of one piece of blue satin.

## Exeter Change, Strand.

Nearly opposite to the Savoy, in the Strand, stood Exeter Exchange, now taken down for the modern improvements. It was originally a handsome building, with an arcade in front, and a gallery above, with shops in both; but, the plan failing, the arcades were filled up, and it since contained two rows of dark shops, with a paved passage between them. The gallery was principally used as lodgings for the shopkeepers; and at the east end was an exhibition of living subjects of natural history. This place took its name from having been built upon the site of the mansion house of the earls of Exeter, a part of which then remained. On this spot formerly stood the parsonage house of the parish of St. Martin; but Sir Thomas Palmer, a creature of the protector Somerset, emulating the infamous example of his patron, obtained it by composition, and began to erect a stately mansion of brick and timber. This afterwards came into the hands of the lord treasurer Burleigh, who finished it in a very magnificent manner, and adorned it with four square turrets. He died here, in 1598; after which it descended to his son, and took the name of Exeter House from his title.

## Church of St. Leonard, Shoreditch.

This church is thus denominated from its dedication to St. Leonard, Bishop of Limoges, in France, and its situation in the hamlet of Shoreditch.

There was a church in this place dedicated to the same saint in very early times, and there are records of a dispute concerning the right of presentation to the rectory, between Henry II. and the prior and canons of the Holy Trinity in London, which being determined in favour of the king, he presented Walter de Wettener.

In the year 1203, king John granted this rectory, by the name of the church of Seordig, to William de Sanctæ Mariæ, bishop of London, as a foundation for the office of chief chantor or precentor of St. Paul's Cathedral, which the bishop confirmed for that purpose; but it was soon after alienated from this office, and conferred upon that of the archdeacon of London, who has held the rectory ever since, and has the right of appointing a vicar: and all the parish is subject to his jurisdiction in ecclesiastical matters, except the liberties of Hoxton and Norton-folgate, which belong to the dean and chapter of St. Paul's.

The old church, which was a very mean heavy pile, stood till the year 1735, when the inhabitants having the year before applied to parliament, it was pulled down, and the present light and elegant edifice was soon after erected in its stead.

To this church there is an ascent by a double flight of plain steps, which lead to a portico of the angular kind, supported by four Doric columns, and bearing an angular pediment. The body of the edifice is plain, but well enlightened, and the steeple light, elegant and lofty. The tower at a proper height has a series of Ionic columns, and on their entablature are scrolls which support as many Corinthian columns on pedestals, and supporting a dome from whose crown rises a series of columns of the Composite order, on the entablature of which rests the spire, standing upon four balls, which give it an additional air of lightness, and on the top is a ball and vane.

## Church of St. Clement Danes, Strand.

At a small distance from Temple-bar, on the north side of the Strand, is situated the parish church of St. Clement Danes.

The first part of this name is derived from its dedication to St. Clement, a disciple of St. Peter, the apostle, but the latter part has been always an object of conjecture. Baker says, it derived this name from having been the place of re-interment of Harold, whose brother Hardicanute had caused his body to be dug up and thrown into the Thames, where it was found by a fisherman, "who buried it in the church-yard of St. Clement, without Temple-bar, then called the church of the Danes." William of Malmesbury mentions a church here, before the arrival of the Danes, which, he says, they burnt together with the monks and abbot, and that they continued their savage and sacrilegious fury throughout the land. He then goes on, " desirous at length to return to Denmark, they were about to embark, when they were, by the just judgment of God, all slain at London, in a place which has since been called the church of the Danes." There is also another reason given for the denomination of this church, namely, that when most of the Danes were driven out of this kingdom, those few that remained, being married to English women, were obliged to live between the Isle of Thorney (Westminster), and Caer Lud (Ludgate), where they built a synagogue, which was afterwards consecrated and called " Ecclesia Clementis Danorum." This is the account given by Fleetwood, the antiquary, recorder of London, to the lord-treasurer Burleigh, who resided in this parish.

The old church was taken down in 1680, and the present structure erected in 1682, under the direction of Sir Christopher Wren; but the steeple was not added to it for some years.

It is a very handsome structure, built entirely of stone. The body of it is enlightened by two series of windows; the lower plain, but the upper well ornamented; and the termination is by an attic, whose pilasters are crowned with vases. The entrance, on the south side, is by a portico, to which there is an ascent of a few steps: the portico is covered with a dome, supported by Ionic columns. On each side the base of the steeple, in the west front, is a small square tower with its dome. The steeple is carried to a great height in several stages; where it begins to diminish, the Ionic order takes place, and its entablature supports vases. The next stage is of the Corinthian order, and above that stands the Composite, supporting a dome, which is crowned with a smaller one, from whence rises the ball and its vane.

This church is a rectory, the patronage of which was anciently in the Knights Templars; but, after passing through several hands, it at length came to the earls of Exeter, in whom it still remains. The length of this church is ninety-six feet, its breadth sixty-three, and its height to the roof forty-eight feet; and the altitude of the steeple is about 140 feet.

Drawn by Tho. H. Shepherd.

ST. LEONARD'S, SHOREDITCH.

Engᵈ by S. Lacy.

ST. CLEMENT DANES, STRAND.

Drawn by Tho. H. Shepherd.

Engᵈ by J. B. Allen.

ST. DUNSTAN IN THE WEST, FLEET STREET.

G

### Church of St. Dunstan, in the West, Fleet Street.

This church is so called to distinguish it from another in Tower Ward, dedicated to the same saint, and called St. Dunstan in the East.

It is a very ancient foundation, in the gift of the Abbot and Convent of Westminster, who, in the year 1237, gave it to King Henry III., towards the maintenance of the foundation of the house called the Rolls, for the reception of converted Jews. It was afterwards conveyed to the Abbot and Convent of Alnwick, in Northumberland, in which patronage it continued till that religious house was suppressed by King Henry VIII. Edward VI. granted the advowson of this church, under the name of a vicarage, to Lord Dudley. Soon after which, the rectory and vicarage were granted to Sir Richard Sackville, and the impropriation has continued ever since in private hands.

This is one of the churches that escaped the fire of London, the flames having stopped within three doors of it; since which time, however, it has been frequently repaired, and the inconveniences that formerly arose from a number of small shops, or sheds, that stood in the front of it have been remedied by their removal.

The church, which is built of brick and stone, consists of a large body, with a very disproportionate square tower. It is ninety feet in length, sixty feet in breadth, thirty-six feet in height, to the roof, and the altitude of the turret is 100 feet. The dial of the clock projects over the street, on the south side of the church, and the clock-house is formed of an Ionic porch, containing two figures erect, carved and painted, and as large as life, which, with knotted clubs, alternately strike the quarters on two bells hung between them: these figures were set up in the year 1671. In a niche at the east end of the church is the statue of Queen Elizabeth, which formerly stood on Ludgate, and, when that gate was taken down, was purchased by alderman Gosling, and placed in its present situation. It is in contemplation to take down the present church, and build another either on its site, or some part contgiuous.

The ground in this neighbourhood appears to have been anciently of a marshy nature, or else within the course of the tide; for, in digging at the end of Chancery lane, and further eastward in Fleet street, in the year 1595, a stone pavement was discovered at the depth of four feet from the surface, which was supported by a number of piles, driven very close to each other.

### Trinity House, Tower Hill.

This is a handsome stone-fronted building, consisting of a main body and two wings; the latter of which project a little. The basement story is of massy rustic work, and in the centre is the entrance, which, as well as all the windows in this story, is arched. On this rises the principal story, of the Ionic order, supporting a plain entablature, on which rests a sloping roof. In the centre of the main body are the arms of the corporation, and, on each side, a circular medallion, containing the profiles of George III. and his consort. Above the windows, in the two wings, are square medallions, in which are groups of genii, exhibiting different nautical instruments, with representations of the four principal light-houses on the coast. This building is seen to great advantage, by being placed on a rising ground, and having an extensive area in front.

## Town Hall, Borough High Street.

At the south extremity of the Borough High Street, formerly stood a church dedicated to St. Margaret on the Hill, the site of which is now occupied by a court of justice, or Town Hall. It is a modern built brick edifice, the front of which is ornamented with stone, and consists of a rustic basement story, above which are a series of Ionic pilasters, and the whole is crowned with a handsome balustrade.

The steward for the city of London holds a court of record here every Monday, for all debts, damages, and trespasses, within his limits.

Besides this court, there are three court-leets held in the borough, for its three liberties, or manors, viz., the great liberty, the guildable, and the king's manor; in which are chosen constables, aleconners, &c.

## Church of St. Paul, Covent Garden.

This church, which is dedicated to St. Paul the Apostle, is remarkable for its majestic simplicity. It is said, on the authority of Lord Oxford, that when the earl engaged Inigo Jones to build it, he told him he wanted a chapel, not much better than a barn; to which the architect replied, "well, then, you shall have the handsomest barn in England." In the front is a plain but noble portico, of the Tuscan order, executed in the most masterly manner; the columns are massy, and the intercolumniation large. Though as plain as possible, the building is happily proportioned. The walls being of brick, were cased with stone about the year 1788, at an expense of £11,000, including the other repairs at that time. The windows are of the Tuscan order, to correspond with the portico, and the altar-piece is adorned with eight fluted columns of the Corinthian order. The roof was entirely of wood, and considered a most inimitable piece of architecture, being supported by the walls alone. Unfortunately, this was destroyed by a fire, which consumed the whole interior of the church, on the 17th of September, 1795; since which it has been rebuilt, and is very little different from the original structure.

The patron of this parish enjoys the unusual privilege of nominating a churchwarden; the rector nominates another, and the parishioners elect a third.

The election of members to serve in parliament, for the city of Westminster, is held in front of this church, on temporary hustings erected for that purpose.

## Buckingham Water Gate, Strand.

On the south side of the Strand are avenues to York Buildings, so called from having been the residence of the archbishops of York, till archbishop Matthew, in the reign of

TRINITY HOUSE, TOWER HILL.

TOWN HALL, BOROUGH HIGH STREET.

Drawn by Tho. H. Shephard.

ST. PAUL'S, COVENT GARDEN

Drawn by Tho. H. Shephard.

BUCKINGHAM WATER GATE, STRAND

James I., exchanged it with the crown for several manors. It was the residence of lord chancellors Egerton and Bacon, after which it was granted to George Villiers, duke of Buckingham, who rebuilt it most magnificently. In 1648 the parliament bestowed it on general Fairfax, whose daughter and heiress marrying the second duke of Buckingham, the house reverted to its true owner, who resided here several years subsequent to the Restoration, but at length disposed of it, and laid several streets out on the site, which go by his name and titles,—" George Street, Villiers' Street, Duke Street, Off Alley, and Buckingham Street."

At the bottom of these streets, next the river, is a very elegant stone WATER GATE to the stairs. The design of this gate is greatly admired, and is every way worthy of its architect, Inigo Jones. It is of the Tuscan order, and ornamented with rustic work, which can never be better introduced, than in buildings by the side of water, and indeed it is a question, with some judges, whether it ought to be made use of any where else. This gate is considered a most perfect piece of building, of such equal and harmonious parts, and so appropriately embellished, that nothing can justly be censured or added.

The stairs have for a considerable time fallen into disuse, from the causeway to them having been so long neglected as to render the approach of the boats almost impossible, except at high water. Near these stairs was erected the high wooden tower, called York Building's Water Works, for raising water for the supply of that neighbourhood. The company, to whom it belonged, was incorporated by act of parliament in the year 1691.

## STATUE OF GUY, EARL OF WARWICK.—LONDON STONE.

The memory of the above mentioned earl is still preserved by a stone statue, restored in 1817, in front of the house at the West corner of Warwick Lane, in Newgate Street. The Lane derives its name from the Inn or house of Richard Nevil, the king-making earl of Warwick. Speaking of his coming to London, to the convention of 1458, Stow says, he was accompanied by " six hundred men, all in red jackets imbroidered with ragged staves before and behind, and was lodged in Warwicke Lane: in whose house there was often six oxen eaten at a breakfast, and every taverne was full of his meate, for hee that had anie acquaintance in that house, might have there so much of sodden and rost meate as he could pricke and carry upon a long dagger."

Against the south wall of St. Swithin's church, Cannon Street, is placed the famous old stone, called London Stone. This stone was much worn away before the fire of London; but it is now cased over with a new stone, cut hollow, so that the old one may be seen.

This stone, which has been carefully preserved for many ages, is of great antiquity, as appears from its being mentioned by the same name so early as in the time of Ethelstan, king of the West Saxons. It formerly stood nearer the channel opposite the same place; and, being fixed upright in the ground, was so well fastened, with bars of iron, that it was perfectly secured from receiving any damage by carriages.

The antiquity of this stone cannot be traced; but, from the most reasonable conjecture, it is supposed to be of Roman origin; for, as the ancient Roman colony extended, from the river Thames, no higher than Cheapside, and Watling Street was the principal street, or Prætorian way, it has been supposed, with great probability, that this stone was the centre, from whence they measured the distances to their several stations throughout England, more especially as these distances coincide very exactly.

Another conjecture is, that as this street was anciently the principal one in the city, as Cheapside is at present, London stone might have been the place where public proclamations and notices were given to the citizens. This conjecture has indeed some argument to support it; for, in the year 1450, when Jack Cade, the Kentish rebel, came through Southwark into London, he marched to this stone, where was a great concourse of people, among whom was the lord mayor. On this stone Jack Cade struck his sword, and said, "Now is Mortimer lord of this city."

It is also said that this stone was set up for the tendering and making of payments by debtors to their creditors, at their appointed days, till, in after times, they were usually made at the font in St. Paul's church, or the Royal Exchange.

These, however, are but conjectures; nor can we say more than that is is very singular so much care should have been taken to preserve the stone, and so little to preserve the history of its origin.

## St. John's Gate, Clerkenwell.

Where St. John's Square is now situated, stood the house or hospital of St. John of Jerusalem, which was founded by Jordan Briset, and Muriel, his wife, who, for that purpose, purchased of the prioress and Nuns of Clerkenwell ten acres of land, on which he erected the said hospital, about the year 1110; but the church belonging to it was not dedicated to St. John the Baptist, till the year 1185.

By the profuse liberality of bigots and enthusiasts, this foundation became the chief seat in England belonging to the Knights Hospitallers; and to such a degree of wealth and honour did they arrive, that their prior was esteemed the first baron in the kingdom, and in state and grandeur vied with the king.

Such was the antipathy of the populace to these imperious knights, that the rebels of Kent and Essex, under the conduct of Wat Tyler and his rabble, in the year 1381, consumed this stately edifice by fire. However, it was afterwards rebuilt in a much more magnificent manner, and continued upon its former system, till it was entirely suppressed by Henry VIII. in the year 1541.

Soon after this foundation was suppressed, the building was converted into a repository of martial stores, and the Royal hunting equipage; and to these purposes it was applied till the year 1550; when Edward Seymour, duke of Somerset and protector of the kingdom, caused the church with its lofty and beautiful steeple, which Stow says was " graven gilt, and inameled, to the great beautifying of the city, and passing all other that he had seen," to be demolished, and the stones thereof used in building his magnificent palace of Somerset House. The priory adjacent was partly restored by queen Mary; the remains of the choir, and some side chapels, were repaired by cardinal Pole, and Sir Thomas Tresham was appointed prior; but it was again suppressed by Elizabeth.

Drawn by Tho. H. Shepherd.

GUY EARL OF WARWICK, WARWICK LANE.

Engraved by J. B. Allen.

LONDON STONE, CANNON STREET.

Drawn by Tho. H. Shepherd.

Engraved by J. B. Allen.

ST. JOHN'S GATE, CLERKENWELL.

CHEAPSIDE, POULTRY, & BUCKLERSBURY.

ALDGATE

Part of the site of this priory is now occupied by St. John's Square, an irregular open place. The southern entrance into it is by the magnificent old gate of the priory, which is still called St. John's Gate. It has a lofty Gothic arch, and on each side, over the gate, are several escutcheons of arms, carved, under which were formerly inscriptions; but these, by length of time, are now entirely defaced. At the north-east corner of the square is the parish church of St. John, Clerkenwell, which was at first erected as a chapel of ease to St. James's. It is a plain brick building, with stone corners; and the patronage of it is in the gift of the lord chancellor.

## CHEAPSIDE, POULTRY, AND BUCKLERSBURY.

The imposing and interesting view which this spot presents to the eye of the perambulator, at once characteristic of Metropolitan activity, commerce, and opulence, renders it truly worthy of the pencil of the artist, whose correct and happy delineation is instantly recognized by all acquainted with the original.

The fine mansion to the right of the foreground is occupied by, and the property of, one who may be truly considered as a personification of the above mentioned characteristics of the place, and whose talents and indefatigable exertions have been crowned with merited success. It was originally built by Sir Christopher Wren, as a residence for the then lord mayor, and since it was purchased by its present occupant, Mr. Tegg, has been restored at a very great expense to its pristine architectural beauty. It must be now pretty well known as a mart for literature throughout the reading world, since the most extensive trade of the Metropolis, in that branch of commerce, is there conducted on such liberal principles as to ensure priority and success. Nearly opposite is the fine old entrance to Mercer's Hall, of which a view has been given in a preceding part of this work.

The vista from this point, where Cheapside, an epitome of the wealth and splendour of the metropolis, terminates, is perhaps unequalled; and the gay and ever moving throng of pedestrians and carriages give indescribable life and animation to the scene. Diverging to the right is Bucklersbury, corrupted from Bucklesbury, and which was named after one Buckle, lord of the manor, who resided and kept his court in a spacious stone building, called the Old Barge, from such a sign being in front of it. The site of his mansion is now occupied by Barge Yard; to which place, according to tradition, boats and barges came from the Thames, up the Walbrook, when its navigation was open. Directly front, and in continuation of this great leading thoroughfare, is the Poultry, from the end of which Lombard Street diverges by a trifling inclination to the right, and Cornhill to the left.

## ALDGATE

Somewhat similar to our preceding View, for bustle and activity, but deficient in architectural splendour and variety, is this part of the High Street, Aldgate.

The name is a corruption of Ealdgate, signifying Old Gate, being originally one of the four principal gates of the city, and that through which the Roman vicinal way led to the

*Trajectus*, or ferry at Old-ford. The earliest mention we can find of it is in a charter granted by King Edgar, about the year 967.

This gate, being in a very ruinous condition, was pulled down in the year 1606, and rebuilt; but it was not completed till 1609.

In digging the foundation, several Roman coins were discovered, resemblances of two of which Mr. Bond, one of the surveyors of the work, caused to be cut in stone, and placed on each side of the east front, where they remained till the demolition of the gates.

In a large square, on the same side of the gate, was placed the statue of king James I. in gilt armour, with a golden lion, and a chained unicorn, both couchant at his feet.

On the west side of the gate was a figure of Fortune, gilt, and standing on a globe, with a prosperous sail spreading over her head, under which was carved the king's arms, with the motto, *Dieu et mon Droit*, and a little below it, *Vivat Rex:* somewhat lower, on the south side, stood Peace, with a dove perched on one hand and a gilded wreath in the other. On the north side of the gate was the figure of Charity, with a child at her breast, and another in her haud. On the top of it was a vane, supported by a gilt sphere, on each side of which stood a soldier holding a bullet in his hand, on the top of the upper battlements. Over the arch of the gate were carved the following words:

*Senatus Populusque* Londinensis

Fecit 1609,

HUMPHREY WELD, *Maior.*

There were two posterns through this gate; that on the south side being made as late as the year 1734. There were likewise apartments over it, which were appropriated to the use of one of the lord mayor's carvers, but had of late years been used as a charity-school.

### SOUTH SEA HOUSE, THREADNEEDLE STREET.

At the north east extremity of Threadneedle Street is the South Sea House. This house stands upon a large extent of ground, running backward as far as Old Broad Street, facing the church of St. Peter-le-Poor. The back front was originally the Excise-office, and then the South Sea Company's office, and it is now distinguished by the name of the Old South Sea House. It is a substantial and handsome building of brick, ornamented with Portland stone. The front, in Threadneedle Street, is very beautiful. The entrance is a gateway, leading into a court, with a piazza, formed of Doric pillars. The walls are remarkably solid, and the interior is very commodious: one room, in particular, is peculiarly lofty, spacious, and elegant.

### EXCISE OFFICE, BROAD STREET.

This handsome, plain, stone building, stands on the east side of Broad Street. It is four stories in height, with an entrance through the middle of it into a large yard, in which is

SOUTH SEA HOUSE, THREADNEEDLE ST.

EXCISE OFFICE, BROAD ST.

H

another building of brick, nearly the size of the principal one. The front building stands on the site of ten almshouses, founded by Sir Thomas Gresham in 1575; and the back one, with the yard, occupies the space on which Gresham College formerly stood. Part of it is in Bishopsgate ward. From the centre of both buildings are long passages and staircases to the galleries, in which are the numerous offices for the commissioners and clerks in the different departments of the excise.

This is the principal office of excise in his majesty's dominions, and the business of it is conducted by nine commissioners, under whom are a great number of officers, both within and without the house. These receive the duties on beer, ale, and spirituous liquors; on tea, coffee, and chocolate; on malt, hops, soap, starch, candles, paper, vellum, parchment, and other exciseable commodities: for the surveying and collecting of which duties a great number of out-door officers are employed in different districts or divisons, throughout the kingdom, to prevent frauds and losses. Before these commissioners all cases of seizure for frauds, committed in the several branches of the revenue under their direction, are tried: and from their determination there is no appeal except to the commissioners of appeal, who are part of themselves, for a rehearing.

### SIR PAUL PINDAR'S HOUSE, BISHOPSGATE STREET.

Nearly opposite to Widegate Street, in Bishopsgate Street, are the remains of the residence of Sir Paul Pindar, for some years past occupied as a liquor shop. Its original ancient Gothic front has been strangely metamorphosed, being stuccoed, coloured, &c. The original owner who was one of the richest merchants of his time, was ruined by his conscientious attachment to Charles I. He died in 1650, aged 84. An old house still remaining in half Moon Street, running from Bishopsgate Street towards Long Alley, and which is easily distinguished by its raised figuring upon the front, was, according to tradition, that of Sir Paul Pindar's gardener.

### MERCER'S HALL AND CHAPEL, CHEAPSIDE,

is situated on the spot that was once occupied by an hospital dedicated to St. Thomas of Acors, or Acons, and was founded for a master and brethren of the Augustine order, by Thomas Fitz-Theobald de Heili, and his wife Agnes, sister to Thomas-a-Becket, who was born in the reign of King Henry II.

On the dissolution of religious houses, in the reign of Henry VIII., this hospital was purchased by the Mercers' Company, who had the gift of the mastership, and was opened by them, immediately, under the name of Mercer's Chapel. They were both destroyed by the fire of London, soon after which the present structure was erected.

The front of this building, next Cheapside, is exceedingly handsome; the door-case is enriched with the figures of two Cupids, mantling the Company's arms, with festoons, &c. Over the door is a balcony, adorned with two pilasters of the Ionic order, and a pediment, with the figures of Faith, Hope, and Charity, and other enrichments. The inner-court is adorned with piazzas, formed of columns of the Doric order. The hall-room and great parlour are wainscoted with oak, and ornamented with Ionic pilasters; and the ceiling is beautifully decorated with fret-work. The chapel is neatly wainscoted, and paved with black and white marble.

The entrance into this hall, from Ironmonger Lane, is decorated with rustic stone pillars, supporting an arch, on the key-stone of which are the Company's arms. The door is panelled, and the upper compartment, on each side, is also filled with the arms carved in wood.

## Skinners' Hall, Dowgate Hill.

On the west side of Dowgate Hill is Skinners' Hall, a very handsome edifice, built with bricks of different colours: the hall room is elegantly wainscoted with oak, and the great parlour is panelled with cedar. The entrance to this building is through an arched doorway, in a modern stone-fronted building, in which are the offices for the clerk and other persons belonging to the Company. In the beginning of the last century, the East India Company had the use of this hall, for which they paid the Company three hundred pounds per annum.

## Church of St. Dionis, Backchurch.

Near the south-west corner of Lime Street, behind the houses in Fenchurch Street, stands the parish church of St. Dionis, Backchurch. It owes its name to being dedicated to St. Dionis, Dionysius, or Dennis, an Athenian areopagate, or judge, who, being converted to Christianity, and afterwards made bishop of Athens, travelled into France, where he suffered martyrdom, by being beheaded, and has been since adopted as the patron saint of the French nation. The epithet of Backchurch was added, from its situation behind a row of houses, to distinguish it from the church of St. Gabriel, which, before the fire in 1666, stood in the middle of Fenchurch Street; wherefore those churches were anciently known by no other appellation but those of Fore and Backchurch.

The oldest authentic mention of this church is in the year 1288, when Reginald de Standon was rector of it. It is one of the thirteen peculiars in the city, belonging to the archbishop of Canterbury. The patronage was formerly in the prior and canons of that church; but, at the dissolution of the priory, it was conferred upon the dean and chapter, who have remained patrons ever since.

The old edifice was destroyed in 1666, and the present structure was erected in 1674, except the steeple, which was not added until ten years after. It is a plain stone building, of the Ionic order, with a tower and turret, in which are ten bells and a set of chimes. The length of the church is sixty-six feet, its breadth fifty-nine, and the height of the roof thirty-four feet; that of the tower and turret is ninety feet.

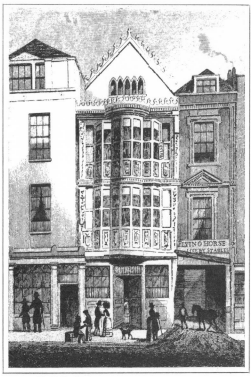

Drawn by Tho. H. Shepherd.

SIR PAUL PINDAR'S HOUSE, BISHOPSGATE STREET.

Engraved by M. Barrenger.

MERCERS' HALL, CHEAPSIDE.

Drawn by Tho. H. Shepherd.

Engraved by M. Barrenger.

SKINNERS' HALL, DOWGATE HILL.

ST. DIONIS BACKCHURCH, FENCHURCH STREET.

ST. JOHN THE BAPTIST, SAVOY.

## Chapel of St. John the Baptist, Savoy.

In the Savoy is the ancient chapel belonging to the hospital, which was originally dedicated to St. John the Baptist; but, when the old church of St. Mary-le-Strand was destroyed by the Protector Somerset, the inhabitants of that parish united themselves to those of the precinct of the Savoy; and this chapel being consequently used as their parish church it acquired the name of St. Mary-le-Savoy.

This structure being built of squared stone, in the Gothic style, has an aspect of great antiquity. Contrary to the general construction of religious edifices, its greatest length is north and south, and the altar is placed at the north end. The roof is remarkably fine, being adorned with carved figures of the Holy Lamb, shields of arms, and other decorations, within elegant circular compartments. It was completely repaired in the year 1721, at the expense of His Majesty King George I., who also inclosed the burial-ground with a wall; since which it has been again repaired and beautified. There are many ancient monuments in this chapel, some of which are very magnificent.

This precinct is extra-parochial, and the right of presentation to the chapel is in the lord high-treasurer, or the commissioners for executing that office.

## Drapers' Hall, Throgmorton Street.

On the north side of Throgmorton Street is Draper's Hall. This is a spacious and noble edifice, built upon the ruins of a palace erected on that spot by Thomas Cromwell, earl of Essex, in the reign of King Henry VIII., on the site of several tenements belonging to the priory of St. Augustine, which he purchased at its suppression. But, the garden belonging to the edifice not being of sufficient extent to gratify his inordinate ambition, he, in an arbitrary manner, without the consent of either landlord or tenant, caused the fences of the neighbouring gardens to be removed twenty-two feet northward, and, having added the ground to his own garden, inclosed it with a high brick wall.

Among the sufferers was Stow's father, who had a garden adjoining to Cromwell's, with a house standing close to the south paling of it. This house was raised from the ground, and, being placed on rollers, was removed back to that distance without the knowledge of the owner, who could not obtain satisfaction for the injury, so greatly was the power of this oppressor dreaded.

This noble mansion being forfeited to the crown, by his attainder and execution for high treason, it was purchased by the company of Drapers, who converted it into a hall for transacting the business of their corporation: and, that building being destroyed by the fire of London, the Company built the present hall, which is a most elegant building, composing the four sides of a quadrangle, each of which is elevated on columns, and adorned with arches formed in a piazza round a square court; and between each arch is a shield, mantling and other fret-work. On the east side is the common hall, the ascent to which is by a grand staircase, and within, it is adorned with a stately screen and fine wainscot.

### STATIONERS' HALL, STATIONERS' HALL COURT.

On the north side of Ludgate Hill, in Stationers' Court, is Stationers' Hall. This building stands on the site of a mansion which anciently belonged to the dukes of Bretagne; after which it was possessed by the earls of Pembroke, and, in Queen Elizabeth's time, by Henry lord Abergavenny. Finally, it belonged to the Stationers' Company, who rebuilt it of wood, and made it their Hall. This building, however, shared in the common calamity of 1666, and was succeeded by the present brick edifice, which was afterwards newly fronted with stone. It is a spacious, convenient building, enlightened by a single series of windows, over each of which is placed a neat medallion. The entrance is from a small paved court, enclosed with a dwarf wall, surmounted by an iron railing. Beneath the Hall, and at the north end of it, are warehouses for the Company's stock.

### CLOTHWORKERS' HALL, MINCING LANE.

On the north side of Tower Street is Mincing Lane, anciently called Mincheon Lane, which is handsomely built, and well inhabited; on the east side of it, near the north end, stands Clothworkers' Hall, a neat brick building, with fluted columns of the same, having Corinthian capitals of stone. The Hall is a lofty room, adorned with wainscot to the ceiling, which is of curious fret-work. The screen at the south end is of oak, with four pilasters, their entablatures and compass pediment of the Corinthian order, enriched with the arms of the Company and palm branches. The west end is adorned with the figures of king James and king Charles I., richly carved, as large as life, in their robes, with regalia, all gilt and highly finished. At this end of the hall is a spacious window of stained glass, on which are the king's arms, as also those of Sir John Robinson, Bart., his majesty's lieutenant of the Tower of London, lord mayor of the city in the year 1663, and president of the Artillery Company.

### GOLDSMITHS' HALL, FOSTER LANE.

At the north-east corner of Foster Lane stands the hall belonging to the Company of Goldsmiths. This spacious building supplies the place of one which was originally erected by Drew Berentin, about the year 1407, but was destroyed by the fire of London. It is an irregular structure, built with brick, and the corners wrought in rustic of stone. The door is large, arched, and decorated with Doric columns, which support a pediment of the arched kind, but open for a shield, in which are the arms of the Company. The hall room is spacious, and both that and the other rooms are well enlightened. It is however proposed to pull down and rebuild it, as part of the improvements connected with the neighbourhood of the New Post Office.

DRAPERS' HALL, THROGMORTON ST.

STATIONERS' HALL, STATIONERS' HALL COURT.

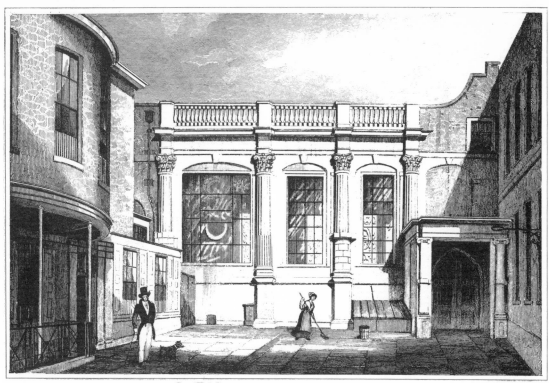

Drawn by Tho. H. Shepherd.

Engraved by W. Wallis.

CLOTHWORKER'S HALL, MINCING LANE.

Drawn by Tho. H. Shepherd.

GOLDSMITH'S HALL, FOSTER LANE.

## Middlesex Hospital.

This hospital was instituted in the year 1745, for the relief of the indigent, sick, and lame, at which time, and for several years after, it was carried on in two convenient houses adjoining to each other, in Windmill Street, Tottenham Court Road. The benefactions of the public having greatly increased, the governors, in 1747, extended their plan to the relief of pregnant wives of the industrious poor; when the great increase of patients soon obliged them to think of enlarging their edifice as well as their plan, and, by the benevolence of the contributors, they were enabled, in 1755, to erect the present building, which at that time was situated in the open fields.

That part of the institution which relates to the admission of pregnant women was altered about fifteen years ago, in consequence of an offer made by an unknown person, through the medium of a respectable surgeon, to advance £3000, and to settle £300 per annum on the hospital, provided the governors would appropriate a ward for the reception and cure of cancerous diseases. Such an offer was not to be rejected, and the obstacle to its adoption was the unwillingness of the governors to narrow the extent of their charity, to the exclusion of some part of those who were already within its scope. It being, however, suggested that delivering married women at home would, in most cases, be a more effectual and beneficial relief to them than obliging them to pass the period of their confinement in an hospital, secluded from their families, it was determined to appropriate the lying-in ward to the desired purpose, and to provide those who might want it with obstetrical assistance, medicine, and nurses, at their own habitations, by which means the managers of this charity were enabled to accept the benevolent offer; and since that period the upper part of the hospital has been devoted solely to the cure of that disease.

Though this building is exceeding plain, yet it has a very decent appearance, and is accommodated with every convenience to answer the charitable purposes for which it was erected.

## Charter House.

This charitable foundation was instituted for the maintenance of a master, a preacher, a head schoolmaster, a second master, and eighty pensioners, consisting of decayed gentlemen, merchants, or others, reduced by misfortunes, who are provided with handsome apartments, and all the necessaries of life, except clothes; instead of which, each of them is allowed a cloak and fourteen pounds per annum. There are also forty-four boys supported in the house, where they have good lodgings, and are instructed in classical learning. From among these, are chosen twenty-nine students at the Universities, who are each allowed twenty pounds per annum, for eight years. Others, who are judged more fit for trades, are put out apprentices, and the sum of forty pounds is given with each of them. As a farther encouragement to the scholars brought up in this foundation, there are nine ecclesiastical preferments in the patronage of the governors, who, according to the constitution of the charity, are to confer them upon those who receive their education in that school. The pensioners and scholars are taken in at the recommendation of the governors, who appoint in rotation.

The Charter House is situated between St. John's Street on the west, Goswell Street on the east, Long Lane on the south, and Wilderness Row on the north. There is scarcely any vestige of the conventual building, which is said to have stood where the garden now is. The present buildings were erected by the Duke of Norfolk; they are very irregular, and have little to recommend them but their convenience and situation. The rooms are well disposed, and the court within, though small, is very neat. In one corner of this court is a handsome chapel, in which, among others, is a very superb monument, erected to the memory of Mr. Thomas Sutton, the founder; on which is his effigy, habited in a gown, and in a recumbent posture. On each side is a man in armour, standing upright, and above, a preacher represented as addressing a full congregation. In the front of these buildings is a very handsome square, and behind, a large garden, which at once contributes to the health and to the pleasure of those who receive the benefit of so valuable a foundation.

## MIDDLE TEMPLE.

The entrance into the Middle Temple, from Fleet Street, is by a very handsome gate, which was built in the style of Inigo Jones, in the year 1684. The front of it, though narrow, is graceful: it is built of brick, with four large stone pilasters of the Ionic order and a handsome pediment. In a course of stone, between the first and second story, is cut the following inscription:—*Surrexit impensis societat. Med. Templi*, M.DC.LXXXIV., and beneath it, just over the gate, is the figure of a Holy Lamb.

The great hall belonging to the Middle Temple is very spacious and beautiful, and is esteemed one of the finest halls in the kingdom. It was originally built in the reign of Edward III., but the present edifice was erected in the reign of Queen Elizabeth, in the year 1572. It is ornamented with paintings by Sir James Thornhill, and contains full-length portraits of those pillars of the law—Littleton and his able but insolent commentator Coke.

In the treasury chamber of the Middle Temple is preserved a great quantity of armour which belonged to the Knights' Templars, consisting of helmets, breast and back pieces, a halbard, and two very beautiful shields, with iron spikes in their centres, of the length of six inches, and each about twenty pounds weight. They are curiously engraved, and one of them richly inlaid with gold; the insides are lined with leather stuffed, and the edges are adorned with silk fringe.

In Garden Court, in the Middle Temple, is a library founded by the will of Robert Ashley, Esq., in the year 1641, who bequeathed his own library for that purpose, and £300 to be laid out in a purchase, for the maintenance of a librarian, who must be a student of the society, and be elected into that office by the benchers.

MIDDLESEX HOSPITAL.

PENSIONER'S HALL, CHARTER HOUSE.

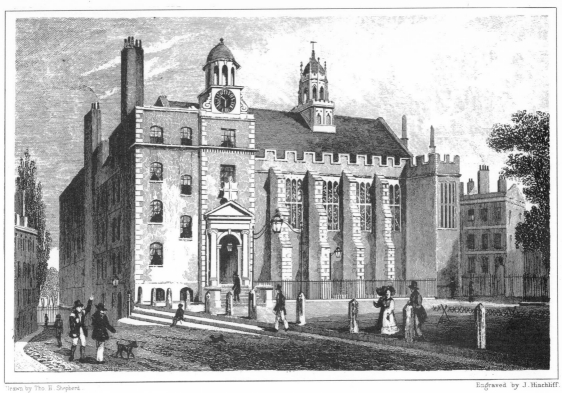

MIDDLE TEMPLE HALL.

CLIFFORD'S INN HALL, FLEET STREET.

The Inner Temple is situated to the east of the Middle Temple, and has a cloister, a large garden, and more spacious walks than the other. In this division there is also a handsome hall.

The chief officer belonging to each of these societies is a treasurer, who is annually elected from among the benchers or senior members, and whose office is to admit students and to receive and pay all cash belonging to the society. Both the Temples, however, are under one master, who, since the reign of Henry VIII., has been a divine, and constituted by letters patent from the crown, without any other induction.

## CLIFFORD'S INN.

East from Chancery Lane, in Fleet Street, is Clifford's Inn, which is so called from having been the city residence of the family of the Clifford's; it was demised, in the year 1345, by Isabel, widow of Robert de Clifford, to certain students of the law; since which time it has continued to be inhabited by gentlemen of that profession. The Gothic hall is castellated at the top, and has a beautiful little clock turret in the centre of the roof. The body is enlightened by three spacious windows, with pointed arches.

It is an inn of chancery, and an appendage to the Middle Temple; but its present occupiers are chiefly attornies and officers of the Marshalsea Court.

## CHURCH OF ST. LAWRENCE, JEWRY, KING STREET.

At the south-west corner of Guildhall Yard is the parish church of St. Lawrence, Jewry, which runs westward, on the north side of Cateaton Street. It is dedicated to Lawrence, a Spanish saint, born at Huesca, in the kingdom of Arragon; who, after having undergone the most grievous tortures, in the persecution under Valerian the emperor, was cruelly broiled alive upon a gridiron, with a slow fire, till he died, for his strict adherence to Christianity; and the additional epithet of Jewry, from its situation among the Jews, was conferred upon it, to distinguish it from the church of St. Lawrence, Pounteney, now demolished.

This church, which was anciently a rectory, being given by Hugo de Wickenbroke to Baliol College, in Oxford, anno 1294, the rectory ceased; wherefore Richard, Bishop of London, converted it into a vicarage, the patronage of which still continues in the master and scholars of that college.

The old church being destroyed by the fire in 1666, it was rebuilt, at the expense of the parishioners, assisted by a very liberal benefaction from Sir John Langham, and the parish of St. Mary Magdalen, Milk Street, was annexed to it.

The present structure is eighty-one feet long, sixty-eight feet broad, forty feet high to the roof, and the altitude of the steeple is 130 feet. The body is enlightened by two series of windows, the lower ones large and uniform, and the upper small. At the east end is a pediment, with niches, supported by Corinthian columns. The lower, which is lofty, is terminated by a balustrade, with plain pinnacles; and within this balustrade rises a kind of lantern, which supports the base of the spire.

### CROSBY HALL.

On the east side of Bishopsgate Street is Crosby Square, so called from Sir John Crosby, Knt., who built a large house here in 1466. This house was the city residence of Richard, Duke of Gloucester, while the measures which eventually secured him the crown were concerting. Part of this house still remains, on the north side of the entrance into the square, which is chiefly built on the garden ground that belonged to the house. The part improperly called Richard III.'s Chapel is still very entire. It is a beautiful Gothic building, with a bow window at one end; the roof, which is of timber, elegantly carved, is very worthy of admiration. This building is now the residence of a packer.

### THE KING'S WEIGH-HOUSE.

The ground on which the church of St. Andrew Hubbard, destroyed by the great fire, formerly stood, with the church yard, in Little Eastcheap, between Botolph Lane and Love Lane, and also the site of the parsonage house, were sold to the City of London, for public uses: some of the purchase money was paid to the parish of St. Mary at Hill, towards the repairs of that church, and the remainder was appropriated to making a provision for the rector and his successors, in lieu of the parsonage house. On one part of the ground was erected the King's Weigh-House, which before stood on Cornhill. The original intent of this Weigh-House was, to prevent frauds in the weight of merchandize brought from beyond sea. It was under the government of a master and four master porters, with labouring porters under them, who used to have carts and horses to fetch the merchants' goods to the beam, and to carry them back; but little has been done in this office of late years, as a compulsive power is wanting to oblige merchants to have their goods weighed.

### COAL EXCHANGE.

This building is situated in Thames Street, nearly opposite to Billingsgate, and is a neat and very convenient structure, for the use of dealers in the important article of coals, consisting of a very handsome front and quadrangle behind, where every branch of the coal business is transacted.

### CHURCH OF ST. MARY, ALDERMARY.

Near the middle of Bow Lane, on the east side, is the parochial church of St. Mary Aldermary. This church, which is a rectory, owes its name to its dedication to the Virgin Mary; and the additional epithet of Aldermary, to Older, or Elder Mary, from its being

ST. LAWRENCE, KING STREET.

HOLMES HALL & SONS PACKERS

CROSBY HALL, BISHOPSGATE STREET.

Drawn by Tho. H. Shepherd.

Engraved by R. Acon.

THE KING'S WEIGH HOUSE, LITTLE EAST CHEAP.

Drawn by Tho. H. Shepherd.

Engraved by R. Acon.

COAL EXCHANGE, THAMES STREET.

the oldest church in this city dedicated to the said virgin. It is one of the peculiars belonging to the Archbishop of Canterbury, and was founded before the conquest, under the Saxon kings.

In the year 1510 Sir Henry Keble, lord mayor of London, bequeathed £1000 towards rebuilding this church. And, in 1626, William Rodoway gave towards the building of the steeple, then greatly decayed, the sum of £3000; and Richard Pierson, about the same year, gave 200 marks towards the same works, with condition that this steeple, thus to be built, should follow its ancient pattern, and go forward and be finished according to the foundation of it laid before by Sir Henry Keble; which, within three years after, was so finished, that, notwithstanding the body of the church was burnt in the fire of 1666, the steeple remained firm and good. That part of it which was consumed was afterwards rebuilt in its present form by the munificence of Henry Rogers, Esq., as appears by a Latin inscription over the west door of the church.

This Gothic edifice is very spacious, it being 100 feet in length and sixty-three in breadth; the height of the roof is forty-five feet, and that of the steeple 135. The body is enlightened by a single series of large Gothic windows. The wall has well-contrived buttresses and battlements; these buttresses run up pilaster fashion, in two stages, not projecting in the old manner from the body of the building. The tower, which is full of ornaments, consists of five stages, each of which, except the lowest, has one Gothic window; and the pinnacles, which are properly so many turrets, are continued at each corner down to the ground, divided into stages as the body of the tower, and cabled with small pillars bound round it, with a kind of arched work, and subdivisions between.

## CHURCH OF ST. MICHAEL, CORNHILL.

This church, standing on the south side of Cornhill, is a rectory, and owes its name to its dedication to St. Michael, the Archangel, and its situation.

The patronage of it appears to have been anciently in the abbot and convent of Eversham, erroneously called Coversham, who, in the year 1133, granted the same to Sparling, a priest, with all the lands thereunto belonging, except those held by Orgar le Proud, at the rent of 2s. a year; in consideration of which grant, the said Sparling covenanted and agreed, not only to pay annually, to the abbot and canons, the sum of 13s. 4d., but likewise to supply the house of the said abbot (when in London) with fire, water, and salt.

Some time afterwards, the rectory reverted to the convent, and they continued patrons of it until the year 1503, when, by a deed bearing date December 3, they conveyed the advowson to the Drapers' Company, in consideration of a perpetual annuity of £5. 6s. 8d., in addition to an ancient pension of 6s. 8d. annually, paid to the abbot and canons, out of the said church; since which time, the patronage has continued to be in the Drapers' Company.

The old church being destroyed by the fire of London, in 1666, the present Gothic structure arose in its stead; the body of which is seventy feet long, sixty broad, thirty-five in height, and 130 feet to the top of the tower. The lower part of the tower occupies the centre of the church; and, on each side, there is a regular extent of building. The prin-ipal door opens in the lower stage of the tower, which rises with angulated corners from the ground, forming a kind of base, terminated at the height of the body of the church. The second stage, which is plain and lofty, has two tall windows, one over the other, properly shaped for the style of the building: this is terminated with a truly Gothic cornice. The third stage is exactly in the form of the two others, only they are plain and this is covered with ornaments; the angulated corners are fluted, and terminated by cherubs' heads, under a cornice; the plain face, between, has four windows, in two series. Above the cornice, over the uppermost of these windows, runs a battlement, on the plain faces of the tower, and from the corners are carried up four beautiful fluted turrets, cased, a part of their height, with Doric turrets; these terminate in pinnacle heads, from within which rises a spire at each corner, crowned with a vane. The tower contains an excellent ring of bells, remarkable for their melody.

## CHURCH OF ST. OLAVE JEWRY, OLD JEWRY.

On the west side of Old Jewry stands the parish church of St. Olave Jewry, of very ancient foundation, and originally called Olave Upwell, from its being dedicated to the saint of that name, and, probably, from a well under the east end, where, at this time, and for many years past, has stood a pump for the use of the public; but this name afterwards gave way to that of Jewry, owing to the great number of Jews that took up their residence in this neighbourhood.

This parish was a rectory, in the gift of the dean and chapter of St. Paul's, till about the year 1181, when it was transferred by them, with the chapel of St. Stephen, Coleman Street, to the prior and convent of Butley, in Suffolk, and became a vicarage. At the suppression of that convent, the impropriation was forfeited to the crown, in whom it has continued to the present time. When the old church was burned down, in 1666, the parish of St. Martin, Ironmonger Lane, was annexed to it; the patronage of which is also in the crown.

The present structure was erected soon after the fire of London, and is built partly of brick, and partly of stone. It is seventy-eight feet long, twenty-four feet broad, thirty-six feet high to the roof, and eighty-eight feet high to the top of the tower and pinnacles. The door is of the Doric order, well proportioned, and covered with an arched pediment. The tower is very plain, on the upper part of which rises a cornice, supported by scrolls, and upon this a plain attic course. On the pillars, at the corners, are placed the pinnacles upon balls; and each pinnacle is terminated at the top by a ball. The body of the church is well enlightened, the floor is paved with Perbeck, and the walls are wainscoted. The

ST. MARY, ALDERMARY.

ST. MICHAEL'S, CORNHILL.

ST. OLAVE JEWRY, OLD JEWRY

Drawn by Tho. H. Shepherd.

## PICCADILLY, FROM COVENTRY STREET

Drawn by Tho. H. Shepherd. Engraved by T. Barber.

## MIDDLE ROW HOLBORN.

pulpit is enriched with carvings of cherubim; the floor of the altar, on which the communion-table stands, is paved with black and white marble, and in the front of the altar are the king's arms.

## PICCADILLY, FROM COVENTRY STREET.

The fine and very interesting street-view here presented, by our artist, forms one of the peculiar characteristics of the metropolis, and therefore determined him to make it the subject of an engraving.

Piccadilly appears to have taken its name originally from a gaming-house for the nobility. Lord Clarendon, in his History of the Rebellion, describes it as "a place called Pickadilly (which was a fair house for entertainment, and gaming, with handsome gravel walks, with shade, and an upper and lower bowling-green, whither very many of the nobility, and gentry of the best quality, resorted, both for exercise and conversation.)" This was in the year 1640: the street was completed in the year 1642, as far as the present Berkeley Street. The first good house built in it was Burlington House; the site of which was chosen by its noble founder, "because he was certain no one would build beyond him." It is on the north side of the street, and fenced in with a brick wall, about 220 feet in length, in which are three gates for the admission of carriages. The front of the house is of stone, and is remarkable for the beauty of the design and workmanship. It has two wings, joined by a circular colonnade, of the Doric order. The front was built by the father of the late Earl of Burlington, and is more modern than the house. The apartments are in fine taste, and the stair-case painted with great spirit, by Seb. Ricci.

## MIDDLE ROW, HOLBORN.

Second to the Strand, if not equal to it, Holborn may be considered one of the great leading thoroughfares, running from east to west of the metropolis. The part here exhibited is perhaps the widest and best of the whole line of street, and from its proximity to the principal Inns of Court, as well as general thoroughfare, displays an extraordinary scene of activity and traffic.

Holborn was first paved in 1417, as appears from an order in the Fœdera, Vol. IX. p. 447, in which king Henry V., taking notice "that the high-way named Holborn, in London, was so deep and miry that many perils and hazards were thereby occasioned, as well to the king's carriages passing that way, as to those of his subjects; he therefore ordained two vessels, each of twenty tons burthen, to be employed at his expense, for bringing stones for paving and mending the same." This shows the gradual improvement of London's suburbs.

### GRAY'S INN HALL, CHAPEL, AND LIBRARY.

Grays Inn occupies the site of the Mansion House of the ancient manor of Portpool, one of the Prebends belonging to St. Paul's Cathedral, which, in the year 1515, becoming the residence of the noble family of Gray, of Wilton, received the name of Gray's Inn, and, in the reign of Edward III., was demised to certain students of the law, by that name. Some time after this, the prior and monks of Shene obtained a licence to purchase the manor of Portpool, by whom the Mansion House and gardens were again demised to the students, at an annual rent of £6. 13s. 4d.; and this grant remained in force until the general suppression of the monasteries. In the year 1541, this Inn was granted by Henry VIII. to the students, and their successors, in fee farm.

The principal entrance to this Inn is in Holborn, though the buildings are situated at some distance from the street. There is another entrance to it in Gray's Inn Lane; part of the west side of which is occupied by the back of the buildings, and the wall that encloses the gardens. The Inn consists of several well-built courts, particularly Holborn Court and Gray's Inn square; the latter of which was built in 1687. The hall, which is used for the commons of the society, is large and commodious; but the chapel is too small: it is a Gothic structure, and is of much greater antiquity than any other part of the building; it being the old chapel belonging to the manor-house. Here is an exceedingly good library, well furnished with books for the use of the students; but the chief ornament of this Inn is the spacious garden behind it, which consists of gravel walks between lofty trees, grass-plats, agreeable slopes, and a long terrace, with a portico at each end. It is open to the public in the summer season.

### LINCOLN'S INN HALL, CHAPEL, AND CHANCERY COURT.

Lincoln's Inn is situated to the south of Holborn, and on the west side of Chancery Lane; being the spot where formerly stood the house of the bishop of Chichester, as also that of the Black Friars; the latter erected about the year 1222, and the former about 1226; but both of them coming to Henry Lacey, earl of Lincoln, he pulled them down, and in their stead erected a stately mansion for his city residence; into which it is said, that, some time before his death, in 1310, he introduced the study of the law.

This mansion afterwards reverted to the bishopric of Chichester, and was devised by Robert Sherbourn, bishop of that see, to Mr. William Syliard, a student there, for a term of years; at the expiration of which, Dr. Richard Sampson, his successor, in the year 1536, passed the inheritance thereof to the said Syliard, and Eustace, his brother; the latter of whom, in 1579, in consideration of the sum of £500, conveyed the house and gardens, in fee, to Richard Kingsmill, and the rest of the benchers.

Drawn by Tho. H. Shepherd.

GRAYS INN HALL CHAPEL AND LIBRARY

Drawn by Tho. H. Shepherd.

LINCOLN'S INN HALL, CHAPEL AND CHANCERY COURT

This Inn principally consists of three rows of large and uniform buildings, forming three sides of a square, most of them occupied by gentlemen of the society. The north side of the square lies open to the gardens, which are very spacious, and adorned with gravel walks, grass-plats, rows of trees, and a very long terrace walk, which is so elevated as to command a fine prospect of Lincoln's Inn Fields. In the centre of the square is a neat fluted Corinthian column, in a small bason, surrounded with iron rails. This column supports a handsome sun-dial, which has four sides, and on the corners of the pedestal are four naked boys, intended to spout water out of Triton shells; but this has been long out of repair.

Behind the north-east side of the square are a good hall and chapel; the latter of which was built by Inigo Jones, about the year 1622, on pillars, with an ambulatory, or walk, underneath, paved with broad stones, and used as a place of interment for the benchers. The outside of the chapel is a very indifferent specimen of Gothic architecture, and the windows are painted with the figures at full length of the principal personages mentioned in the Scriptures. On the twelve windows, on the north side, are Abraham, Moses, Eli, David, and the prophets Daniel, Isaiah, Jeremiah, Ezekiel, Amos, and Zachariah, with John the Baptist, and St. Paul; and on the south side are the rest of the apostles. Under these figures are the arms of a great number of gentlemen belonging to this society.

The hall is an extremely fine room, and is used not only for the commons of the society, but for sittings, out of term, before the lord Chancellor. At the upper end of it is Hogarth's picture of St. Paul before Agrippa and Festus.

Between the chapel and Chancery Lane are several ranges of chambers, called the Old Buildings. Here is a very good library, which consists of a good collection of books in most languages, and a great number of manuscripts, of a parliamentary, judicial, legal, and public nature, the greatest part of which were bequeathed by lord Hale, with a strict injunction that no part of them should be printed.

The gate to Lincoln's Inn, from the west side of Chancery Lane, is of brick, and not undeserving of notice. It was built by Sir Thomas Lovel, once a member of this inn and afterwards treasurer of the household to Henry VII.

On the east side of the gardens is a new range of buildings, called the Stone Buildings, from having stone fronts. When these were erected, a plan was in agitation for rebuilding the whole inn, in the same style of elegant simplicity; but this design has been long laid aside.

## CHRIST CHURCH, SPITALFIELDS.

Spitalfields derives its name from having been built upon the fields and grounds belonging to St. Mary's, Spital, which stood on the east side of Bishopsgate Street. When, by the revocation of the edict of Nantes, Louis XIV. compelled his protestant subjects to fly to foreign lands for shelter and protection, a considerable number of them sought refuge in this country; the greater part of whom settled on this spot, and established here the manufacture of silk in all its branches; and the neighbourhood is still, in a great measure, peopled by their descendants

Spitalfields was, originally, a hamlet belonging to the parish of St. Dunstan, Stepney; but, from the great increase of inhabitants, it was, in the year 1723, made a distinct parish; and the church is one of the fifty ordered to be built by act of parliament.

This building is situated on the south side of Church Street; it was begun in 1723, and finished in 1729; and, from being dedicated to our Saviour, is called Christ church, Middlesex.

It is a very handsome edifice, built of stone, with a very high steeple, in which is a fine ring of bells. The body of the church is solid and well-proportioned. It is 111 feet in length, and eighty-seven in breadth; the height of the roof is forty-one feet, and that of the steeple 234 feet. It is ornamented with a Doric portico, to which there is a handsome ascent by a flight of steps; and upon these the Doric order arises, supported on pedestals. The tower, over these, rises with arched windows and niches, and, on its diminishing for the steeple, is supported by the heads of the under corners, which form a kind of buttresses: from this part rises the base of the spire, with an arcade; its corners are, in the same manner, supported with a kind of pyramidal buttresses, ending in a point; and the spire, in which are three series of square windows, crowned with pediments, is terminated by a vase and vane.

This church is made a rectory, but is not to be held in *commendam ;* and the patronage, like that of its mother church, is in the Principal and Scholars of King's Hall and Brazennose College, Oxford.

At the west end of the church is a neat brick building, in which are two charity schools; the one for girls, the other for boys, erected in 1782, and supported by voluntary contributions.

## CHURCH OF ST. DUNSTAN IN THE EAST.

At the west end of Thames Street, on the north side, is Idol Lane, between which and St. Dunstan's Hill stands the beautiful church of St. Dunstan in the East. This church is dedicated to St. Dunstan, archbishop of Canterbury; and the addition of the East is given to distinguish it from St. Dunstan in Fleet Street.

It suffered greatly by the fire of London, in 1666; the body of the church was repaired in a short time, though the steeple was not erected till about 1678. It is built in the style called modern Gothic, eighty-seven feet in length, sixty-three in breadth, and thirty-three in height, to the roof: the steeple, which is constructed in the same style as the body of the church, is 125 feet high. The tower is light, supported by out works at the angles, and divided into three stages, terminating at the corners by four handsome pinnacles, in the midst of which rises the spire, on the crowns of four pointed arches; a bold attempt in architecture, and one proof, among many, of the great geometrical skill of Sir Christopher Wren, who planned and built this elegant tower.

The patronage of this rectory was anciently in the prior and canons of Canterbury, who, in the year 1365, granted the same to Simon Islip, their archbishop, and his successors, in

CHRIST CHURCH, SPITALFIELDS.

ST DUNSTAN'S IN THE EAST.

CORNHILL, AND LOMBARD STREET, FROM THE POULTRY.

whom it still remains. It is one of the thirteen peculiars in this city, belonging to the archi-episcopal see of Canterbury.

## CORNHILL AND LOMBARD STREET, FROM THE POULTRY.

Another very picturesque street view is here presented to the eye of the passenger, by a combination of architectural splendour, in the Tower of the Royal Exchange, the beautiful Tower of St. Michael, Cornhill, and numerous church spires in the surrounding neighbourhood; heightened by other buildings, gay shops, and an ever-moving throng of carriages and pedestrians. Cornhill was so called from its being in ancient times a market for corn. The Ward is bounded on the east by Bishopsgate Ward, on the north by Broad Street Ward, on the west by Cheap Ward, and on the south by Langbourn Ward.

Its extent is very small; for, beginning at the south-east corner of the church of St. Martin Outwich, it winds through several courts and alleys, to the western extremity of Cornhill, whence it returns, in as tortuous a direction, to St. Peter's Alley, in Gracechurch Street, and then, turning northward, it extends about fifty feet into Bishopsgate Street, and afterwards passes, by the east side of Merchant Taylors' Hall, to its commencement at the church.

This Ward is divided into four precincts, and is governed by an alderman, six common council-men, four constables, sixteen inquest men, and a beadle. The principal street in this Ward is very spacious, and consists of large houses, well inhabited. The uniformity of appearance, in most of these buildings, arises from the many fires which have happened on both sides of this street, whereby the old houses were destroyed, and those erected in their stead being all in a more modern style.

Lombard Street is so called from having been the residence of the Lombards, the great money-lenders of ancient times, and who came originally from the Italian republics of Genoa, Lucca, Florence, and Venice. Owing to the abuses committed by this body of men, queen Elizabeth compelled them to quit the country. Lombard Street after having been long a kind of exchange, became, as it still continues to be, the residence of bankers of eminence.

## CHURCH OF ST. JAMES CLERKENWELL.

The parish church of St. James Clerkenwell is situated on the north side of Clerkenwell-green. On the spot where this church stands, was anciently a priory, founded by Jordan Briset, a wealthy baron, who, about the year 1100, gave to his chaplain fourteen acres of land, in a field adjoining Clerk's or Clerkenwell, whereon he built a monastery; which was no sooner erected, and dedicated to the honour of God and the assumption of the Virgin Mary, than he placed therein a certain number of black nuns, of the order of St. Benedict, in whom, and their successors, it continued till it was suppressed by Henry VIII., in the year 1539.

Some time after the dissolution of the convent, the ground came to the inheritance of Sir William Cavendish, who, being created duke of Newcastle, built a large brick mansion, on the north-west side of the church, which for many years was called Newcastle House, the site of which is now occupied by modern buildings.

The church belonging to the old priory not only served the nuns as a place of worship, but also the neighbouring inhabitants, and was made parochial on the dissolution of the nunnery, when it appears to have been dedicated to St. James the Less; for in the old records it is styled " Ecclesia Beatæ Mariæ de fonte Clericorum." In 1623, the steeple of the church being greatly decayed, a part of it fell down, whereupon the parish contracted with a person to rebuild it. This person raised the new work upon the old foundation; but, before it was entirely finished, it fell down, and destroyed a part of the church, both of which were, however, soon after rebuilt.

The old church was a very heavy structure, partly Gothic, which was the original form, and partly Tuscan. It was taken down in the year 1788, and the old materials sold for £825; after which the present edifice was, in pursuance of an act of parliament obtained for that purpose, erected in its stead. It is a lofty brick edifice, strengthened at the corners with rustic quoins of stone, and enlightened by two series of windows. The tower is of stone, and erected upon the west end of the church, which is faced with stone, in order to give it a corresponding appearance. The first two stages above the roof are square, and contain the bells. Above these are two open octangular towers, with pilasters of the Doric order at each corner, and from the uppermost rises a ball and vane.

## CHURCH OF ST. MARGARET PATTENS, ROOD LANE.

At the south-east angle of Rood Lane stands the parochial church of St. Margaret Pattens. This church received its name from its dedication to St. Margaret, virgin and martyr; and its situation, which, at the time of its foundation, was a lane, occupied only by makers and dealers in pattens. This lane, however, was afterwards called Rood Lane, on account of a rood, or cross, set up in the church-yard of St. Margaret, when the church was pulled down to be rebuilt. This cross or rood was blessed in a particular manner, and privileged by the pope with many indulgencies, for the pardon of the sins of those who came to pray before it, and to make their offerings towards the rebuilding of St. Margaret's church. But the church being finished in the year 1538, soon after the Reformation, some people unknown assembled, without noise, in the night of the 22nd of May, in that year, who broke the rood to pieces, and demolished the tabernacle in which it was erected.

The old church was destroyed in 1666, after which the present one was immediately erected, and the parish of St Gabriel Fenchurch was united to it. It is built part of stone, and part of brick, and consists of a plain body, sixty-six feet in length, fifty-two feet broad, and thirty-two feet in height. The windows are arched, with port-hole windows over them. Above the front door is a large Doric window, with a cherub's head, and a large festoon over it; and, above these is a pediment, which stretches from the steeple to the end of the church.

Drawn by Tho. H Shepherd.    Engraved by J. Henshall.

Drawn by Tho. H Shepherd.    Engraved by J. Henshall.

ST JAMES'S CLERKENWELL.

ST MARGARET PATTENS, ROOD LANE.

Drawn by Tho. H. Shepherd.

ST GILES'S CRIPPLEGATE, FORE STREET.

Drawn by Tho. H. Shepherd.

BARBER SURGEON'S HALL, MONKWELL STREET.

FISHMONGER'S HALL, THAMES STREET.

Drawn by Tho. H. Shepherd.

Engraved by J. Greig.

CORDWAINER'S HALL, DISTAFF LANE.

The tower rises square to a considerable height, and is terminated by four plain pinnacles crowned with balls, and a balustrade, within which rises a very solid spire, terminated by a ball and vane.

The original foundation of this church was in or before the year 1325; for the first rector upon record is Hamo de Chyrch, presented by lady Margaret Nevil, on the 14th of June, in that year. And the patronage thereof remained in the family of the Nevils 'till the year 1392, when it came to Robert Rikeden, of Essex, and Margaret, his wife; who, in 1408, conveyed it, by agreement, to Richard Whittington and other citizens of London, together with the advowson of St. Peter, Cornhill, and the manor of Leadenhall, &c., which agreement the said Whittington and others confirmed in 1411, to the mayor and commonalty of London; in whom the right of presentation has ever since remained.

## CHURCH OF ST. GILES, CRIPPLEGATE.

This church is so called from being dedicated to a saint of that name, born at Athens, who was abbot of Nismes, in France. It was founded about the year 1090, by Alfune, the first master of St. Bartholomew's Hospital.

The old church was destroyed by fire, in the year 1545; after which the present structure was erected, and is one of the few that fortunately escaped the dreadful conflagration in 1666.

This ancient edifice may very properly be numbered amongst the best of our Gothic buildings. It is 114 feet in length, 63 feet in breadth, 32 feet high, to the roof, and 122 feet to the top of the turret. The body of the church is well enlightened by two rows of windows, which are truly of the Gothic order, and the spaces between have buttresses for the support of the wall. The tower is well-proportioned, the corners of it are supported by a kind of buttress-work, and at each corner is a small turret. The principal turret, in the centre, is light and open; it is strengthened by buttresses, and crowned with a dome, from whence rises the vane.

The patronage of this church was originally in private hands, till it descended to one Alemund, a priest, who granted the same (after his death, and that of Hugh, his only son) to the dean and chapter of St. Paul's, whereby they became not only ordinaries of the parish, but likewise patrons of the vicarage, from that time to the present.

## BARBER-SURGEON'S HALL, MONKWELL STREET.

This building was designed by that great architect Inigo Jones, and, though of a simple construction, is exceedingly elegant, and considered as one of his master-pieces. The grand entrance from Monkwell-street is enriched with the company's arms, large fruit and other decorations. The court-room has a fret-work ceiling, and is adorned with several beautiful paintings, particularly a very handsome piece, by Hans Holbein, of King Henry VIII. uniting the barbers and surgeons into one company, which contains portraits of eighteen of the most eminent members of the company at that time. The theatre belonging to the hall, at the time these companies were united, contained some chirurgical curiosities ; but, since the barbers and surgeons have been made separate bodies, the latter have taken those curiosities away, and the theatre has ever since been shut up and deserted.

### FISHMONGERS' HALL, THAMES STREET.

At a small distance from the bridge, on the west side of this ward, fronting the Thames, stood Fishmongers' Hall, a very handsome building, erected since the destruction of the old hall, by the great fire, and commanding a fine view of the river and the bridge ; but which has recently been taken down, in consequence of building the new bridge.

The front entrance to this hall was from Thames Street, by a passage leading into a large square court, paved with flat stones, and encompassed by the great hall, the court-room for the assistants, and other grand apartments with galleries. These were of a handsome construction, and supported by Ionic columns, with an arcade. The back front, or that next the Thames, had a grand double flight of stone steps, leading to the first apartments from the wharf. The door was adorned with Ionic columns, supporting an open pediment, in which was a shield, with the arms of the company. The windows were ornamented with stone cases, and the quoins of the building wrought with a handsome rustic.

In the great hall was a wooden statue of Sir William Walworth, armed with his dagger ; and also another of St. Peter : the former belonged to this company, and the latter is, with great propriety, adopted as its patron saint. In the court-room were several pictures of the various species of sea and river fishes : and the arms of the benefactors to the company were emblazoned in painted glass in the different windows.

### CORDWAINERS' HALL, DISTAFF LANE.

On the north side of Distaff Lane is Cordwainers' Hall ; a handsome convenient building, consisting of several rooms, the principal of which contains portraits of King William and Queen Mary. A new stone front has been added to this building ; over the centre window of which is a medallion, representing a country girl, spinning with a distaff, in allusion to the name of the lane ; and at the top is a carving of the company's arms.

Gerard's-hall-Inn, on the south side of Basing Lane, is built upon the remains of a mansion-house, formerly belonging to the ancient family of Gysors, some of whom served the principal offices in the magistracy.

### CHURCH OF ST. EDMUND, THE KING, LOMBARD STREET.

This church received its name from being dedicated to Edmund, the Saxon King, who was murdered by the Danes, in the year 870 ; and though the origin of its foundation cannot be ascertained with any degree of certainty, yet, from several circumstances, it is reasonable to suppose, that it was originally built during the time of the Saxon heptarchy.

Drawn by T. H. Shepherd.

ST. EDMOND THE KING, LOMBARD STREET.

Engraved by A. Cruse.

ST. ANTHOLIN, FROM WATLING STREET.

Drawn by Tho. H. Shepherd.

Engraved by A. Cruse.

ST. MARTIN OUTWICH, BISHOPSGATE STREET

The old church was destroyed by the fire of London, after which the present structure was erected on its ruins. The situation of this building differs from most other churches in London; for, instead of east and west, it stands full north and south; by which the altar is placed at the north end of the church. It is sixty-nine feet long, thirty-nine feet broad, and thirty-two feet high to the roof, which is flat. At the south end is a square tower, from which projects a dial over the street; and upon the tower is a short spire, with its base fixed on a broad lantern.

This church is a rectory, the patronage of which is now in the Archbishop of Canterbury. In the year 1175, there was a dispute between the Dean and Chapter of St. Pauls, and the prior and canons of the Trinity convent, within Aldgate, concerning the patronage; which was determined by Gilbert, Bishop of London, in favour of the latter.

## CHURCH OF ST. ANTHOLIN, WATLING STREET.

At the south-west corner of Sise-lane, on the north side, and near the west end of Watling-street, stands the parish church of St. Anthony, commonly called St. Antholin, or St. Antlin.

This church is so called from its dedication to St. Anthony, an Egyptian hermit, and founder of the order of Eremites of St Anthony. The time of its foundation is not certainly known; but that it is of great antiquity appears from its being in the gift of the canons of St. Paul in the year 1181. It was rebuilt by Thomas Knolles, Lord Mayor of London, in the year 1399: and again, in 1513, by John Tate, mercer. In 1616 it was repaired and beautified at the expense of one thousand pounds, raised by the contribution of several munificent inhabitants; but, being destroyed by the fire of London, it was rebuilt in the year 1682, in the same manner it now appears.

It is built of stone, of the Tuscan order; and is sixty-six feet in length, fifty-four in breadth, forty-four in height, and the altitude of the steeple is one hundred and fifty-four feet. The roof is a cupola of an elliptic form, enlightened by four port-hole windows, and supported by columns of the Composite order. The steeple consists of a tower, and a very neat octangular spire, ornamented with apertures in three stages. The windows at the base of the spire have regular cases, and are crowned with pediments supporting urns. Those of the middle stage have shields, with more free ornaments, which also support their vases; and the crown of the spire with the decorations under the vane are exceedingly handsome.

## CHURCH OF ST. MARTIN OUTWICH, BISHOPSGATE-STREET.

Opposite the South Sea House, and partly in Bishopsgate-street, stands the Parish church of St. Martin Outwich. This church, which is dedicated to St. Martin, bishop of Tours, in France, about the year 376, is of great antiquity. It derives its additional name of Outwich from the family of Oteswich. Stow names four of them, who were buried here, viz. Martin, Nicholas, William, and John, who were proprietors of it. In the year 1325, John de

Warren, earl of Surrey, presented to this living; but he dying without issue, and leaving his estates to the crown, the advowson was purchased, in 1387, by the above family, who, in the sixth year of the reign of Henry II., gave it, with four messuages, seventeen shops, and the appurtenances, in the said parish, to the master and wardens of the Tailors and Linen armourers, and to their successors, to be employed for the perpetual help and relief of the poor brethren and sisters of the said company: by virtue of which grant, the company of Merchant-Tailors have ever since enjoyed the right of patronage to this church.

The old church, which was built in 1540, was one of the few that escaped the fire of London; but the ravages of time, assisted by the injuries it sustained from a fire in Bishopsgate-street, in 1765, had affected it so much, that it was taken down, in 1795, and the present structure, the first stone of which was laid on the 4th of May, 1796, has been erected in its stead; which afforded an opportunity of enlarging the entrance into Thread-needle-street, by taking off the angle, which before projected into that street. It is a plain neat building of brick, except the east end, which is of stone; above which rises a low circular tower, surmounted by a dome. It is a rectory.

### INN-HOLDERS' HALL, GREAT ELBOW LANE.

On the north side of Thames Street, a little east from Joiners' Hall Buildings, is Great Elbow Lane, in which is a very handsome and convenient hall, belonging to the company of Inn-holders. This company was incorporated by king Henry VIII., on the 21st of December, 1515, by the name of "The master, wardens, and company, of the art or mystery of Inn-holders of the city of London." It is a livery company, the thirty-second on the city list, and is governed by a master, three wardens, and twenty assistants. The fine on admission is £10.

### GIRDLERS' HALL, BASINGHALL-STREET.

On the east side of Basinghall-street is Girdlers'-hall, a handsome and convenient build-ing, finished in 1681, well wainscoted within, and with a skreen of the Composite order. This company was incorporated in the twenty-seventh of Henry VI., on the sixth of August, 1449; and re-incorporated, with the pinners and wire-drawers, by queen Elizabeth, on the 12th of October, 1568, by the name of "The master and wardens, or keepers, of the art or mystery of the Girdlers of London." It is a livery company, governed by a master, three wardens, and twenty-four assistants; and the fine on admission is £10.

### DYERS' HALL, LITTLE ELBOW LANE.

At a small distance from Inn-holders' Hall, in Little Elbow Lane, is a neat building, used as a hall by the Dyers' company. Their hall, which was formerly situated near Old Swan-lane, in Thames-street, being destroyed by the conflagration in 1666, and a number of warehouses erected in its place, the company have converted this house into a hall to

Drawn by Tho. H. Shepherd.

Engraved by J. Greig.

INNHOLDER'S HALL, COLLEGE STREET.

GIRDLER'S HALL, BASINGHALL STREET.

Drawn by Tho. H. Shepherd.

Engraved by J. Greig

DYER'S HALL, COLLEGE STREET

ALLHALLOWS. BREAD STREET.

ST. JAMES'S, GARLICK HILL.

ST. MARY, ALDERMANBURY.

transact their affairs in. This company was incorporated by king Edward IV., in the year 1472, by the name of "The wardens and commonalty of the mystery of Dyers of London." Their charter is that of keeping swans on the River Thames. This was originally one of the twelve principal companies, but it is now numbered as the thirteenth. It is governed by two wardens, and thirty assistants, and the livery fine is £15.

### CHURCH OF ALLHALLOWS, BREAD STREET.

This church received its name from being dedicated to all the saints, and its situation. It is a rectory of very ancient foundation, the patronage of which was originally in the prior and canons of Christ-church in Canterbury, who remained patrons of it till the year 1365, when it was conveyed to the archbishop of Canterbury and his successors, in whom it still continues, and is one of the peculiars belonging to that see in the city of London.

The old church being destroyed by the fire of London, in 1666, the present edifice was erected in 1684, at the expense of the public; and serves not only for the accommodation of the inhabitants of its own parish, but likewise for those of St. John the Evangelist, which is annexed to it by act of parliament. This church consists of a plain body, of the Tuscan order, seventy-two feet in length, thirty-five in breadth, and thirty in height to the roof; with a square tower eighty-six feet high, divided into four stages, with arches near the top. The inside is handsomely wainscoted and pewed, the pulpit finely carved, the sounding board veneered, a neat gallery at the west end, and a spacious altar-piece well adorned and beautified.

### CHURCH OF ST. JAMES'S, GARLICK HILL.

At the south-east corner of Garlick-hill stands the parochial church of St. James. This church is so called from its dedication to the above saint, and its vicinity to a garlick market, which was anciently held in the neighbourhood, and called Garlick Hythe, from being a wharf on the bank of the river. It is a rectory, the patronage of which appears to have been in the abbot and convent of Westminster, till the suppression of their monastery; when coming to the crown, Queen Mary, in the year 1553, granted the same to the bishop of London and his successors, in whom it still remains. The earliest mention of this church is, that it was rebuilt by Richard de Rothing, sheriff, in 1326.

The old church being destroyed by the fire of London, the present edifice was begun ten years after, and thoroughly completed in 1682. It is built of stone, seventy-five feet long, forty-five feet broad, and forty feet high to the roof: the altitude of the steeple is ninety-eight feet. The tower is divided into three stages, in the lowest of which is a very elegant door with coupled columns of the Corinthian order. In the second is a large window, over which is another, of a circular form, not opened. In the third story is a window larger than the former; and the cornice above this supports a range of open work in the place of battlements, on a balustrade. Above this is the turret, which is composed of four stages, and decorated with columns, scrolls, and ornaments. From the body of the church projects a very handsome dial, on the top of which is a statue of St. James, to whom the church is dedicated.


## CHURCH OF ST. MARY, ALDERMANBURY.

On the west side of the street, between Love-lane and Addle-street, stands the parish church of St. Mary, Aldermanbury, which is of ancient foundation; as is evident from a sepulchral inscription, in the old church, bearing the date of 1116. The patronage was formerly in the dean and chapter of St. Pauls, who, in the year 1331, with the consent of Stephen, bishop of London, appropriated it to the adjoining hospital of Elsing Spital; but with a proviso, that the dean and chapter should have the patronage of both, and that, upon the appointment of a custos to this church and hospital, he was to swear fealty to the dean and chapter, and to pay them an ancient pension of a mark a year, due from this church, and six shillings and eightpence yearly, for the hospital, as granted by the founder, William de Elsing, in testimony of its subjection to the church of St. Paul. It was also agreed that the custos should find a priest to serve the cure, who was to be approved by the dean and chapter. Hence it appears that this church was, at that time, a curacy, as it still continues: but, after the dissolution of the hospital, the patronage was granted to the parishioners, who have ever since presented to it.

The old church being destroyed, by the dreadful fire in 1666, the present structure was finished ten years after. It is built of stone, and very plain; the body is well enlightened, and the corners are wrought with rustic. It is seventy-two feet long and forty-five broad; the roof is thirty-eight feet high, and the steeple about ninety feet. It has a plain solid tower, constructed in the same manner as the body, and the angles in the upper stage strengthened with rustic; the cornice is supported by scrolls, and above it is a plain Attic course. In this rises a turret, with a square base that supports the dial. This turret is arched, but the corners are massy, and its roof is terminated in a point, on which is placed the vane.


## WATERMAN'S HALL, ST. MARY'S HILL.

Waterman's Hall, which formerly stood in Cold Harbour, was removed into this ward in the year 1786. Its present situation is on the west side of St. Mary's Hill. It is a neat building, partly of stone, and partly of brick. The principal entrance, which is at the south end, is through a rustic basement story, above which rise four pilasters of the Ionic order, supporting a plain triangular pediment. Above the door are the arms of the company.

WATERMAN'S HALL, ST. MARY'S HILL.

PAINTER STAINER'S HALL, LITTLE TRINITY LANE.

WINCHESTER HOUSE, WINCHESTER STREET.

## PAINTER-STAINER'S HALL, LITTLE TRINITY LANE.

On the west side of Little Trinity Lane is Painter-stainer's Hall. This hall is adorned with a handsome screen, arches, pillars, and pilasters of the Corinthian order, painted in imitation of porphyry, with gilt capitals. The panels are of wainscot, and the ceilings are embellished with a great variety of historical and other paintings, exquisitely performed; amongst which are the portraits of king Charles II. and his queen Catharine, by Mr. Houseman; a portrait of Camden; a view of London on fire in 1666; and a fine piece of shipping by Monumea.

In the court room are some fine pictures, most of which are portraits of the members of the company; and in the front of the room is a fine bust of Mr. Thomas Evans, who left five houses in Basinghall Street to the company.

Camden, the Antiquarian, gave the Painter-stainer's Company a silver cup and cover, which they use every St. Luke's day at their election; the old master drinking to his successor out of it. On the cup is the following inscription :—GUL. CAMDENOS CLAREN-CEUX FILIUS SAMPSONIS PICTORIS LONDINENSIS DONO DEDIT.

## WINCHESTER HOUSE, WINCHESTER STREET.

The remains of this building stand in the south-west corner of Winchester Street, near Broad Street, having been originally erected by the old marquis of Winchester, in the reign of Edward VI.

The upper part of this fabric is more modern than the lower, but yet appears in a decayed state. The old walls still retain their mullioned windows surrounded with quoins; and strong bars of iron are inserted in the bricks, which prevent the several parts of the building from separating. This mansion has for a considerable time been in the occupation of several packers.

## CHURCH OF ST. JAMES, WESTMINSTER.

On the south side of Piccadilly is the parish church of St. James, Westminster.

This is also one of the churches that owes its rise to the increase of buildings; for the church of St. Martin in the fields being too small for the inhabitants, and too remote from those in this quarter, Henry Jermyn, earl of St. Alban's, with other persons of distinction in that neighbourhood, erected this edifice at an expense of about £7000. It was built in the reign of king Charles II., and, though a large fabric, was considered as a chapel of ease to St. Martin's. It was consecrated in 1684, and dedicated to St. James, in compliment to the name of the duke of York, and the next year, when that prince had ascended the throne, the district for which it was built was by act of parliament separated from St. Martin's, and made a distinct parish. The walls are brick, supported by rustic quoins of stone; and the

windows, which are large, are also cased with stone.   The tower at the west end rises regularly from the ground to a considerable height, and is crowned with a neat well-constructed
spire.

In this church is a most beautiful baptismal font, of white marble, by Grinlyn Gibbons.
It is supported by a column, representing the tree of the knowledge of good and evil, on which
is the serpent offering the fruit to our first parents, who are standing beneath.   On the font
are three pieces of sculpture : St. John baptizing Christ; Philip baptizing the Eunuch; and
Noah's Ark, with the dove bearing the olive-branch.

Over the altar is some exquisite carving in wood, by the same artist, representing a
pelican feeding its young, between two doves: there is also a very elegant festoon, with
large fruit, flowers, and foliage.   This parish is a rectory in the gift of the bishop of London.

### CHURCH OF ST. PETER-LE-POOR, BROAD STREET.

On the west side of Broad Street, nearly opposite to the back entrance of the South Sea
House, is situated the parish church of St. Peter-le-poor.   This church is of very ancient
foundation, as appears from a register of it so far back as the year 1181.   It was dedicated
to St. Peter the Apostle, and is distinguished from other churches of that name by the additional epithet of Le Poor, which Stow conjectures was given to it from the ancient state
of the parish, though, in his time, there were many fair houses in it, possessed by rich merchants and others.

The old church projected a considerable distance beyond the line of the houses, and was
a great obstruction to the passage of the street, in consequence of which, an act of parliament
was passed, in 1788, for taking it down and rebuilding it, further back, taking in the site of
a court behind.   This desirable object was completed in 1791, at an expense of upwards of
£4000, of which the city of London subscribed 400 : the remainder was raised by annuities
in the parish.   The west end of this new church is elegantly simple : the door is in the
centre, between double Ionic columns; the ends of the front are adorned with pilasters of
the same order, between which and the columns is a blank window on each side.   Above
the door is a moulded pediment, with a plain tympanum, over which rises a square tower,
in two stories; the first plain, for the clock and bells, the second ornamented with double
Corinthian pilasters at the corners, on each of which stands a handsome vase.   The whole
is surmounted with an elegant bell-shaped dome, terminated by a weathercock.   It is a
rectory, the advowson of which appears to have been always in the dean and chapter of St.
Paul's.

### NORTHUMBERLAND HOUSE, STRAND.

At the south-west corner of the Strand, opposite to the end of St. Martin's Lane, stands
Northumberland House, which was erected on the site of the hospital of St. Mary Rounceval,
a cell to the priory of the same name, in Navarre, founded and endowed by the earl of

Drawn by Tho. H. Shepherd.

ST. JAMES'S PICCADILLY.

ST. PETER LE POOR, BROAD STREET.

Drawn by Tho. H. Shepherd.

NORTHUMBERLAND HOUSE, CHARING CROSS.

Pembroke, in the reign of Henry III. This hospital was suppressed, with other alien priories, by Henry V.; but was re-founded, in 1476, by Edward IV. After the general suppression of religious houses by Henry VIII., Edward VI., in the year 1549, granted the chapel, with its appurtenances, to Sir Thomas Cawarden. After this it came into the possession of Henry Howard, earl of Northampton, who, in the reign of James I., erected three sides of the quadrangle. After the death of this nobleman, it became the property of his relation, the earl of Suffolk, and was then known by the name of Suffolk House.

In the reign of Charles I. Algernon, earl of Northumberland, lord high admiral of England, married the daughter of the earl of Suffolk, and, about the year 1642, became proprietor of this house; from which time it has borne its present name.

This earl, finding it inconvenient to reside in the apartments built by lord Northampton, on account of their nearness to the street, completed the quadrangle by building the fourth, or south side, which is at such a distance from the street as to avoid the noise of the carriages, &c., and enjoys all the advantages of retirement. This part was built under the direction of Inigo Jones, as the other three sides had been under that of Bernard Janssen. It was in a conference held in one of these apartments, between the earl of Northumberland, general Monk, and some of the leading men of the nation, that the restoration of Charles II. was proposed, as a measure absolutely necessary to the peace of the kingdom.

The front next the street was begun to be rebuilt by Algernon, duke of Somerset, who became possessed of it in 1748, in right of his mother, the daughter and heiress of the earl of Northumberland; and from him it descended to his son-in-law, and daughter, the late duke and duchess of Northumberland, by whom the new front was completed, and such improvements made as have rendered this building an object of admiration for its elegance and grandeur.

The front of this building, next the street, is exceedingly magnificent. In the centre of it is a grand arched gate, the piers of which are continued up to the top of the building, with niches on each side from the ground, decorated with carvings, in a sort of Gothic style. They are connected at the top, by uniting to form an arch in the centre, opening from the top of the house to a circular balcony, standing on a small bow window over the gate beneath. Over the arch, on a pedestal, is a carved lion, the crest of the duke of Northumberland's arms. The building, on each side the centre, is of brick, containing two series of regular windows, five on each side, over a like series of niches on the ground story. At each extremity is a tower, with rustic stone corners, containing one window each in front corresponding with the building. These towers rise above the rest of the front, first with an arched window, above that a port-hole window, and the top terminated with a dome, crowned with a vane. The centre is connected with the turrets over the building, by a breast-work of solid piers, and open lattice-work, alternately, corresponding with the windows beneath, which have stone-work under them, carved in like manner.

The four sides of the inner court are faced with Portland stone, and the two wings, which extend from the garden front towards the river, are above 100 feet in length. The principal door of the house opens to a vestibule, about eighty-two feet long, and upwards of twelve

L

feet wide, properly ornamented with columns of the Doric order.   Each end of it communicates with a stair-case leading to the principal apartments, which face the garden.   They consist of several spacious rooms, fitted up in the most elegant manner.   The ceilings are embellished with copies of antique paintings, or fine ornaments of stucco, richly gilt.   The chimney-pieces are of curious marble, carved and finished in the most correct taste.   The rooms are hung either with beautiful tapestry, or the richest damasks, and magnificently furnished with large glasses, settees, marble tables, &c., with frames of exquisite workmanship, richly gilt.   They also contain a great variety of pictures, executed by the most distinguished masters, particularly Raphael, Titian, Paul Veronese, Salvator Rosa, Rubens, Vandyke, &c. Among these is the Cornaro family, painted by Titian, which was sold to Algernon, earl of Northumberland, in the reign of Charles I., by Vandyke, for 1000 guineas.   In some of the rooms are large chests, embellished with old genuine Japan, which, being great rarities, are esteemed invaluable.

The gallery or ball-room, in the east wing, is decorated in a very elegant manner.   It is 106 feet long, and 27 feet wide.   The ceiling is carved and ornamented with figures and festoons, richly gilt.   The flat part of the ceiling is divided into five compartments, ornamented with fine imitations of some antique figures ; particularly a flying Fame blowing a trumpet ; a Diana ; a triumphal car drawn by two horses ; a Flora ; and a Victory holding out a wreath of laurel.   The entablature is Corinthian, and of most exquisite workmanship. The whole building, both in the interior and exterior, has within these few years undergone a complete repair, at an immense expense.

## Serjeant's Inn, Chancery Lane,

Is the only remaining inn of court for the judges and serjeants of the law, and contains chambers wholly for the accommodation of these gentlemen ; whereas, in that in Fleet Street, each one possessed a distinct house.   The degree of a serjeant being the highest in the law, except that of a judge, it is conferred by the sovereign on those of the profession most eminently distinguished for their abilities and probity ;  and this order is held so honorable, that none are admitted to the dignity of a judge but the members of it.   According to the opinion of some of our ablest lawyers, among whom may be named Sir Edward Coke, this degree is of very ancient standing, and it is expressly mentioned in a statute of the third of Edward I., cap. xxix.

The Rolls-chapel is the place for keeping the rolls or records in chancery.

This house was founded by king Henry III. in the place where stood a Jew's house, forfeited to that prince in the year 1233.   In this chapel all such Jews and infidels as were converted to the Christian faith were ordained, and in the buildings belonging to it were appointed a sufficient maintenance ; by which means a great number of converts were baptized, instructed in the doctrines of christianity, and lived under a learned christian appointed to govern them ;  but, in the year 1290, all the Jews being banished, the number of converts

Drawn by Tho.H.Shepherd.

Engraved by W.H.Bond.

SERJEANTS' INN HALL, CHANCERY LANE.

Drawn by Tho.H.Shepherd.

Engraved by W.H.Bond.

STAPLES INN HALL, HOLBORN.

decreased, and, in the year 1377, the house, with its chapel, was annexed by patent to the keeper of the rolls of chancery.

The chapel, which is of brick, pebbles, and some free-stone, is sixty feet long, and thirty-three feet in breadth; the doors and windows are Gothic, and the roof covered with slate. In this chapel the rolls are kept in presses fixed to the sides, and ornamented with columns and pilasters of the Ionic and Composite orders. These rolls contain all the records, as charters, patents, &c., since the beginning of the reign of Richard III., those before that time being deposited in the record-office in the Tower; and these being made up in rolls of parchment, gave occasion to the name.

## Staples' Inn, Holborn.

Within the bars, on the south side of Holborn, is Staples' Inn, which is an inn of chancery, and a member of Gray's Inn, and consists of two large courts, surrounded with good buildings.

This inn is said to have been anciently a hall for the accommodation of wool-staplers, whence it derived its appellation. It was, however, an inn of chancery in the year 1415, though how long before is unknown. In the year 1529, the benchers of Gray's Inn purchased this place of John Knighton, and Alice his wife, by the name of "All that messuage, or Inn of Chancery, commonly called Staple Inn;" since which time it has continued to be an appendage to Gray's Inn.

## The Monument, Fish Street Hill.

This noble piece of architecture was erected by an act of parliament to commemorate the great and dreadful conflagration of the city in 1666. It was begun by Sir Christopher Wren in 1671, and finished by him in 1677, at an expense of £14,500.

It is a round fluted pillar of the Doric order, built of Portland stone, 202 feet in height from the ground, the exact distance of the spot where the fire began. The diameter of the shaft or body of the column is fifteen feet; the ground plinth or lowest part of the pedestal is forty feet in height. Over the capitol is an iron balcony, encompassing a cone thirty-two feet high, supporting a blazing urn of gilt brass. In the place of this urn, which was set up contrary to Sir Christopher's opinion, was originally intended a colossal statue, in gilt brass, either of king Charles II., as founder of the new city, after the manner of the Roman pillars, which were terminated with the statues of their Cæsars; or else an erect figure of a woman, crowned with turrets, holding a sword and cap of maintenance, with other ensigns of the city's grandeur and re-edification.

Within is a large staircase of black marble, containing 345 steps, each ten inches and a half broad, and six inches thick. The west side of the pedestal is adorned with curious emblems, by the masterly hand of Mr. Cibber, father of the poet-laureat, denoting the destruction and restoration of the city, in which the eleven principal figures are done in alto,

and the rest in basso relievo.   The first female figure represents the city of London, sitting
among the ruins, in a languishing posture, with her head dejected, hair dishevelled, and her
hand carelessly lying on her sword.   Behind is Time, gradually raising her up: at her side
a woman, representing Providence, gently touching her with one hand, and with a winged
sceptre in the other, directing her to regard the goddesses in the clouds, one with a cornucopia, denoting plenty, the other with a palm branch, the emblem of peace.   At her feet a
bee-hive, showing that by industry and application the greatest misfortunes are to be over-
come.   Behind Time are citizens exulting at his endeavours to restore her;  and beneath,
in the midst of the ruins, is a dragon, who, as supporter of the city arms, with his paw endeavours to preserve the same.   Still farther at the north end is a view of the city in flames;
the inhabitants in consternation, with their arms extended upwards, as crying out for
succour.   Opposite the city, on an elevated pavement, stands the king, in a Roman habit,
with a laurel on his head, and a truncheon in his hand;  and, approaching her, commands
three of his attendants to descend to her relief;  the first represents the sciences, with a
winged head and circle of naked boys dancing thereon, holding Nature by the hand, with
her numerous breasts, ready to give assistance to all;  the second is architecture, with a plan
in one hand, and a square and pair of compasses in the other:  and the third is Liberty,
waving a hat in the air, showing her joy at the pleasing prospect of the city's speedy recovery.   Behind the king stands his brother, the duke of York, with a garland in one hand
to crown the rising city, and a sword in the other for her defence.   The two figures behind
are Justice and Fortitude;  the former with a coronet, and the latter with a reined lion;  and
under the royal pavement, in a vault, lieth Envy, gnawing a heart, and incessantly emitting
pestiferous fumes from her envenomed mouth.   In the upper part of the plinth the re-
construction of the city is represented by builders and labourers at work upon houses.

On the other three façades of the plinth are Latin inscriptions;  that on the north side is
thus rendered:—" In the year of Christ, 1666, September 2, eastward from hence, at the
distance of 202 feet (the height of this column), a terrible fire broke out about midnight;
which, driven on by a high wind, not only wasted the adjacent parts, but also very remote
places, with incredible noise and fury.   It consumed eighty-nine churches, the city gates,
Guildhall, many public structures, hospitals, schools, libraries, a vast number of stately
edifices, 13,000 dwelling houses, and 400 streets.   Of the twenty-six wards it utterly destroyed fifteen, and left eight others shattered and half burnt.   The ruins of the city were
436 acres, from the tower by the Thames side to the Temple church;  and from the north-
east along the wall to Holborn-bridge.   To the estates and fortunes of the citizens it was
merciless, but to their lives very favorable, that it might in all things resemble the last conflagration of the world.   The destruction was sudden;  for, in a small space of time, the city
was seen most flourishing, and reduced to nothing.   Three days after, when, in the opinion
of all, this fatal fire had baffled all human counsels and endeavours, it stopped, as it were
by a command from heaven, and was on every side extinguished."

The inscription on the south side is translated thus:—

" Charles the Second, son of Charles the Martyr, king of Great Britain, France, and

THE MONUMENT, FISH STREET HILL.

ST. AUSTIN, WATLING STREET.

SESSIONS HOUSE, CLERKENWELL GREEN.

Ireland, defender of the faith, a most gracious prince, commiserating the deplorable state of things, whilst the ruins were yet smoking, provided for the comfort of his citizens, and ornament of his city, remitted their taxes, and referred the petition of the magistrates and inhabitants to parliament; who immediately passed an act, that public works should be restored to greater beauty with public money, to be raised by an impost on coals : that churches, and the cathedral of St. Paul's, should be rebuilt from their foundations with all magnificence ; that the bridges, gates, and prisons should be new made, and sewers cleansed ; the streets made straight and regular ; such as were steep levelled, and those too narrow to be made wider ; and that the markets and shambles should be removed to separate places. They also enacted that every house should be built with party-walls, and all in front raised of equal height, and those walls all of squared stone or brick ; and that no man should delay building beyond the space of seven years. Moreover, care was taken, by law, to prevent all suits about their bounds. Also, anniversary prayers were enjoined ; and, to perpetuate the memory hereof to posterity, they caused this column to be erected. The work was carried on with diligence, and London is restored, but whether with greater speed or beauty may be made a question. At three years' time, the world saw that finished which was supposed to be the business of an age."

The inscription on the east side is in English, thus :

"This pillar was begun, Sir Richard Ford, knight, being lord mayor of London, in the year 1671. Carried on in the mayoralties of Sir George Waterman, knt., Sir Robert Hanson, knt., Sir William Hooker, knt., Sir Robert Viner, knt., Sir Joseph Sheldon, knt., lord mayors. And finished, Sir Thomas Davies being lord mayor, in the year 1677."

The prevailing opinion of the citizens of London, and of the generality of protestants of all denominations, after this terrible devastation, was, that it had been occasioned by the contrivances of the papists ; for which reason, the following inscription was engraved round the pedestal.

"This pillar was set up in perpetual remembrance of the most dreadful burning of this protestant city, begun and carried on by the treachery and malice of the popish faction, in the beginning of September, in the year of our Lord, 1666, in order to the carrying on their horrid plot for extirpating the protestant religion, and old English liberty, and introducing popery and slavery."

This inscription was expunged in the time of James II., but was restored in the next reign ; and, by a recent resolution of the court of common-council, it is again ordered to be expunged.

The cornice of the pedestal is adorned with the king's arms, the sword, mace, cap of maintenance, &c., enriched with trophies ; and at each angle are winged dragons, the supporters of the city arms.

This monument is, undoubtedly, the noblest modern column in the world ; and, in some respects, may vie with the most celebrated of antiquity. In height it greatly exceeds the pillars of the emperors Trajan and Antoninus, the stately remains of Roman grandeur, as well as that of Theodosius, at Constantinople.

## CHURCH OF ST. AUSTIN, WATLING STREET.

At the corner of the Old Change, and Watling Street, stands the parish church of St. Austin, called in old records *Ecclesia Sancti Augustini ad portum*, because it stood near the gate leading out of Watling Street into St. Paul's church-yard.

It is a rectory, the patronage of which appears to have been always in the dean and chapter of St. Paul's; for it is mentioned in their books, in the year 1181, when Ralph de Diceto was dean.

The present edifice is erected on the site of the old church, which was destroyed by the fire of London. It is a substantial structure, built with stone, and well pewed and wainscoted within: the pulpit is finely embellished, and the altar-piece is spacious and beautiful, with a very handsome pediment in the front, supported by pillars, in imitation of porphyry, and on the top of the pediment are the king's arms.

The length of this church is fifty-one feet, the breadth forty-five feet, the height of the roof thirty feet, and that of the steeple 145 feet.

After the fire of London, this church was made parochial for the parish of St. Austin and that of St. Faith, which was united to it.

## SESSIONS' HOUSE, CLERKENWELL GREEN.

On the west side of Clerkenwell Green is the sessions' house for the county of Middlesex. The former sessions' house was situated in the middle of St. John Street, and was called Hicks's-hall, from its founder, Sir Baptist Hicks, by whom it was erected in the year 1611, and given for the perpetual use of the magistrates of the county. This building having become very ruinous, and being also extremely inconvenient, an act of parliament was obtained in the year 1779 for erecting a new one; and, a convenient spot of ground having been purchased on Clerkenwell Green, the first stone of the present edifice was laid on the 20th of August in that year, and it was opened for business in 1782.

The east and principal front of it, towards Clerkenwell Green, is composed of four three-quarter columns, and two pilasters, of the Ionic order, supported by a rustic basement. The county arms are placed in the tympanum of the pediment. Under the entablature are two medallions, which represent Justice and Mercy. In the former, Justice holds the scales and sword; and in the latter, Mercy grasps the blunted sword and the sceptre, capped with the British crown, on which, as emblematic of the mildness of the British laws, rests a dove, with an olive-branch in its mouth. In the centre, between Justice and Mercy, is a medallion of his majesty, George III., in profile, decorated with festoons of laurel and oak leaves, the emblems of strength and valour. At each extremity is a medallion, containing the Roman fasces and sword, the insignia of authority and punishment. The extent of this building is 110 feet from east to west, and 78 feet from north to south.

LYON'S INN HALL.

BARNARD'S INN HALL.

FLEET STREET.

The hall is thirty-four feet square, and terminates at the top in a circular dome, enlightened by six circular windows, each four feet eleven inches in diameter. This dome is panelled in stucco, and the spandrils under it are decorated with shields and oak-leaves. The sides of the hall are finished with pilasters of the composite order, crowned with an entablature, the frieze of which is ornamented with foliage and medallions, representing the caduceus of Mercury, and the Roman fasces.

From the hall a double flight of steps leads up to the court, which is in the form of the Roman letter D, and is thirty-four feet by thirty, and twenty-six feet high, with spacious galleries on the sides for the auditors.

The rooms on each side of the entrance are appropriated to the meetings of the magistrates. In one of them is the original portrait of Sir Baptist Hicks, which was brought from the old sessions' house, with the arms and ornaments which decorated the chimney of the dining room there; and in the other is a good copy of the picture.

## LYON'S INN HALL.—BARNARD'S INN.

Opposite to the New Inn, on the south side of Wych Street, is Lyon's Inn, which is a house of chancery, belonging to the Inner Temple. It was anciently a common inn, having the sign of the lion, and is said to have been in the possession of the students and practitioners of the law ever since the year 1420.

On the south side of Holborn is Barnard's Inn, which is also an inn of Chancery, and an appendage to Gray's Inn. It was anciently denominated Mackworth's Inn, and was given to the society in the year 1454, by the executors of John Mackworth, dean of Lincoln.

## FLEET STREET.

It appears, from Fabian and others, that this was the principal part of the Saxon city; and that in king Ethelred's reign, London had more building from Ludgate towards Westminster, and little or none where the chief or heart of the city now is. This might have arisen from the incursions of the Danes, as the gates identify the more ancient city.

The very interesting and picturesque view of this street, seen from the point where the engraving was taken, represents St. Dunstan's church (since taken down); proceeding westward, on the left, the newly erected handsome banking-house of Messrs. Hoare and Company, on the opposite side the way, and that fine object, Temple Bar, in the front distance.

## THE TOWER OF LONDON

stands on the celebrated eminence called Tower Hill; and, though said to be of very ancient date, cannot be traced with any certainty beyond the time of William the Conqueror, who built what is now called the White Tower, and enlarged the whole, which at present covers twelve superficial acres; its ramparts are surrounded by a deep and wide ditch, proceeding north on each side of the fortress, nearly in a parallel line, and meeting in a semicircular projection.    The slope is faced with brick work, and the walls have been so much mended that the original stone is scarcely to be seen.    Cannon are placed at intervals round the wall, though the interior is completely lined with old houses.

The principal entrance into the Tower is by the west gate, large enough to admit coaches and heavy carriages.    This gateway itself is entered by an outer gate, opening to a strong stone bridge built over the ditch.

The Traitor's Gate is a low arch through the wall, on the south side, on which there are several old decayed towers, intermixed with modern brick offices and ragged fragments of patched curtains; and this gate communicates by a canal with the river Thames.

Besides these, there is an entrance for foot passengers over the draw-bridge to the wharf, opened every morning.    The points of a huge portcullis may still be seen over the arch of the principal gate, and great ceremony is used at opening and shutting it night and morning. This mass of buildings is remarkable on several accounts.

The principal buildings within the Tower walls are, the White Tower and the Chapel of St. John, where the records are lodged within the same; the Church of St. Peter Ad Vincula infra Turrim, the Ordnance Office, the Record Office, the Jewel Office, the Horse Armoury, the Grand Storehouse, in which is the small armoury, and the Menagerie.    Here are likewise apartments for state prisoners.    The White Tower, or interior fortress, is a large square irregular building, almost in the centre of the Tower, consisting of three lofty stories, having under them commodious vaults for salt-petre, &c.: on the top, covered with lead, is a cistern or reservoir, from which, in case of necessity, the whole garrison might be supplied with water.

The palace within the Tower was in the south-east angle of the walls, and was used by the kings of England, nearly 500 years, only ceasing to be so on the accession of queen Elizabeth, who, after being confined as a prisoner by queen Mary, had, probably, no longing to renew her residence in the Tower.

On a long platform before the Tower, on the Thames' side, sixty-one pieces of cannon used to be planted, and fired on rejoicing days; but these were removed in 1814, and those on the ramparts are used in their stead.

After passing the spur-guard, in a spacious enclosure, at the right hand, is the repository for wild beasts, &c., presented to the British sovereign from foreign potentates, which are shown to the public by the keepers for a shilling each person; for this fee the beholders are informed of the names, genealogies, &c., of the different animals, which are well worth seeing, as they are kept remarkably clean and healthy in capacious dens.    It is a necessary caution, however, not to go within the rails, or to attempt to play tricks, as the beasts whelped in the Tower are much more fierce than those brought over wild.

Having passed the bridge, the wardens wait at the principal gate, to afford information to strangers, and to conduct them to view the many and valuable curiosities with which the Tower abounds.    These are so various, that the minute description of them would furnish

THE TOWER OF LONDON, FROM TOWER HILL.

PREROGATIVE WILL OFFICE, DOCTOR'S COMMONS.　　　　BEN JOHNSON'S HEAD, DEVEREUX COURT, STRAND.

a volume; we can, therefore, only mention, that the Horse Armoury contains the representations of sixteen English Monarchs on horseback, and in complete armour. The Small Armoury contains complete stands of arms, bright, clear, and flinted, for 150,000 men; besides cannon and pikes, swords, &c., innumerable, ranged in regular order. The Jewel Office contains the imperial crown, placed on the heads of the Kings of England at their coronation, the Prince of Wales's crown, golden spurs and bracelets, the crown jewels, and a great quantity of curious old plate. The Ordnance Office, burnt 1789, has been rebuilt in a way so as to prevent the recurrence of such an accident. The Record Office is opposite the platform, but, like the Ordnance Office, is not a place of mere curiosity, access being confined to such persons as may have particular business to transact there.

The chapel, dedicated to St. Peter Ad Vincula, may be seen, by applying to the pew-opener, at any time, for a small fee.

## PREROGATIVE WILL OFFICE, DOCTOR'S COMMONS.

This court is thus denominated from the prerogative of the Archbishop of Canterbury, who, by a special privilege beyond those of his suffragans, can here try all disputes that happen to arise concerning the last wills of persons within his province, who have left goods to the value of five pounds and upwards, unless such things are settled by composition between the metropolitan and his suffragans; as in the diocese of London, where it is ten pounds. To this court belongs a judge, who is styled Judex Curiæ Prerogativæ Cantuariensis; and a registrar, who hath convenient rooms in his office, for the disposing and laying up safe all original wills and testaments. This registrar also hath his deputy, besides several clerks.

## BEN JONSON'S HEAD, DEVEREUX COURT, STRAND.

Ben Jonson, one of the most considerable dramatic poets of the seventeenth century, whether we consider the number or the merit of his productions, was the son of a clergyman in Westminster, where he was born in the year 1574, about a month after the death of his father. He was descended of a Scottish family; for it appears that his father had been possessed of an estate in Scotland, which he lost in the reign of Queen Mary. The family name was Johnson, but for some reason, which is not known, our poet always wrote it without the *h*. His education was begun at a private school, in St. Martin in the Fields, whence he was removed to Westminster-school, and placed under the tuition of the great Camden; but, his mother having married a bricklayer, Ben was taken home, and obliged to work at his father-in-law's trade. This was an indignity his mind could not submit to; he therefore enlisted as a soldier, and was sent over to the Low Countries, where he distinguished himself by killing one of the enemy in single combat, and carrying off the spoils in sight of both armies.

On his return to England, he entered himself of St. John's College, Cambridge; but, his finances not permitting him to prosecute his studies, he joined a company of players. While he belonged to this company, a quarrel took place between him and one of his associates, which produced a duel, and Ben killed his antagonist; for which he was condemned, and narrowly escaped execution.

Shakspeare is said to have introduced him to the world, by bringing a play of his on the stage, and performing a principal part in it himself. Thus encouraged, his genius ripened apace, and, from 1598 to 1603, he furnished the stage with a new play regularly every year. Afterwards, he became more slow in his productions, though he still continued to write. In 1619, he obtained the degree of master of arts, at Oxford, and was made poet-laureat to James I., with a salary of one hundred marks per annum, and a tierce of wine. As we do not find his economical virtues any where recorded, it will not appear surprising that this sum was too little for his wants; for which reason, on the accession of Charles I., he petitioned for, and obtained, an increase of his allowance, from marks to pounds. Still his extravagance exceeded his income, and, quickly after, we learn that he was very poor and sick, lodging in an obscure alley. Charles was again applied to, and sent him ten guineas, which was so much below his wishes, that he said, on receiving it, " His majesty has sent me ten guineas, because I am poor and live in an alley; go and tell him that his soul lives in an alley."

He died on the 16th of August, 1637, and was buried in Westminster-abbey, where a marble monument is erected to his memory, with this laconic inscription: O Rare Ben Jonson!

### CHURCH OF ST. ANNE, SOHO.

The parish of St. Anne was separated from that of St. Martin in the Fields by an act of parliament passed in the year 1661; previous to which, a piece of ground was laid out, under the authority of the bishop of London, in Kemp's field, now King-street, for the site of a church and church-yard, and also for a glebe for the support of a rector. But, the inhabitants not being empowered by this act to raise money for accomplishing their purpose, the building of the church was long interrupted, and at length a second act was obtained, to enable them to raise the sum of five thousands pounds, for the completion of the church, rectory house, &c., and on the 25th of March, 1685, the church and cemetery were consecrated by the bishop of London.

The walls of this church are of brick, with rustic quoins of stone, and at the east end is a large modillion cornice and triangular pediment. This church has been since repaired, and a handsome painted glass window has been put up at the east end. The tower and steeple at the west end were also rebuilt at the same time.

The interior of the building is handsome. The roof is arched and divided into panels. It is supported by columns of the Ionic order; and the gallery is raised on those of the Tuscan order. The organ is the gift of King William III.

The parish is a rectory in the gift of the bishop of London.

Drawn by Tho. H. Shepherd.

ST. ANNE'S, SOHO.

Engraved by J. Tingle.

FORE STREET, AND CRIPPLEGATE CHURCH.

Drawn by Tho. H. Shepherd.

Engraved by J. Tingle.

ST. MARY, WHITECHAPEL.

Against the tower is a tablet erected to the memory of Theodore Anthony Newhoff, king of Corsica, who died in this parish in the year 1756, soon after his liberation from the King's-bench prison by an act of insolvency. The malice of fortune pursued this unfortunate man even after death. The friend who sheltered him in the last days of his wretched existence was himself so poor as to be unable to defray the cost of his funeral, and his remains were about to be consigned to the grave by the parish, when a Mr. Wright, an oilman, in Compton-street, declared he for once would pay the funeral expenses of a king; which he actually did. The marble was erected and the epitaph written by the honourable Horace Walpole. It is as follows :—

> The grave, great teacher, to a level brings
> Heroes and beggars, galley slaves and kings.
> But Theodore this moral learn'd ere dead,
> Fate pour'd its lessons on his living head,
> Bestow'd a kingdom, and denied him bread.

## CHURCH OF ST. MARY, WHITECHAPEL.

This church is of some antiquity, as appears by Hugh de Fulbourn being rector thereof in the year 1329. It was originally a chapel of ease to the church of St. Dunstan, Stepney, and is supposed to have obtained the epithet of White from having been white-washed or plastered on the outside.

The first church erected on the spot, after it ceased to be a chapel of ease of Stepney parish, was dedicated to St. Mary Matfelon, and the township acquired the appellation of Villa Beatæ Mariæ de Matfelon; a name which has given birth to many conjectures respecting its signification, but which is probably derived from the Hebrew word Matfel, which signifies both a woman lately delivered of a son, and a woman carrying her infant son; either of which significations is applicable to the Virgin Mary and her holy babe.

The old church being in a very ruinous condition, it was taken down in 1673, and the present edifice was soon after erected in its stead. This is a coarse and very irregular building; the body, which is formed of brick, and ornamented with stone rustic work at the corners, is ninety-three feet in length, sixty-three feet in breadth; and the height of the tower and turret is eighty feet. The principal door is ornamented with a kind of rustic pilasters, with cherubs' heads by way of capitals, and a pediment above. The body is enlightened with a great number of windows, which are of various forms, and different sizes, a sort of Venetian, oval and square. The square windows have ill-proportioned circular pediments; and the oval, or more properly elliptic windows, some of which stand upright, and others cross-ways, are surrounded with thick festoons. The steeple, which is of stone, rises above the principal door, and is crowned with a plain square battlement, in the centre of which rises a small turret, with its dome and vane. It was some time since thoroughly repaired.

### CHURCH OF ALLHALLOWS STAINING, MARK LANE.

This church is believed to be of Saxon origin, because of the additional epithet of Stane now corruptly called Staining; which our antiquaries are of opinion was given to it on, account of being built with stone, to distinguish it from some of the other churches in this city, of the same name, that were built of wood. The first authentic mention of it is in the year 1329, when Edward Camel was incumbent thereof.

It was anciently a rectory, under the patronage of the De Walthams, and others, till about 1369, when Simon, bishop of London, upon the petition of the abbot and convent of Grace, near the Tower, appropriated it to them and their successors, with power to convert the profits to their own use, and to supply the cure with either a monk or a secular priest, removable at their pleasure. This curacy devolving with the abbey to the crown, it was sold on the 7th of October, 1607, by king James I. to George Bingley, and others, to be held of the crown, in soccage; and, coming afterwards to the Lady Slany, was by her bequeathed to the company of Grocers, who have since held the advowson.

This church escaped the fire in 1666; but it was in so ruinous a state, that the body of it fell down three years after, and the whole was rebuilt, at the expense of the parishioners, as it now appears. It is a very plain edifice, enlightened with Gothic windows; but the front, which is of free-stone, is of the Tuscan order. It has a square tower, crowned with a small turret. The length of the church is seventy-eight feet, its breadth thirty-two, and its height twenty-four; and the altitude of the tower is seventy feet.

### CHURCH OF ST. MARTIN ORGAR, ST. MARTIN'S LANE, CANNON STREET.

The church of St. Martin Orgar stood on the east side of St. Martin's-lane, near Cannon-street, and was so denominated from its dedication to St. Martin, and from Ordgarus, who was supposed to be the founder of it. It was also a rectory, the patronage of which was granted by Ordgarus, with the consent of his wife and sons, to the Dean and Chapter of St. Paul's, about the year 1181, in whom it still remains; and, since the union of this parish to that of St. Clement, they present alternately with the bishop of London.

The remains of this church being found capable of repair, after the fire in 1666, a body of French protestants, in communion with the church of England, obtained a lease of the tower and ruinous nave, from the minister and church-wardens, which being confirmed by parliament, they repaired it, and converted it into a place of worship for their own use.

### CHURCH OF ST. NICHOLAS, COLE-ABBEY, OLD FISH STREET.

On the south side of Old Fish-street, at the corner of Labour-in-vain-hill, stands the parish church of St. Nicholas, Cole-abbey; which is so denominated from being dedicated to St. Nicholas, Bishop of Mera; but the reason of the additional epithet is not known;

ALLHALLOWS STAINING, MARK LANE.

ST. MARTIN, ORGAR, MARTIN'S LANE, CANNON ST.

ST. NICHOLAS, COLE ABBEY, FISH STREET.

ALLHALLOWS, LONDON WALL.

some conjecturing it to be a corruption of Golden-abbey, and others, that it is derived from Cold-abbey, or Coldbey, from its cold or bleak situation. It is known that there was a church in the same place, before the year 1377, when, according to Stow, the steeple, and south aisle, which were not so old as the rest of the church, were rebuilt; but, the last structure being consumed in the great conflagration in 1666, the present church was built in its place, and the parish of St. Nicholas, Olave, united to it.

This edifice consists of a plain body, built of stone, well enlightened by a single range of windows. It is sixty-three feet long, and forty-three feet broad, thirty-six feet high to the roof, and one hundred and thirty-five to the top of the spire.

The tower is plain, but strengthened with rustic at the corners; and the spire, which is the frustrum of a pyramid, and covered with lead, has a gallery, and many openings. This was the first church built and completed after the fire.

The advowson of this rectory was anciently in the Dean and Chapter of St. Martin's-le-Grand; but, upon the grant of that collegiate church to the abbot and canons of Westminster, the patronage devolved to that convent, in whom it continued till the dissolution of their monastery; when, coming to the crown, it remained therein till Queen Elizabeth, in the year 1560, granted the patronage thereof to Thomas Reeve and George Evelyn, and their heirs, in soccage, who conveying it to others, it came at last to the family of the Hackers, one whereof was Colonel Francis Hacker, commander of the guard that conducted King Charles I. to and from his trial, and at last to the scaffold; for which, after the Restoration, he was executed as a traitor, when the advowson reverted to the crown, in whom it still continues.

## Church of Allhallows, London Wall.

A little to the east of where Beth'lem Hospital formerly stood, is the parish church of Allhallows, London Wall. The patronage of this church, which is a rectory, was anciently in the prior and convent of the Holy Trinity, near Aldgate, who presented Thomas Richard de Sanston to it, in 1335.

At the dissolution of religious houses, in the time of Henry VIII., this church, with the priory to which it belonged, was surrendered to the crown, in whom the advowson still remains. The old church escaped the fire of London, but became so ruinous, that in 1765 the parishioners obtained an act of parliament to empower them to pull it down, together with the parsonage house, and to enable them to raise money by annuities to rebuild it.

The present church is built of brick and stone, and, though plain, is very neat. It is longer than the old church, and the rector's house stands at the north-east corner of the church-yard.

## WESTMINSTER HALL

Was built by William Rufus as a banqueting-house to the palace, which then stood in Old Palace-Yard; but old Westminster Hall was pulled down, and the present edifice erected in its stead, in the year 1397. This ancient building is of stone, the front ornamented with two towers, adorned with carved work. The hall within is reckoned the largest room in Europe, being 270 feet in length and seventy-four in breadth. The pavement is of stone, and the roof of chestnut-wood. It was formerly covered with lead, but, this being found too weighty, it has been slated for many years past. On entering the hall to the right, is the entrance to the Court of King's Bench, and on the left are stairs leading to various offices. The Court of Common Pleas is on the west side, nearly in the middle of the hall, and was established by Magna Charta in the year 1215, being before ambulatory, in following the king. The Court of Chancery is so called from the Latin word Cancelli, or a screen, within which the judges sat to determine causes, without being annoyed by the spectators. The Court of King's Bench, situated on the right directly on entering the Hall, is so called from a high bench on which our ancient monarchs usually sat in person, whilst the judges to whom the judicature was deputed in their absence sat on lower benches at their feet.

The delapidated state of the exterior of this fine Hall was long a subject of regret with the antiquary, as the figures, arms, and other decorations that originally adorned the gate and walls, were fast sinking to decay. These, however, as well as the various courts and offices, have been recently repaired and restored by Mr. Soane. The front and other parts of the exterior, have likewise undergone a complete repair by the same architect, and which has given occasion for much animadversion and severe criticism.

A dark passage from the south-east corner of the Hall formerly led to St. Stephen's Chapel Yard and Old Palace Yard. From this part the beautiful ancient cloisters might be observed, with their rich-groined arches and sculptured key-stones. Before this Hall was anciently a handsome conduit or fountain, with numerous spouts; whence, on occasions of rejoicing, streams of wine issued to the populace; at other times the inhabitants received the waste water from this source for their domestic uses.

## CHURCH OF ST. JOHN THE EVANGELIST, WESTMINSTER.

The parish of St. Margaret being greatly increased in the number of houses and inhabitants, it was judged necessary to erect one of the fifty new churches within it. This church, being finished, was dedicated to St. John the Evangelist; a parish was taken out of St. Margaret's, and the parliament granted the sum of two thousand five hundred pounds, to be laid out in the purchase of lands, tenements, &c., for the maintenance of the rector; but, besides the profits arising from this purchase, it was also enacted, That, as a farther

Drawn by Tho. H. Shepherd. Engraved by W. Watkins.

WESTMINSTER HALL.

Drawn by Tho. H. Shepherd. Engraved by W. Watkins.

ST. JOHN'S CHURCH, WESTMINSTER.

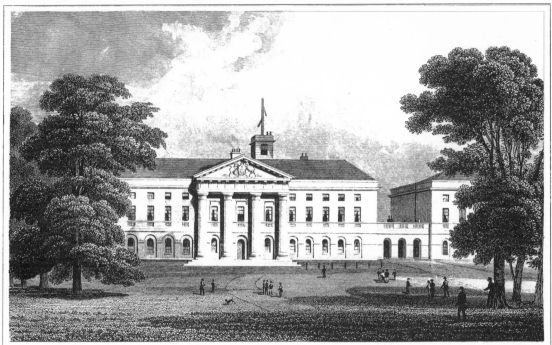

THE DUKE OF YORK'S SCHOOL, CHELSEA.

EARL SPENCER'S HOUSE, GREEN PARK.

provision for the rector, the sum of one hundred and twenty-five pounds should be annually raised, by an equal pound rate upon the inhabitants.

This church was begun in 1721, and finished in 1728, and is remarkable only for having sunk while it was building, which occasioned an alteration in the plan. On the north and south sides are magnificent porticos, supported by vast stone pillars, as is also the roof of the church. At each of the four corners is a beautiful stone tower and pinnacle: these additions were erected, that the whole might sink equally, and owe their magnitude to the same cause. The parts of this building are held together by iron bars, which cross even the aisles.

The advowson of this church is in the Dean and Chapter of Westminster: and, to prevent this rectory being held in commendam, all licenses and dispensations for holding it are, by act of parliament, declared null and void.

## The Royal Military Asylum, Chelsea,

For the children of the soldiers of the regular army, is near the Royal Hospital, and adjoining the King's Road. This building is environed on all sides with high walls, and a handsome iron railing before the grand front. This edifice, built of brick, forms three sides of a quadrangle, with an elegant stone balustrade. The centre of the western front has a noble portico of the Doric order, consisting of four immense columns, supporting a large and well-proportioned pediment; on the frieze of which is inscribed, "The Royal Military Asylum for the Children of the Soldiers of the Regular Army." Over this inscription are the royal arms. Here are seven hundred boys, and three hundred girls; the boys wear red jackets, blue trowsers, &c.; and the girls red gowns, blue petticoats, straw bonnets, white aprons, &c.; it is commonly called "the Duke of York's school," from his late Royal Highness having been the chief promoter and patron of the institution.

## Spencer-House, Green Park.

From Cleveland Row, Piccadilly, is a passage leading to the Green Park. The Wilderness, with the Ranger's Lodge, the Lawn, the Water, the Walks, and the extensive prospects, render which extremely beautiful. The east side is ornamented with the houses of many of the nobility, with gardens before them. SPENCER HOUSE is one of the most worthy of notice; the Park front of this mansion is ornamented to a high degree, though the pediment in it is considered too lofty, and has not the grace and majesty of the low Grecian pediment. The statues on the pediment, and the vases at each extremity, must be mentioned with approbation, as they are in a good style, and judiciously disposed. The interior of Spencer House is not inferior to the outside; but its chief ornament is THE LIBRARY.

## The Albany, Piccadilly.

Adjoining to Burlington-House is the Albany Hotel, first inhabited by Lord Melbourne, and exchanged with him by the late Duke of York. When his Royal Highness quitted possession, the next proprietors built on the gardens, and converted the whole into chambers for the casual residence of the nobility and gentry who had not settled residences in town. The name of the Albany was given to this house in compliment to the Prince Duke, whose second title is Duke of Albany. Here also stood the house of the Earl of Sutherland, whose advice ruined his sovereign James the Second. The present structure is the work of the late Sir William Chambers.

## Shaftesbury House, Aldersgate Street.

On the east side of the street, nearly opposite to Westmoreland buildings, is Shaftesbury, or, as it is sometimes called, Thanet-house. This edifice, which is by the masterly hand of Inigo Jones, is built with brick, and ornamented with stone, in a very elegant taste. The front is adorned with Ionic pilasters, from the volutes of which hang garlands of foliage. These pilasters are doubled on each side of the centre window, over which is an arched pediment, opened for the reception of a shield. The door is arched, and from each side of it springs an elegant scroll, for the support of a balcony. This structure had been let out for mechanical uses, and was going fast to decay, when, in the year 1750, the London Lying-in-hospital was instituted. The promoters of that charity, having hired this house, repaired it thoroughly, and preserved it for a time, from the fate of its opposite neighbours. The increase of that institution having rendered a larger building necessary, they quitted Shaftesbury-house, in 1771, and were succeeded by the General Dispensary, which still occupies the back part of it. The front is divided into tenements, and let to respectable shopkeepers.

## Broad Street, Bloomsbury, and Church of St. Giles.

This magnificent edifice, seen to great advantage from Broad St., Bloomsbury, is exceeding lofty, and the whole of it is built of Portland stone. The area of the church within the walls is sixty feet wide, and seventy-five in length, exclusive of the recess for the altar. The roof is supported with Ionic pillars of Portland stone on stone piers, and is vaulted underneath. The outside of the church has a rustic basement, and the windows of the galleries have semicircular heads, over which is a medallion cornice. The steeple is one hundred and sixty feet high, and consists of a rustic pedestal, supporting a Doric order of pilasters, and over the clock is an octangular tower with three quarter Ionic columns, supporting a balustrade with vases; on this tower stands the spire, which is also octangular and belted.

Drawn by Tho. H. Shepherd.

Engraved by R. Acon.

THE ALBANY, PICCADILLY.

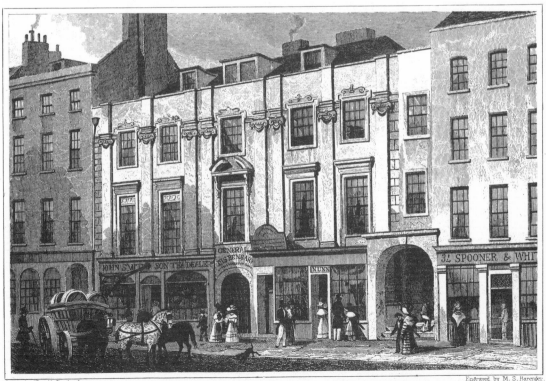

Drawn by Tho. H. Shepherd.

Engraved by M. S. Barenger.

SHAFTESBURY HOUSE, ALDERSGATE STREET

BROAD STREET, BLOOMSBURY.

HOLBORN BRIDGE.

The author of the Review of the Public Buildings says, " The new church of St. Giles is one of the most simple and elegant of the modern structures : it was raised at a very little expense, has very few ornaments, and little beside the propriety of its parts, and the harmony of the whole, to excite attention, and challenge applause, yet still it pleases, and justly too. The east end is both plain and majestic, and there is nothing in the west to object to but the smallness of the doors, and the poverty of appearance that must necessarily follow. The steeple is light, airy, and genteel ; argues a good deal of genius in the architect, and looks very well, both in comparison with the body of the church, and when it is considered as a building by itself in a distant prospect.

The expense of erecting this church amounted to ten thousand and twenty-six pounds, fifteen shillings and nine-pence, including the eight thousand pounds granted by parliament. It is a rectory in the gift of the crown.

Over the north-west door into the church-yard is a curious piece of sculpture, representing the Day of Resurrection. It contains a great number of figures, and was set up about the year 1686.

## HOLBORN BRIDGE, CHURCH OF ST. ANDREW, &c.

It would be difficult, perhaps, to select any single point of the metropolis better calculated to convey to the mind of a stranger some idea of its unceasing bustle and traffic than the part of Holborn Bridge from which our view of this scene is taken. Here, what was formerly Fleet Market, but is now called Farringdon Street, terminates to the north, and pours forth its living stream from Fleet Street ; which, running parallel, may be considered as dividing with Holborn the principal communication and traffic from east to west.

The church of St. Andrew, on the left of the view, was one which escaped the fire of London, but was found so ruinous that it was entirely rebuilt in 1687, except the tower, which was not erected till 1704. The body of the church is one hundred and five feet long, sixty-three feet broad, and forty-three feet high, and the height of the tower is one hundred and ten feet. The body is well built, and enlightened by two series of windows, and on the top of it runs a handsome balustrade. The tower rises square, and consists only of two stages, crowned with battlements and pinnacles at the corners. The first stage, which is plain, has the dial : in the upper stage there is a very handsome window to each front ; tall, arched, and decorated with Doric pilasters, which support a lofty arched pediment, decorated within by a shield. The cornice, that crowns the tower, is supported by scrolls ; and the balustrade that rises above this has a very firm base. Each corner of the tower has an ornamental pinnacle, consisting of four large scrolls, which, meeting in a body, support a pine-apple ; and from the crown of the fruit rises a vane. The inside is extremely neat, and well finished. Over the communion-table is a large painted window, the lower part of which represents the Messiah and his disciples at the Last Supper ; and in a compartment above is represented his resurrection from the grave. The church stands at an advantageous distance from the street, from which it is separated by a wall that incloses the church-yard, and the entrance to it is by large and elegant iron gates.

The church is a rectory, the patronage of which was originally in the gift of the Dean and Canons of St. Paul's, who transferred it to the Abbot and Convent of Bermondsey, who continued patrons of it till their convent was dissolved by Henry VIII., when that prince granted it to Thomas Lord Wriothesley, afterwards Earl of Southampton, from whom it descended by marriage to the late Duke of Montague, in whose family the patronage still remains.

## CHURCHES OF ST. MILDRED, BREAD STREET, AND ST. BARTHOLOMEW THE GREAT, WEST SMITHFIELD.

Bread Street, in which the father of Milton resided as a scrivener, contains the parish church of St. MILDRED: the front of free-stone, the other parts of brick. The roof is covered with lead, and the floor paved with Purbeck stone. The pulpit and the altar-piece are handsomely adorned; and the communion-table stands upon a foot-piece of black and white marble.

On the east side of Smithfield, and at the north end of Duck Lane, stands the parish church of St. Bartholomew the Great. This church was originally a parish church adjoining to that of the priory of St. Bartholomew; but, when the latter was pulled down to the choir, that part was annexed by the king's order for the enlargement of the old church; in which manner it continued till queen Mary gave the remnant of the priory church to the Black Friars, who used it as their conventual church till the first year of queen Elizabeth, when the friars were turned out, and the church was restored, by act of parliament, to the parish.

The present church is the same as it stood in the reign of Edward VI., except the steeple, which, being of timber, was taken down in the year 1628, and a new one, of brick and stone, erected. It is a spacious edifice of the Gothic and Tuscan orders, one hundred and thirty-two feet long, fifty-seven broad, and forty-seven high; and the altitude of the tower is seventy-five feet.

## CHURCH OF ST. MARY, LAMBETH.

A church stood on the present site till the year 1374, about which time it was rebuilt, there being commissions still preserved, dated in that year, and in 1377, for compelling the inhabitants of Lambeth to contribute to the rebuilding of their new church and tower. The tower, which is of free-stone, still remains; the other parts of the structure appear to have been built at different times. In its present form it consists of a nave, two aisles, and a chancel; the nave being separated from the aisles by octagonal pillars and pointed arches. The walls are built of flint, mixed with stone and brick; and both the tower and the body of the church are crowned with battlements. It is dedicated to the Virgin Mary, and is a rectory in the gift of the Archbishop of Canterbury.

Drawn by Tho.H.Shepherd.

Engraved by T.Higham.

ST. MILDRED, BREAD STREET.

ST. BARTHOLOMEW, THE GREAT. WEST SMITHFIELD.

Drawn by Tho.H.Shepherd.

Engraved by T.Higham.

ST. MARY, LAMBETH.

WESTMINSTER BRIDGE.

LONDON DOCKS, LOOKING WEST.

In the south-east window of the middle aisle is a painting of a man followed by a dog, which is said to have been put up in compliance with the will of a pedlar, who left a small piece of ground to the parish, on condition that a picture of him and his dog should be put up and preserved in its present situation. Whether this tradition be true or not, there is a piece of ground on the Surrey side of Westminster-bridge called Pedlar's Acre, which contains about an acre and nine poles, and belongs to Lambeth parish. Mr. Lysons is of opinion that this tradition originates in a rebus upon the name of the donor, and gives a similar instance from the church of Swaffham, in Norfolk, in which there is a portrait of John Chapman, a great benefactor to the parish, and in different parts of the church the device of a pedlar and his pack. By whatever means Pedlar's Acre became the property of the parish, it must have happened prior to 1504, when it was let for two shillings and eight-pence per annum. It is now estimated at several hundred pounds a year.

In this church were interred the mild and amiable prelates, Tunstal, of Durham, and Thirleby, of Ely; who, being deprived of their sees for their conscientious attachment to the Catholic religion, lived the remainder of their days under the protection, rather than in the custody, of Archbishop Parker, who revered their virtues, and felt for their misfortunes. The body of Thirleby was found in digging a grave for Archbishop Cornwallis. His long and venerable beard, and every part was entire, and of a beautiful whiteness; a slouched hat was under his left arm, and his dress was that of a pilgrim, as he esteemed himself to be upon earth.

### WESTMINSTER BRIDGE

Is a structure of that simplicity and grandeur, that, whether viewed from the water, or by the land-passenger, it fills the mind with admiration. This bridge is regarded by architects as one of the most beautiful in the world. It was begun in the year 1738, and finished in 1750, and cost £389,500. The whole of the superstructure is of Portland stone, except the spandrils of the arches. It is 1223 feet long, and 44 feet wide; has fifteen large semicircular arches. The central arch is seventy-six feet wide; the other arches decreasing in width five feet. The quantity of stone used in this bridge is said to have been nearly double to what was employed in St. Paul's Cathedral.

Before this bridge was built, the houses in this part of Westminster were very ruinous. Many of these were probably built about Le Wolstaple, held in New Palace-Yard. Henry the Sixth had no less than six wool-houses in this place; and the conflux of people towards this wool-market caused such an increase, that in time the royal village of Westminster became a town.

### LONDON DOCKS.

To form these Docks, great part of the parish of Wapping has been excavated; and these excavations extend from the Thames almost to Ratcliff Highway, and are enclosed by a wall of brick, lined with warehouses. St. George's Dock covers the space from Virginia-

Street almost to Old Gravel-Lane in one direction, and is capable of holding 500 ships, with room for shifting.

Another, called Shadwell Dock, adjoining, will hold about fifty ships; and the entrance to both is by three basons, capable of containing an immense quantity of small craft. The inlets from the Thames into the basons are at the Old Hermitage Dock, Old Wapping Dock, and Old Shadwell Dock. The foundation of the entrance bason to these was laid on the 26th of June 1802, by the Chancellor of the Exchequer, with the first stone of a tobacco warehouse. Since the conclusion of the late peace with France, this busy scene has undergone various changes and improvements.

## RUSSELL SQUARE

Is considerably larger than any other in London, Lincoln's-Inn-Fields excepted. The south side is graced by a pedestrian statue, in bronze, of the late duke of Bedford, by Mr. Westmacott: his grace reposes one arm on a plough; the left hand holds the gifts of Ceres. Children playing round the feet of the statue, personify the four seasons. To the four corners bulls' heads are attached, in a very high relief; the cavity beneath the upper mouldings has heads of cattle in recumbent postures. On the carved sides are rural subjects in basso relievo: the first is the preparation for the ploughman's dinner; his wife, on her knees, attends the culinary department; a youth is also represented sounding a horn; two rustics and a team of oxen complete the group. The second composition is made up of reapers and gleaners; a young woman in the centre is delineated with the agreable features and general comeliness of a village favourite.

These enrichments, the four seasons, and the statue of the duke, are cast in bronze, and are very highly finished. The pedestal is of Scotch granite; and with the superstructure, from the level of the ground to the summit of the monument, measures twenty-seven feet. The principal figure is nine feet high. The only inscription in front is, " Francis, Duke of Bedford; erected 1809."

## BLOOMSBURY SQUARE.

The north side of this Square is embellished with a statue of the late Right Hon. Charles James Fox. The work consists simply of a statue of colossal dimensions, being to a scale of nine feet in height, executed in bronze, and elevated upon a pedestal of granite, surmounting a spacious base, formed of several gradations: the whole is about seventeen feet in height. Dignity and repose appear to have been the leading objects of the artist's ideas; he has adopted a sitting position, and habited the statue in the consular robe, the ample folds of which, passing over the body, and falling from the seat, give breadth and effect to the whole. The right arm is extended, the hand supporting Magna Charta; the left is in repose. The head is inclined rather forward, expressive of attention, firmness, and complacency: the likeness of Mr. Fox is perfect and striking. The inscription, which is in letters of bronze, is, " CHARLES JAMES FOX, erected M.DCCC.XVI." This statue, and the statue of the late duke of Bedford, by the same artist (Westmacott), at the other extremity of Bedford-Place, form two grand and beautiful ornaments of the metropolis.

Drawn by Tho. H. Shepherd.                                                    Engraved by C. Motram.

RUSSELL SQUARE, AND STATUE OF THE DUKE OF BEDFORD.

Drawn by Tho. H. Shepherd.                                                    Engraved by C. Motram.

BLOOMSBURY SQUARE, AND STATUE OF FOX.

Drawn by Tho. H. Shepherd.

Engraved by R. Acon.

COMPTER, GILTSPUR STREET.

Drawn by Tho. H. Shepherd.

Engraved by R. Acon.

NEWGATE, OLD BAILEY.

## NEWGATE, OLD BAILEY, AND GILTSPUR STREET COMPTER.

Between Snow-hill and Ludgate-hill runs the street called the Old Bailey, which many of our antiquaries are of opinion is a corruption of Bale-hill, an eminence whereon was situated the Bale, or Bailiff's-house, wherein he held a court for the trial of malefactors ; and this opinion seems to be corroborated by such a court having been held here for many centuries, in which there is a place of security, where the sheriffs keep their prisoners during the session, which still retains the name of the Bale-dock.

On the east side of the Old Bailey, and contiguous to the place where the Newgate of the city formerly stood, is the gaol for the county of Middlesex, which, from being appropriated to the same uses, also bears the name of Newgate. It is a massy stone building, consisting of two parts, that on the north being formerly appropriated for debtors, and that on the south for felons, between which is a dwelling-house, occupied by the keeper. The whole of the front is formed of rustic work, and at the extremities of each face are arched niches for statues.

Contiguous to this building, and only separated from it by a square court, is Justice-hall, commonly called the Sessions-house.

This was formerly a plain brick edifice ; but it has since been rebuilt entirely of stone, and is brought so much forwarder than the old one as to be parallel with the street. On the north side, or front, are two flights of steps leading to the court-room, which has a gallery on each side for the accommodation of spectators. The prisoners are brought to this court from Newgate by a passage that closely connects the two buildings ; and there is a convenient place under the Sessions-house in front, for detaining the prisoners till they are called upon their trials. There are also rooms for the grand and pettit jury, with other necessary accommodations.

Opposite to the north end of the Old Bailey is Giltspur-street, which leads into Smithfield. On the east side of Giltspur-street, in a line with Newgate, is Giltspur-street Compter. It is composed of three pavilions, crowned with triangular pediments, and connected by two galleries with flat roofs. The whole of this building, like Newgate, is of rustic stone work, but, having arched windows to the front, it has a lighter appearance.

The corner opposite the north end of this building is remarkable for being the spot where the fire of London terminated : which event is commemorated by the figure of a bloated boy on the corner house, bearing an inscription, purporting that this dreadful conflagration was a punishment for the sin of gluttony.

## LUNATIC HOSPITAL, ST. LUKE'S.

This hospital was first established by voluntary contributions, in the year 1751, for the reception of lunatics, and was intended not only in aid of, but as an improvement upon Beth'lem-hospital, which, at the time of this institution, was incapable of receiving and providing for the relief of all the unhappy objects for whom application was made. With this view, a house was erected on the north side of Moorfields, and called St. Luke's-hospital, from the name of the parish: but the utility of the institution was so evident, and benefactors increased with such rapidity, that the governors soon determined to extend its benefits to a much larger number of patients, and for that purpose purchased the piece of ground on which the present edifice (the foundation stone of which was laid on the 20th of July, 1782) was erected, at an expense of forty thousand pounds.

The north and south fronts of this building, which are of brick, ornamented with stone, are exactly the same. The centre and ends project a little, and are higher than the intermediate parts. The former is crowned by a triangular pediment, under which is inscribed in large letters, " Saint Luke's Hospital for Lunatics." The two latter are surmounted with an attic balustrade, which conceals the roof. The whole building is divided into three stories; and the spaces between the centre and ends are formed into long galleries; the female patients occupying the western galleries, and the male the eastern. Between the hospital and the street is a broad space, separated from the street by a wall, in the centre of which is the entrance, leading to the door by a flight of steps, under a roof supported by Tuscan columns.

The simple grandeur of the exterior of this building, the length of which is four hundred and ninety-three feet, produces an effect upon the mind which is only superseded by a knowledge of the propriety, decency, and regularity, which reign within, notwithstanding the unhappy state of its inhabitants.

Behind the house are two large gardens, one for the men, the other for the women; where such of the patients as can be permitted with safety are allowed to walk and take the air. Those in a more dangerous state, who are obliged to be confined with strait waistcoats, have, with very few exceptions, the range of the galleries, in which there are fires, so protected by iron bars, reaching from the floor to the breast of the chimney, that no accident can possibly occur; and in those cells where the most dangerous and hopeless patients are confined, every thing which can contribute to alleviate their miserable state is attended to. In short, the system of management in this hospital is such, that nothing which can add to the comfort, or tend to the cure of the patients admitted into it, is neglected.

### CITY OF LONDON LYING-IN HOSPITAL.

This building consists of a centre and two wings; the latter of which project a little from the main building. In the front of the centre is a neat plain pediment. In this part of the building is a chapel, with a handsome organ, and the top of it is crowned with a light open turret, terminated by a vane. The wards for the patients are in the wings, and are eight in number; each of which is so formed as to contain ten beds: behind the building are regular and convenient offices. In the front of the left wing is this inscription: ERECTED BY SUBSCRIPTION, MDCCLXXI.; and in the front of the other wing are these words, SUPPORTED BY VOLUNTARY CONTRIBUTIONS. On a slip of

CITY OF LONDON LYING-IN HOSPITAL.

LUNATIC HOSPITAL, ST. LUKE'S.

GROCERS' HALL, POULTRY.

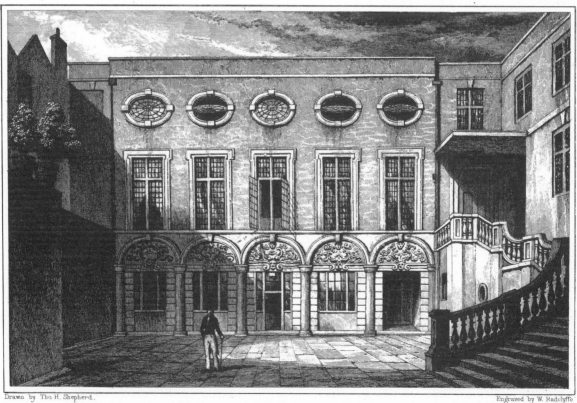

BREWER'S HALL, ADDLE STREET.

stone, in the centre, and also on the south side, are these words, THE CITY OF LONDON LYING-IN HOSPITAL.

Though this is a plain building, yet it is very neatly constructed. It stands in an airy and pleasant situation, and is well adapted to the purposes for which it was erected. There is a public baptism of the children born in it, on the last Sunday in every month, to which persons may be admitted by tickets, on application to any subscriber.

This charity was formerly kept in Shaftesbury-house, Aldersgate-street; where it was instituted in the year 1750, by voluntary contributions.

## GROCERS' HALL, POULTRY.

At the north end of Grocers'-hall-court is Grocers'-hall. This building is situated on a spot of ground, purchased by the Grocers' company, in the year 1411, of Robert Fitz-Walter, for three hundred and twenty marks. The present structure, which has been recently new fronted and beautifully ornamented, is well designed and executed, for the purposes of a common-hall; stately, ornamental, and so capacious, that for many years, it served for the uses of the Bank of England, which was kept in this hall till there was an office built on purpose, in Threadneedle-street. This hall contains a portrait and statue of Sir John Cutler (who is said to have built the parlour and dining room over it), created a baronet in 1660, of Sir John Moor, Lord Mayor, 1681; and Sir John Fleet, Lord Mayor 1692. William Pitt, Earl of Chatham, and the Right Hon. William Pitt his son, were both members of this Company.

The Grocers' Company, anciently denominated, pepperers, were incorporated by letters-patent of King Edward III. in the year 1345: formerly they had the management of the king's beam in the city, with a right of appointing a master weigher and four porters to attend it.

This company at one time held the highest rank among the city companies; for in the reign of Henry IV. there were no less than twelve of the aldermen, at the same time, belonging to it. It has also been dignified with the names of five kings enrolled among its members.

## BREWERS' HALL, ADDLE STREET.

At the eastern entrance to Addle-Street, is Brewers'-Hall, with a large paved court. The front of this building is on the north side, composed of a rich basement, approaching to the Tuscan order.

The Brewers' Company, which is the fourteenth among the city companies, was incorporated by King Henry VI. in the year 1438, by the name of " The master, and keepers or wardens, and commonalty of the mystery or art of Brewers of the city of London." King Edward IV. not only confirmed that charter, but granted them a further power to make bye-laws.

### CHURCH OF ST. CATHERINE CREE, LEADENHALL.

At the south-east angle of Cree-church-lane, in Leadenhall-street, stands the church of St. Catherine Cree. This church received its name from being dedicated to St. Catherine, an Egyptian virgin; and is distinguished from other churches of the same name, by the addition of Cree, or Christ, from its situation in the cemetery of the conventual church of the Holy Trinity, which was originally called Christ-church.

The present structure was erected in 1630, but repaired and beautified in 1805. It is built of stone, in a mixed style. It has rounded battlements on the top, and a square tower, with battlements of the same kind. This tower is crowned with a square turret, over which is a dome, and from its summit rises the weathercock. The length of the church is ninety feet; the breadth fifty-one; the altitude of the roof, which is square, supported by pilasters and columns of the Composite order, is thirty-seven feet; and that of the steeple is seventy-five feet.

At the west end of this church, adjoining to the steeple, stands a pillar of the old church, as originally erected. This pillar, from the base to the chapiter, upon which the arch was turned, being eighteen feet high, and but three to be seen above ground, shows the height to which the floor of the new church has been raised above that of the old.

This church is a curacy; and the parishioners have the privilege of choosing their own minister, who must be licensed by the Bishop of London.

### CHURCH OF ST. MILDRED, POULTRY.

This church is a rectory, and derives its name from its dedication to St. Mildred, a Saxon princess, and its situation. It appears to be of ancient foundation, for John de Asswel was collated to it in the year 1325; and in the eighteenth of Edward III. we find it with the Chapel of Corpus Christi and St. Mary de Coneyhope annexed, which chapel stood at the end of Coneyhope-lane, or the Rabbit-market, now called Grocers'-hall-court: but being suppressed by King Henry VIII. on account of a fraternity founded therein, it was purchased by one Thomas Hobson, a haberdasher, who turned the chapel into a warehouse.

The old church, which had been rebuilt in 1450, was burnt down in 1666, after which the present structure was erected, and the parish of St. Mary Colechurch united to it.

It is a plain substantial stone building, enlightened by a series of large windows, and strengthened with rustic at the corners. The tower is crowned with a plain course, without pinnacles, or any other ornament. The length of this church is fifty-six feet, its breadth forty-two feet, the height of the roof thirty-six feet, and that of the tower seventy-five feet. Within, it is paved with Purbeck stone, the chancel with the same, mixed with black marble. There is a handsome gallery at the west end, and a good pulpit.

The patronage of this church was in the convent and prior of St. Mary Overy's, in Southwark, till the suppression of that religious house, when it came to the crown; since which time, the lord chancellor presents to the living.

ST. CATHERINE CREE, LEADENHALL STREET.

ST. MILDRED, POULTRY.

Drawn by Tho. H. Shephard.

LOCK HOSPITAL, HYDE PARK CORNER.

Drawn by Tho. H. Shephard.

CHRIST'S HOSPITAL, NEWGATE STREET.

## Christ's Hospital.—The Lock Hospital.

Christ's Hospital was founded by Edward the Sixth. Of the ancient buildings remaining, there is an old cloister of the Grey Friars, part of their priory. It serves for a place of recreation for the boys, especially in rainy weather. The reparations which this part underwent by Sir Christopher Wren have nearly deprived it of its ancient appearance.

The new Grammar-school, which it is now proposed to remove for further improvements, is a very commodious structure, well adapted to its intention. The Writing-school, at the end of the great hall, is very lofty and airy, and was founded by Sir John Moore, Knt. and Alderman of the City; and contains a desk at which three hundred boys may sit and write. This school rests upon columns, and the space beneath is allotted for play and exercise. Sir John Moore's statue, in white marble, at full length, is placed in the front of the building. The expenditure of the whole establishment of this hospital has been estimated at £30,000 per annum.

Many great and gross abuses having existed in the disposal of the funds of this hospital, it induced Mr. Waithman, then one of the Common Council, but since Alderman of Farringdon without (a man who for talent, indefatigable perseverance, undaunted courage, and consistency, has ever been one of the brightest ornaments of the city of London) to institute an enquiry, the result of which made it evident, that instead of being a benefit to the children of the poor and friendless, it was engrossed almost exclusively by the rich. It had long been known that presentations, instead of being given, had been regularly sold by some of those who had the disposal of them. It even appeared, that a clergyman in Middlesex, with a living not less than £1200 per annum, had solicited and received a presentation for one of his sons from a member of the county.—On Thursday, Jan. 25, 1810, Mr. Waithman brought in the report of the committee appointed to consider of the conduct of the governors of Christ's Hospital, which stated, that upon consulting Mr. Samuel Romilly and Mr. Bell, they recommend the petitioning of the Lord Chancellor; and the committee was therefore requested to prepare a petition accordingly. Unhappily the inefficiency of this enquiry appeared very striking, after waiting some years for its aid; as at a meeting of the Common Council, in the beginning of January, 1816, Mr. Waithman said, the way in which the Hospital Committee managed was, that the members of it were for life, and they elected new ones to fill up the vacancies occasioned by death in their own number. The children were admitted by the almoners; and, in many instances, the children of persons possessing six, seven, eight, nine, ten, eleven, and even some of £1200 a year had been admitted: yet when an enquiry was instituted into these abuses, he found not one commoner or alderman to stand by his side, or to support him. The great fault lay in the composition of this committee, four or five of whom managed the whole of the affairs of the hospital. The committee ought to be elected annually. He then moved, that this memorial be referred to the committee for enquiring into the affairs of Christ's Hospital.

Sir W. Curtis, and others interested in upholding the abuses, proposed referring it to the committee of City Lands, and Mr. Waithman, again foiled in his laudable efforts, withdrew his motion.    Much good has however been since effected by his unceasing exertions.

It is remarkable, that since this perversion of these noble funds has been increasing, a circumstance not sufficiently noticed will appear evident in its object to the judicious observer. As testimonies to the original design of this foundation, a statue of a Blue Coat Boy in each of the four corners of the cloisters had, within the recollection of several persons living, the following painted notice underneath:

" This is Christ's Hospital, where poor Blue Coat Boys are harboured and educated."

What sacrilegious hand removed this salutary land-mark, set up by the piety of our ancestors, we cannot at this distance of time point out.    It would seem that some reasons, not the most commendable, must have been felt for getting rid even of these dumb witnesses; or that modern pride and false refinement could not bear the implication that the objects of this charity were still, as they were originally termed,   " The children of poor distressed men and poor distressed women."

However, that the public may be satisfied with the excellent mode of education pursued in this national institution, the various specimens of the boys' performances are exhibited at stated times in the great hall.

In a niche over the avenue into the hospital, from the passage leading from Newgate-Street to the west door of Christ's Church, is the statue of Edward the Sixth.    That of Charles the Second embellished the former entrance of the hospital from Newgate-Street, opposite Warwick-Lane, called Grey Friars.

The LOCK HOSPITAL, Grosvenor Place, Pimlico, an engraving of which accompanies the preceding subject, is a spacious and extensive range of Buildings, appropriated for Syphilitic Maladies, Supported by voluntary contributions.

### CHURCH OF ST. SWITHIN, LONDON STONE, CANNON STREET.

At the south-west angle of St. Swithin's-Lane, in Cannon-street, stands the parish church of St. Swithin.    This church is so called from its being dedicated to St. Swithin, Bishop of Winchester, and chancellor to King Egbert, who died in the year 806.    By ancient records it appears that there was a church on this spot, dedicated to the same saint, before the year 1331; but how long it was standing before that time is uncertain: however, the old structure was destroyed by the fire of London, and the present edifice erected in its stead.

This is a plain solid and strong building of stone, sixty-one feet long, and forty-two broad; the roof is forty feet, and the steeple one hundred and fifty feet high.    The body is well enlightened, and the windows are arched and well proportioned.

The patronage of this church appears to have been anciently in the prior and convent of Tortington, in the diocese of Chichester, in whom it continued till the dissolution of their monastery; when coming to the crown, Henry VIII., in the year 1540, granted the same, together with a stately mansion, on the north side thereof, where Oxford-court now stands,

Drawn by Tho. H. Shepherd.

Engraved by J. Tingle.

ST. SWITHIN, LONDON STONE, CANNON STREET.

Drawn by Tho. H. Shepherd.

Engraved by J. Tingle.

ST. MICHAEL, QUEEN HYTHE.

to John Earl of Oxford, who soon after disposing of the same, it passed through several hands, and was, at length, purchased by the company of Salters, in whom the patronage still remains.

Against the south wall of St. Swithin's church is placed the famous old stone, called London-stone. This stone was much worn away before the fire of London; but it is now cased over with a new stone, cut hollow, so that the old one may be seen. See a full account of this stone in a preceding part of the Work.

## CHURCH OF ST. MICHAEL, QUEENHITHE.

On the north side of Thames-street, directly opposite to Queenhithe, is situated the parish church of St. Michael, Queenhithe; so called from its dedication to St. Michael the Arch-angel, and its situation near that hithe. It was formerly called St. Michael de Cornhithe, all the corn brought to London from the western parts of the country being landed here.

The earliest authentic mention of this church is in the year 1404, when Stephen Spilman, who had served the offices of alderman, sheriff, and chamberlain, died and left part of his goods to found a chantry here.

The old church being destroyed by the fire of London, the present structure was erected in its stead. It consists of a well-proportioned body, enlightened by two series of windows; the first a range of tall arched ones, and over them another range of large port-hole windows, above which are cherubs' heads, and underneath festoons that adorn the lower part, and fall between the tops of the under series. The tower is plain, but well proportioned, and is terminated by a spire crowned with a vane in the form of a ship. The length of this church is seventy-one feet, its breadth forty, and its height to the roof, which is flat and covered with tiles, is thirty-nine feet. The altitude of the tower and spire is one hundred and thirty-five.

The patronage of this church is in the Dean and Chapter of St. Paul's, but it is subject to the arch-deacon. On its being rebuilt, the parish of Trinity the Less was annexed to it; and, the patronage of the latter being in the Dean and Chapter of Canterbury, they and the Dean and Chapter of St. Paul's present alternately to the united living.

## CHRIST CHURCH, NEWGATE STREET,

Is situated behind the houses on the north side of Newgate Street, and was the church belonging to the Grey Friars, which was given for a parish church by Henry VIII., after the Reformation, in lieu of the two churches of St. Ewen in Newgate Market and St. Nicholas in the Shambles.

That the old church of the Grey Friars was a magnificent structure is confirmed by Weever, in his "Funeral Monuments," who informs us, that here were buried four queens, four duchesses, four countesses, one duke, two earls, eight barons, thirty-five knights, &c.;

P

in all, six hundred and sixty-three persons of quality were interred here before the dissolution of the convent. In the choir were nine tombs of alabaster and marble, besides a great number of marble grave-stones.

This church, three hundred feet long, eighty-nine broad, and sixty-four feet, two inches high, was burnt down in the great fire of London, since which, only the choir, or east end, has been rebuilt, with a tower added to it: this tower is square and of considerable height, crowned with a light and handsome turret, neatly adorned: the interior is correspondent. There are very large galleries in the north, south, and west sides, for the use of the scholars of Christ's Hospital, with a stately organ in the centre. Here the Spital sermons have been preached in the Easter week, since they were discontinued at St. Bride's, Fleet Street; and an annual sermon is also preached on St. Matthew's day, before the Lord Mayor, Aldermen, and Governors of Christ's Hospital, after which, the senior scholars deliver Latin and English orations in the great hall, preparatory to their being sent to the university.

## CHRIST CHURCH, SPITALFIELDS,

Was begun in 1723, as one of Queen Anne's fifty new churches, and finished in 1729. It is situated on the south side of Church Street, and at its western extremity, its principal entrance facing Union Street.

This is a stately edifice, built of stone, the height of the roof forty-one feet, and of the steeple 234. To the Doric portico there is a handsome ascent by a flight of steps. The steeple contains twelve bells, and excellent chimes, which perform four times a day. Sir Robert Ladbroke's monument, in this church, is a beautiful specimen of Mr. Flaxman's abilities.

The tower has arched windows and niches, and, on its diminishing for the steeple, is supported by the heads of the under corners, which form a kind of buttresses; from this part arises the base of the spire, with an arcade. Its corners are in the same manner supported with a sort of pyramidal buttresses, ending in a point; the spire terminates with a vase and fane.

## ST. MARY, SOMERSET.

This church and tower are built of stone, with which it is also paved, having two aisles; the roof within is flat, adorned with a cornice, and between the windows with fret work of cherubim, &c. It is finely wainscoted with oak, about ten feet high; it has a neat wainscot gallery at the west end, supported by four stone columns of the Tuscan order. There are also two spacious inner door-cases, and handsome pews; the pulpit is enriched with cherubim and the sound-board veneered.

The tower is square, well-proportioned, and high, crowned at each corner with very handsome vases on pedestals, between which are four tall pyramidal columns.

CHRIST CHURCH, AND PART OF CHRIST'S HOSPITAL

BOW CHURCH, CHEAPSIDE.

ST. MARY MAGDALEN, OLD FISH ST.

## Church of St. Mary-le-bow, Cheapside.

This church took its name from being dedicated to the Virgin Mary, and received the additional epithet of Le Bow from being the first church in London built upon stone arches, at that time called bows. It was founded in or before the reign of William the Conqueror, and was at first called New Mary church, but afterwards obtained the name of De Arcubus, or Le Bow, in Westcheap.

In the history of the ancient edifice, we find that, in the year 1271, a great number of people were destroyed, and many more maimed, by the falling of the steeple; after which it remained without one for many years, but was gradually repaired by the donations and legacies of charitable persons; so that, in 1469, the common-council ordained that Bow-bell should be rung at nine of the clock every night; and, in the year 1512, it was finished upon the old plan, with stone brought from Caen, in Normandy; that is to say, with arches and five lanterns, one at each corner and one at the top, upon the arches, which were intended to have been glazed, and to have lights placed in them every night, in the winter, to give light to the passengers in the street: and thus it continued till it was destroyed, with the other buildings in the city, by the fire in 1666.

The present noble structure was built by the great Sir Christopher Wren, and is chiefly admired for the elegance of its steeple, which is built entirely of Portland-stone, and was finished in 1680. It is extremely light in its appearance, and, though very high and full of openings, secure, by the geometrical proportion and lightness of its several parts. The length of this church is sixty-five feet, its breadth sixty-three feet, the height of the roof thirty-eight feet, and that of the steeple two hundred and twenty-five feet.

The tower is square from the ground, and in this form rises to a considerable height, but with more ornament as it advances. The principal decoration of the lower part is the entrance, which is a noble, lofty, and well-proportioned arch, on two of the sides faced with a bold rustic, and raised on a plain solid course from the foundation. Within the arch is a portal of the Doric order, the frieze ornamented in tryglyphs, and with sculpture in the metopes: over this arch is an opening, with a small balcony, which answers to a window on the other face. The first stage is terminated by an elegant cornice, over which rises a plain course, whence a dial projects. Above this, in each face, is a large arched window, with coupled Ionic pilasters at the sides near the corners. The cornice over the windows supports an elegant balustrade, with attic pillars over the Ionic columns, supporting turrets, each composed of four handsome scrolls, which join at the top, where are placed urns with flames. From this part the steeple rises circular. There is a plain course to the height of half the scrolls, and upon this is raised a circular range of Corinthian columns, while the body of the steeple is continued round and plain within them. These support a second balustrade, with very large scrolls, extending from it to the body of the steeple. Above these is placed a series of composite columns, and from the entablature rises another set of scrolls, supporting the spire, which rests upon four balls, and is terminated by a globe, whence rises a vane, in the form of a dragon. In this steeple are twelve bells, said to be superior in harmony to any set in England.

The author of the Critical Review of the Public Buildings, says, " The steeple of Bow-church is a master-piece in a peculiar style of building : it is, beyond question, as perfect as human imagination can contrive or execute ; and, till we see it outdone, we shall hardly think it to be equalled."

In digging the foundation of this church, Sir Christopher Wren discovered that part of the ancient Roman colony which ran from the Thames northward. On opening the ground a foundation appeared, firm enough for the intended fabric, which, on inspection, was found to consist of the remains of a temple, or church, of Roman workmanship, entirely buried under the level of the present street. On this he determined to erect the new building; and, as the old church stood about forty feet backward from the high street, by purchasing the ground of one private house, in front, not then rebuilt, he was enabled to bring the steeple forward, so as to range with the houses in Cheapside. Here, to his great surprise, he sunk about eighteen feet through made ground, and then imagined that he was come to the natural soil and hard gravel; but, on farther inspection, it appeared to be a Roman causeway, of rough stone, close and well rammed with Roman brick and rubbish at the bottom, all firmly cemented. On this causeway, which was four feet thick, Sir Christopher determined to lay the foundation of the tower and steeple, as being most proper to bear a weighty and lofty structure. Some alarm having arisen as to the safety of the latter, it has, within these few years, undergone a complete repair.

### CHURCH OF ST. MARY MAGDALEN, OLD FISH STREET.

On the north side of Knight-rider Street, at the west corner of the Old Change, stands the parish church of St. Mary Magdalen, Old Fish-street; so called from its dedication to that saint, and its ancient situation in the fish-market, the principal part of which was in that street.

This church was a vicarage, in the tenure of the canons of St. Paul's, in the year 1181 ; but for some ages past it has been a rectory, in the gift of the dean and chapter of St. Paul's. The old edifice was destroyed by the fire of London; and the present structure was erected in the year 1685.

This is a small but well-proportioned church, built with stone, and enlightened by a single series of arched windows, each ornamented with a cherub and scrolls, supporting a cornice which runs round the building; but these windows are so high from the ground that the doors open completely under them. The tower is divided into two stages, in the upper of which is a large window on each side. From the top of the tower the work diminishes, in the manner of high steps, on each side ; and on the top of these is a turret, with a very short spire, on which is placed a vase, with flames.

COOPERS' HALL, BASINGHALL ST.

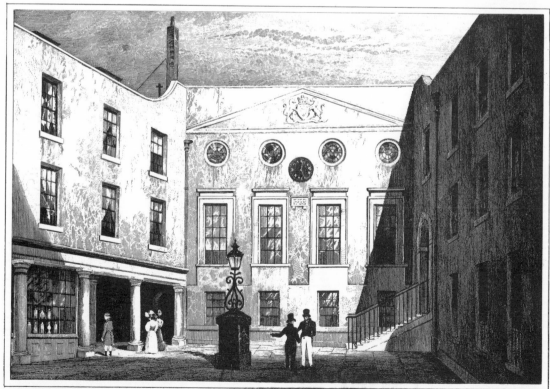

APOTHECARIES' HALL PILGRIM ST.

BLACKFRIARS.

To this parish is annexed that of St. Gregory, the church of which stood at the south-west corner of St. Paul's cathedral. It is a rectory of very ancient foundation, and took its name from Pope Gregory the Great, who sent Austin, the monk, to convert the English nation to Christianity. The patronage of it is in the dean and chapter of St. Paul's, who are both patrons and ordinaries. After its destruction by the fire of London, the ground on which it stood was laid into St. Paul's charch-yard.

## COOPERS' HALL, BASINGHALL STREET,

Is a stately well-built edifice of brick, nearly opposite to Sambrook court, in Basinghall Street. The interior forms a very handsome room, wainscoted to the height of fourteen feet, and paved with marble, and was used for the drawing of the lottery.

The company was incorporated in 1501, by letters patent of King Henry VII., under the title of " The Masters, Wardens, and Assistants of the company of Coopers of London and suburbs thereof;" and in the succeeding reign was empowered, by an act of parliament, to search and gauge all beer, ale, and soap vessels, within the city of London and two miles round its suburbs, for which they were allowed a farthing for each cask. They are governed by a master, three wardens, and twenty assistants.

## APOTHECARIES' HALL.

Within the precinct of Blackfriars, on the east side of Water-lane, stands Apothecaries' Hall.

This is a handsome building, with a pair of gates in front that lead into a paved court; at the upper end of which is a flight of stairs leading into the hall-room, which is built with brick and stone, and adorned with columns of the Tuscan order. The ceiling of the court-room and of the hall are elegantly ornamented with fret-work; the wall is wainscoted fourteen feet high, and adorned with the bust of Dr. Gideon Delaun, apothecary to king James I., and with several pieces of exceedingly good painting; among which are portraits of king James I., and of the gentleman who procured their charter, and who had been obliged to leave France for religion.

In this building are two large laboratories, one for chemical and the other for galenical preparations; where great quantities of the best medicines are prepared for the use of apothecaries and others; particularly for the surgeons of the royal navy, who here furnish their chests with all useful and necessary medicines.

This company was incorporated at first with the grocers, in the year 1606; but, such a connection not answering the purposes of their incorporation, they were separated by another charter granted by king James I. in the year 1617, and incorporated by the name of " The Masters, Wardens, and Society of the art and mystery of Apothecaries of the city of London :" at which time there were no more than 104 apothecaries' shops within the city and suburbs of London.

The members of this company, who by divers acts of parliament are exempt from ward and parish offices, are governed by a master, two wardens, and twenty-one assistants.

## CHURCH OF ST. SEPULCHRE, SNOW HILL.

This church, which is so dedicated in commemoration of our Saviour's sepulchre or grave at Jerusalem, is now a spacious building, but not so large as of old time, part of the site of it being let out upon a building lease. It is supposed to have been founded about the year 1100, at which time a particular devotion was paid to the holy sepulchre; and was so decayed in the reign of Edward IV. as to require rebuilding. Roger, bishop of Salisbury, in the reign of Henry I. gave the patronage of this church to the prior and convent of St. Bartholomew, in West Smithfield, who established a perpetual vicarage in it, and held it till their dissolution, when it fell to the crown. King James I., in the seventh year of his reign, granted the rectory and its appurtenances, and the advowson of this vicarage, to Francis Philips, and others; after which the parishioners purchased the rectory and its appurtenances, and held them in fee-farm of the crown. And the advowson of the vicarage was purchased by the president and fellows of St. John Baptist College, Oxon, who continue patrons thereof.

The present structure was much damaged by the fire of London in 1666. The outward walls and tower were, however, capable of reparation; and the middle aisle of the church was at the same time made with an arched roof, which was not so originally.

This church, in its present situation, measures 126 feet in length, exclusive of the broad passage at the west end; the breadth, exclusive of the north chapel, is fifty-eight feet. The height of the roof in the middle aisle is thirty-five feet; and the height of the steeple, to the top of the pinnacles, is 146 feet. The body of the church is enlightened with a row of very large Gothic windows, with buttresses between, over which runs a slight cornice; and on the top a plain and substantial battlement work, in the style of the public buildings in the reign of Edward IV. The steeple is a plain square tower, crowned with four pinnacles.

## CHURCH OF ST. OLAVE, TOOLEY STREET.

Though it cannot be ascertained at what time a church was first situated on this spot, yet it is mentioned as early as the year 1281. However, part of the old church falling down in 1736, and the rest being in a ruinous condition, the parishioners applied to parliament for a power to rebuild it, which being granted, the remains of the old building were taken down in the year 1737, and the present structure finished in 1739. It consists of a plain body, strengthened with rustic quoins at the corners; the door is well-proportioned, without ornament, and the windows are placed in three series; the lowest is upright, but considerably broad; those above them circular, and the others on the roof are large and semi-circular. The tower consists of three stages, the uppermost of which is considerably diminished: in this is the clock,

Drawn by Tho. H. Shepherd.

Engraved by S. Lacey.

ST. SEPULCHRE'S, SKINNER STREET.

Drawn by Tho. H. Shepherd.

Engraved by S. Lacey.

ST. OLAVE, TOOLEY STREET.

ST. BARTHOLOMEW'S HOSPITAL.

STOCK EXCHANGE

and in the stages below are large windows.    The top of the tower is surrounded by a plain substantial balustrade, and the whole has an air of plainness and simplicity.

This parish is a rectory, the patronage of which is in the gift of the crown.

### St. Bartholomew's Hospital, West Smithfield.

On the east side of Smithfield is the magnificent hospital of St. Bartholomew, which appears to have been the first establishment of this nature in London, having been founded in the year 1102, by Rahere, minstrel to Henry I., who, quitting his gay life, founded a priory of black canons, which he dedicated to St. Bartholomew, and became himself the first prior. He afterwards obtained from the king a piece of waste ground, on which he built an hospital for a master, brethren, and sisters, and for the relief of the diseased and maimed poor, which he placed under the care of the priory.

Both the priory and hospital were surrendered to Henry VIII., who, in the last year of his reign, refounded the latter, and endowed it with an annual revenue of 500 marks, on condition that the city should pay an equal sum ; which proposal being accepted, the new foundation was incorporated by the name of " The Hospital of the Mayor, Commonalty, and Citizens of London, Governors for the Poor, called Little St. Bartholomews, near West Smithfield."   Since this time the hospital has received considerable benefactions from charitable persons, by which means the governors have been enabled to admit all indigent persons maimed by accident, at any hour of the day or night, without previous recommendation ;   and the sick on Thursdays, on which days a committee of governors sit to examine persons applying for admission.   The patients, whether sick or maimed, are provided with lodging, food, medicine, and attendance, and have the advice and assistance of some of the most eminent physicians and surgeons in the kingdom.

Notwithstanding the old building escaped the dreadful fire in 1666, yet the chief part of its revenues being in houses, the hospital was greatly injured by that calamity.   In the year 1729, the hospital became so ruinous that there appeared an absolute necessity for rebuilding it ; and a subscription was entered into by many of the governors and other charitable persons, among whom was Dr. Ratcliffe, for defraying the expense, upon a plan then prepared, containing four detached piles of stone building, to be connected by gateways, and to form a quadrangle.

The first stone of this building was laid on the 9th of June, 1730, by Sir George Brocas, the lord mayor, in the presence of several aldermen and governors ; and the eastern side of the square, which completed the whole, being finished in 1770, it is now one of the most pleasing structures in London, when viewed from the area within, which it surrounds, and where only it can be seen to advantage.

That part which opens to Smithfield, and which may be esteemed the principal front, is allotted for the public business of the hospital.   It contains a large hall for the general courts of the governors ; a counting house for the meetings of committees ; rooms for examining, admitting, and discharging patients ; with other necessary offices.   In this part of the building is a stair-case painted and given by the late Mr. Hogarth, consisting of two pictures, representing the good Samaritan and the pool of Bethesda; which, for truth of colouring and expression are thought to equal any thing of the kind in Europe.

In the hall is a full-length portrait of Henry VIII., and another of Dr. Ratcliffe, who bequeathed £500 per annum to the hospital, for the improvement of the diet, and £100 per annum to purchase linen for the patients. There is also a fine portrait of Percival Pott, esq., many years an eminent surgeon to this hospital, painted by Sir Joshua Reynolds.

The centre of the great quadrangle has been ornamented with a curious cylindrical pump, enclosed within a handsome iron railing, for the use of the hospital. The water is drawn from a very deep spring on the spot, evidently connected with another spring, which supplies Whitbread's brewery in Chiswell Street, because when much water was drawn at either place, the other failed.

## STOCK EXCHANGE, CAPEL COURT,

Is opposite the east entrance to the Bank, at the upper end of Capel Court, which derived its name from the house of Sir William Capel, a lord mayor in 1503. This is a neat plain building, fronted with stone to the attic story, which is of brick, and erected in 1801, by Mr. James Peacock, the architect. The expense was defrayed by a subscription among the principal stock-brokers of £50 transferable shares. No person is allowed to transact business here unless ballotted annually by a committee: persons so chosen subscribe fifteen guineas each. Under the clock, at the south end, is a tablet, exhibiting the names of such defaulters as have not been able or willing to make their payments good, for the purchase or transfer of stock, and who are not allowed to become members any more. On the east side, a recess is appropriated for the commissioners for the redemption of the national debt, who make their purchases four times a week. The hours of business here are from ten to four; and there are three entrances besides that in Capel Court.

## KING'S BENCH PRISON, ST. GEORGE'S FIELDS.

At the south-west corner of Blackman Street, in the road to the Obelisk, St. George's Fields, is situated the King's Bench Prison, for debtors, and every one sentenced by the Court of King's Bench; but those who can purchase the liberties have the benefit of walking through Blackman Street, a part of the Borough, and in St. George's Fields. This building is surrounded by a very high wall. Prisoners in any other jail may remove hither by Habeas Corpus. This prison contains at least 300 rooms: the number of people confined here is greater; and decent accommodations are much more expensive than in the Fleet.

KING'S BENCH PRISON.

PRINCIPAL ENTRANCE.

SADDLER'S WELLS THEATRE

## Sadler's Wells' Theatre, Spa Fields.

Near the east end of the New River Reservoir is a small summer theatre, called Sadler's Wells; the amusements of which, like those of all the minor theatres, are limited to the representation of burlettas, ballets, pantomimes, and various feats of activity. This place of entertainment originated in the salubrious qualities of a well, formerly famed for the extraordinary cures effected by it, in certain diseases, but which was filled up, by the authority of government at the Reformation, to check the impositions of the priests of the priory of Clerkenwell, who extorted money from the people, by making them believe that the virtues of the water proceeded from the efficacy of their prayers. The concourse of visitors had induced the proprietors to have music at their house, and concerts were constantly performed there: but the well being closed, the place declined, the music ceased, and the virtues of the water were forgotten. This once celebrated well was again discovered in the year 1683, by one of the labourers of Mr. Sadler, who had rebuilt the music house there, and renewed the former concerts; since which time it has continued to be opened, with performances of different descriptions, according to the talents or the taste of its managers. The present building, wholly of brick, was erected in 1765, and has since undergone many alterations. Under the excellent management of Mr. Charles Dibdin, the performances here have been improved beyond any precedent in places of this description. The inside has been lately rebuilt at the expense of £1500, in a very splendid style, forming a neat semi-circle, and the aquatic exhibitions produce a very striking effect.

## West India Docks, Isle of Dogs.

If, with natural advantages alone, the Thames is of the greatest importance to the City of London, to what immense extent must its value be increased by the modern improvements on it! The great increase of trade in the port of London required additional convenience for loading and unloading vessels, and hence the various extensive docks which have been constructed on the north banks of the Thames were undertaken.

Those appropriated for the use of the West India trade are wholly on the Isle of Dogs; a name given to it on account of the noise the King's hounds made when the court was kept at Greenwich. The northern one is for receiving loaded vessels inwards, covering an extent of thirty acres, and affording accommodation for from 2 to 300 ships, such as are used in that trade, at one time. The southern one, which is appropriated to loading vessels outwards, occupies a space of twenty-four acres. The openings into these docks are at Blackwall and Limehouse, and there is an extensive range of warehouses all round them for storing West India produce, the whole of which must be landed here.

South from these docks, and in a line parallel to them, is a canal across the Isle of Dogs, by which ships are enabled to avoid a very circuitous passage round that peninsula, in their course up and down the river, on payment of a small sum in proportion to their bulk.

### St. Katherine Docks, Tower.

On the site of the present great commercial establishment, which, as docks, afford facilities and advantages of the first importance to the metropolis, formerly stood the collegiate church and hospital of St. Katherine, situated on the east side of the Tower, in a small open space called St. Katherine's Square: it belonged originally to an hospital founded in 1148, by Matilda, consort to King Stephen. The old foundation was dissolved and refounded, in 1273, by Queen Eleanor, relict of Henry III. Queen Philippà, consort to Edward III., was a great benefactress to this hospital, as was King Henry VI., who not only confirmed all the former grants, and made several additional ones, but gave an ample charter to it. It was exempt from the jurisdiction of the Bishop of London, till its suppression by Henry VIII., soon after which, Edward VI. annexed it to that diocese; leaving the patronage, however, in the hands of the Queens of England, according to the disposition of its re-foundress. The church, which was a very handsome Gothic building, and collegiate, has a master, whose situation is a valuable sinecure, and three brethren, who have forty pounds each; three sisters, who have twenty pounds; and ten beads-women, who have eight pounds per annum each; and six poor scholars. This church being pulled down to make way for the present docks, a splendid building in lieu of it, has been erected in the Regent's Park, of which an engraving and description is given in the other volume of the present work.

### Church of St. Clement, East Cheap.

In Clement's lane, at the western extremity of Eastcheap, stands the parish church of St. Clement, Eastcheap.

This church was dedicated to St. Clement, disciple of St. Peter, the Apostle, who was ordained Bishop of Rome in the year 93; and it received the addition of Eastcheap from its situation, and to distinguish it from other churches dedicated to the same saint. The date of its foundation is lost; but William de Southlee appears to have been rector of it prior to the year 1309; and, before the suppression of religious houses, it was in the gift of the abbot and convent of St. Peter's, Westminster. But, in the first year of her reign, Queen Mary gave the advowson thereof to the Bishop of London, whose successors have continued patrons of it from that time to the present.

The old church was burnt down in 1666, and the present building was erected in 1686. It is a neat, though plain, structure, of the Composite order, having a square tower, finished with a balustrade round the top. The length of this church is sixty-four feet, its breadth forty feet, the height of the roof thirty-four feet, and that of the tower eighty-eight feet. It is a rectory, and the living was considerably augmented by the parish of St. Martin Orgar being annexed to it.

WEST INDIA IMPORT DOCK, POPLAR.

ST. KATHARINE'S DOCKS, FROM THE BASIN.

ST. CLEMENT'S CHURCH, CLEMENT'S LANE.

ST. BENNET FINK, THREADNEEDLE STREET.

IRONMONGERS' HALL, FENCHURCH STREET.

### CHURCH OF ST. BENNET FINK, THREADNEEDLE STREET.

This church is so called from its dedication to St. Benedict, an Italian saint, and founder of the order of Benedictine monks; and it received the additional name of Fink from one Robert Fink, who rebuilt it. It is of ancient foundation, and, though at present only a curacy, yet was originally a rectory; John de Branketree being rector thereof, before the year 1323. The patronage of this church, which was formerly in the family of the Nevils, falling to the crown, King Edward IV. gave it to the Dean and Chapter of Windsor; and, the impropriation being in the said dean and chapter, it is supplied by one of the canons, who is licensed by the Bishop of London.

The old church being destroyed by fire, in 1666, the present building was erected in 1673. The body is of an elliptical form, enlightened by large arched windows, which reach to the roof. This is encompassed with a balustrade, and crowned with a lantern; a dome rises upon the whole extent of the tower, and on its top is a turret. The church-yard was given to the parishioners, as a free burial place, without any expense.

### IRONMONGERS' HALL, FENCHURCH STREET.

On the north side of Fenchurch-street is a very noble hall, erected in the year 1748, by the Ironmongers, for transacting their affairs as a body corporate. This edifice is entirely fronted with stone, and the whole lower story is wrought in rustic. The centre part of the building projects a little; and in this are a large arched entrance and two windows, with two others on each side. Over this rustic story rises the superstructure, which has a light rustic at the corners, to keep up a correspondence with the rest of the building: the part which projects is ornamented with four Ionic pilasters, coupled, but with a large intercolumniation. In the middle is a very noble Venetian window, and over it a circular one. In each space, between the pilasters, is a smaller window, with an angular pediment; and over these are also circular ones; but the sides have arched windows, with square ones over them. The central part is crowned with a pediment, supported by these pilasters, and in its plane are carved the arms of the company, with handsome decorations in relievo. The rest of the building is terminated by a balustrade crowned with vases.

The Ironmongers' company was incorporated by charter from King Edward IV. in the year 1464, and is the tenth of the twelve principal companies in this city. It was incorporated by the name and style of "The master and keepers, or wardens, and commonalty of the art or mystery of Ironmongers of London." And, by virtue of the said charter, the government of this fraternity is now in a master, two wardens, and a court of assistants, which consists of the whole livery, and represents the commonalty or whole freedom.

## Fleet Prison, Farringdon Street.

On the east side of what was called Fleet Market, but now Farringdon Street, is the Fleet Prison. The body, inclosed with houses, and very high walls, is a handsome lofty brick building, of a considerable length, with galleries in every story, which reach from one end of the house to the other. On each side of these galleries are rooms for the prisoners. All manner of provisions are brought into this prison every day, and cried as in the public streets. Here also is a coffee-house, a tap, and an ordinary, with a large open area for exercise. This prison is properly that belonging to the Courts of Chancery and Common Pleas; and the keeper is called the Warden of the Fleet, a place of considerable confidence and emolument, arising from the fees, the rent of the chambers, &c.

Probably the most authentic statement respecting the economy of this prison is to be found in the evidence of Nicolas Nixon, Esq., delivered before the Committee of the House of Commons, he being then the Deputy and sole Acting Warden. The other officers within the prison, besides his clerk, were three turnkeys, one watchmen, and one scavenger, all paid by the wardens.

Nothing can be publicly sold within the prison without the authority of the Warden or his Deputy. The beer and ale coming into the prison and sold at the tap are on the credit of the Deputy. The license for selling wine has been many years discontinued. The sale of all spirituous liquors within the prison is prohibited by Act of Parliament. There is a penalty on their admission. The cook and the racket-master, being officers of the prisoners, are elected by them; they are elected twice a year. The priority of chummage, or admission to rooms in the prison, is by rotation, or seniority, among such prisoners as have paid their entrance fees. A few among the very oldest prisoners are exempted from chummage, i. e. from having any others put into their rooms. When a prisoner cannot pay for his clearance out of prison, the fees are always paid by some of the charitable societies. Prisoners who are supersedable have their rooms taken from them. The distinction between the Master's side and the Common side is, that for the former the entrance fee is paid; for the latter no fee at all. Prisoners who swear they are not worth five pounds in the world, are allowed the benefit of the begging grate, and take it in rotation, each man twenty-four hours. Besides this, there are sometimes charitable donations, which are distributed among the very poorest prisoners. The £500 per ann., granted by the act, is distributed among the poor prisoners indiscriminately. Some of the poor prisoners wait upon the wealthy ones, and gain some relief that way. The room rents on the Master's side are fifteen pence each; they are in general paid for weekly, but a prisoner cannot be turned out of a room for non-payment, unless a quarter's rent be accumulated. The racket-masters, who are paid so much per game, make about a guinea a week each, by their situations. The pastime has been approved by the Court as healthful.

At eleven, oil, candles, and fires, are ordered to be put out in the coffee-house and tap; but riots and irregularities are frequently complained of. Every thing practicable is done

Drawn by Tho. H. Shepherd.

Engraved by J. Henshall.

FARRINGDON ST. AND THE FLEET PRISON.

Drawn by Tho. H. Shepherd.

FOUNDLING HOSPITAL, GUILDFORD STREET.

to repress those. Since the passing of what is called the "'Three Months Act," the prisoners are less moral than they were before; for prisoners in general contrive to procure money to maintain them during the three months, and they are less careful of their behaviour. Strangers are obliged to quit the prison between ten and half-past ten o'clock. Two clubs are established in the prison; one on Monday nights in the tap-room; the other on Thursday nights in the coffee-room. Strangers are admissible to both.

The prison is well secured against fire, all the rooms but those on the top gallery being arched with brick. The chapel is very badly attended; there are no means of enforcing the rule for the attendance of the prisoners. The prison gates are locked during Divine Service; at other times, upon an average, the key turns about once in a minute. The number of prisoners within the walls, and in the rules for the then last three years, averaged about three hundred. The Court of Common Pleas sends an officer of their own four times a year to visit the prison, immediately before each term. The circumference of the rules is about three-fourths of a mile. Prisoners are entitled to this on giving sufficient security to the warden. There are day rules in Term time, every day the Court sits. The ordinary expence of a day's rule to a prisoner is two pounds seven shillings for the whole, if the charge be under £500; in addition to this, four shillings and sixpence are paid for each day. Several of the prisoners live most luxuriously within the walls, as well as in the rules, and this they all seem inclined to do, as far as their means will admit.

The ground on which this prison, and the buildings up to Skinner-Street, now stand, formed the eastern shore of the Town Ditch, denominated Fleet Ditch, which was navigable for small vessels nearly as high as Holborn Bridge, before the Fire of London. In 1733 it was completely arched over between that place and the south end of Fleet Market. Still, on the south side of Fleet-Street, a "genuine and muddy ditch" was scarcely concealed from the public eye by a range of stone buildings, consisting of the watch-house, &c., for St. Bride's parish, built upon an arch over the ditch. The Obelisk, at the north end of New Bridge Street, erected in the mayoralty of John Wilkes, Esq., in 1775, marks the extent of this ditch till that period, when it was completely filled up, and when the fine range of buildings between that and the water side rose in its stead.

## FOUNDLING HOSPITAL, LAMB'S-CONDUIT STREET.

The Foundling hospital is a handsome building, and consists of two large wings directly opposite to each other, one of which is for the boys, and the other for the girls. They are built of brick, in a plain, but regular, substantial, and convenient manner, and with handsome piazzas. At the farthest end is the chapel, which is joined to the wings by an arch on each side, and is very elegant within. In the front is a large piece of ground, on each side whereof is a colonnade of great length, which also extends towards the gates that are double, with a massy pier between them, so that coaches may pass and repass at the same time. These colonnades are now enclosed, and contain ranges of workshops, where the children are taught to spin, weave, and exercise other handicrafts. The large area between the gates and the hospital is adorned with grass plats, gravel walks, and lamps erected upon handsome posts; besides which there are two convenient gardens.

In erecting these buildings, particular care was taken to render them neat and substantial, without any costly decorations; but the first wing of the hospital was scarcely inhabited when several eminent masters in painting, carving, and other of the polite arts, were pleased to contribute many elegant ornaments, which are preserved as monuments of the abilities and charitable benefactions of the respective artists. Among these are several fine paintings by Hogarth, Hayman, Wilson, Gainsborough, &c.

The altar-piece in the chapel, which is most beautifully executed, is accounted one of Mr. West's best productions. It was painted for Macklin's Bible, and the subject is, " Except ye become as little children," &c.

The first organ was presented by Mr. Handel, and was rendered particularly useful in the infancy of the institution, by that gentleman performing on it at certain times for the benefit of the charity; but this organ having become defective, through time and use, a new one was put up in its stead.


## Church of St. George, Hanover Square.

West of St. James's parish is that of St. George, Hanover Square, the church of which stands in Great George Street.

This parish was taken out of St. Martin's in the Fields. The commissioners for building the fifty new churches appointed by virtue of an act of parliament passed in the reign of Queen Anne, observing the want of one in this part of the town, on account of the great increase of buildings and inhabitants, erected this elegant structure, which was finished in 1724, and in compliment to the reigning monarch was dedicated to St. George the Martyr. It has a plain body, with an elegant portico; the columns are Corinthian, of a large diameter, and the pediment has an acroteria, but without further ornament. The tower is elegantly adorned at the corners, with coupled Corinthian columns that are very lofty; these are crowned with an entablature, which, at each corner, supports two vases; and over these the tower still rises, till it is terminated by a dome, crowned with a turret, that supports a ball, over which is a vane.

It is a rectory, the patronage of which is in the Bishop of London.

The ground on which this church stands was given by Lieutenant General William Stewart, who also bequeathed four thousand pounds to the parish, towards erecting and endowing a charity school


## Church of St. George, Bloomsbury.

To the east and north of St. Giles's parish is that of St. George, Bloomsbury, the church of which stands in Hart-street.

ST. GEORGE'S, HANOVER SQUARE.

ST. GEORGE'S, BLOOMSBURY.

INTERIOR QUADRANGLE, SOMERSET HOUSE.

This is one of the fifty new churches appointed to be built by act of parliament within the bills of mortality. The name of St. George was given to it in honour of his late majesty; and it received the additional epithet of Bloomsbury from its situation in the ancient village of Lomesbury, corruptly called Bloomsbury, to distinguish it from others of the same name. It is likewise farther distinguished by standing north and south.

Mr. Walpole calls this building a master-piece of absurdity. The portico on the south side is of the Corinthian order, and makes a very good figure in the street, but has no affinity with the church, which is plain and heavy, and might have corresponded with a Tuscan portico. The tower and steeple on the west side is a very extraordinary structure. On the top, standing on a round pedestal or altar, is a colossal statue of George I., supported by a square pyramid; at the corners of which, near the base, are a lion and unicorn, alternately, the first with his heels in the air, and between them are festoons: these animals, being very large, are injudiciously placed over very small columns, which makes them appear monsters. The under part of the tower is not less heavy than the church, but in style is wholly unconnected with it.

This church was erected at the public expense, and consecrated in January, 1731. A district, for its parish, was, by authority of parliament, taken out of that of St. Giles, and the sum of three thousand pounds was given towards the support of its rector, to which one thousand two hundred and fifty pounds being added, by the inhabitants of St. Giles's parish, both sums were ordered to be laid out in the purchase of lands, tenements, &c., in fee simple, as a perpetual fund for the maintenance of the rector and his successors; but the poor of this parish, and that of St. Giles in the Fields, are to be maintained by the joint assessment of both parishes, in the same manner as before their being divided.

This church is a rectory, in the gift of the crown, but cannot be held in commendam; and all licenses to that effect are made void by the act of parliament for separating this parish from St. Giles's. The following epitaph, intended for the architect of this church, is a severe but humorous critique on his bad taste:—

> "Lie heavy on him earth, for he
> Laid many a heavy load on thee."

## Canonbury Tower, Islington.

Canonbury House, the manorial residence, was originally built for a mansion house for the priors of St. Bartholomew. This edifice was of considerable extent, covering nearly the whole site of ground now called Canonbury Place, and having a small park, with garden grounds and domestic offices. A large old house, having a *tower of brick*, about seventeen feet square, and sixty feet high, which, both externally and within doors, retains much of its primitive appearance, together with a considerable part of the wall that encompassed the park and garden-ground, form at this time the most prominent remains of this once splendid dwelling.

R

Stow says, " William Bolton (who was prior of St. Bartholomew) builded anew the manor of Canonbury at Islington, which belonged to the canons of that house." Mr. Lysons thinks it probable that this part of the premises was built by some of the owners of Canonbury, since the Reformation ; but from Bolton's rebus (a bolt in a tun) appearing in several parts of the wall, originally connected with the Old Brick Tower, and which is evidently of the same materials and workmanship, there can be no doubt of its having been erected by him. Part of this wall still incloses the ground attached to the Canonbury Tavern on the East, dividing it from the open fields, and on the north by the side of Hopping Lane. The western wall branched off from the above, somewhat behind the site of Compton Terrace, towards Canonbury Lane. For the erection of the original mansion house we may, without doubt, refer to the date 1352 (1362) inscribed on the building.

The most considerable part of the old mansion appears to have been much altered by Sir John Spencer, who came to reside here in the year 1599, previously to which time it was probably rented of him by various individuals. It has been many years divided into several houses, and forms a considerable part of the white-fronted buildings in Canonbury Place. Two of these houses contain some interesting remains of ancient grandeur.

## CHURCH OF ST. MARY, ISLINGTON.

This church is situate on the east side of the Upper Street, and nearly in the centre of the village. Though perhaps not formed according to strict architectural rule, it is allowed to be a very light and handsome edifice. It is built with brick, strengthened and adorned with stone groins, cornices, &c., in plain rustic. It contains a nave, chancel, and two aisles, and is adorned at the west end with an elegant spire of Portland stone. The floor is vaulted considerably above the level of the church-yard. The west door is ornamented with a portico of a semicircular form, consisting of a dome, supported by four Tuscan columns, to which there is an ascent of five steps, arranged also semicircularly. The two side doors are from a Vetruvian model, and have a very neat appearance. At the east end is a Venetian window, divided into three compartments, by pillars of the Ionic order; but the intercolumns are filled up with stone, and covered on the inside with the painted decorations of the altar. The roof is spanned from the walls of the church without the support of pillars, and is covered with Westmoreland slates.

The steeple consists of a tower, rising square to the height of eighty-seven feet, terminated by a cornice supporting four vases at the corners ; upon this is placed an octagonal balustrade, from within which rises the base of the spire in the same form, supporting eight Corinthian double columns, with their shafts wrought in rustic. Upon these the dome rests, and from its crown the spire is continued with perforations, and is terminated by a ball and vane.

The ceiling of the church was originally vaulted, and disposed in parabolical compartments, having a circle in the centre, and was enriched with mouldings of wreathed flowers, &c., in stucco. The galleries are supported by Tuscan pillars, and are painted on the front

CANONBURY TOWER, ISLINGTON.

ST MARY ISLINGTON.

OLD QUEENS HEAD,

ISLINGTON.

in imitation of oak wainscot. They contain between sixty and seventy pews, framed of fir, and at the west end is a very handsome and good toned organ, in a mahogany case, placed here in 1772. It was opened by Dr. Worgan.

The pews in the area of the building, which were originally ninety-one in number, together with the screen which divides the church from the vestibule, are framed of oak wainscot; and in the christening pew is a neat marble font. The pulpit, reading desk, &c., are of mahogany, and the sounding board is supported by two Corinthian columns. The altarpiece is composed also of the same wood, divided into compartments by pillars and their entablature of the Doric order. The Decalogue, &c., is painted in golden letters on a black ground; and above the pediment, in the place of the window, is a chaste and appropriate painting of the Annunciation, having on each side emblems of the law and the gospel in *chiaro-'scuro*. These were painted by Mr. Nathaniel Clarkson, a parishioner. The church throughout exhibits an elegant plainness, but the beauty of the interior has been much impaired by some alterations which were made in 1818, when the building was newly roofed. The ceiling is far inferior, in construction and design, to the one which it was thought necessary to remove, and the filling the lobby with pews, and thereby preventing access to the galleries and the middle of the church from the side doors, has darkened and encumbered the entrance, and is attended with some inconvenience to the congregation.

In the Tower is a good peal of eight bells; the six which were in the old church being recast in 1774, and two smaller ones added by subscription to complete the octave. The tenor weighs sixteen cwt., and was recast in 1808, in order to improve the tone.

## The Old Queen's Head, Islington.

The Old Queen's head public house, lately pulled down and rebuilt, is described by an antiquarian, "as one of the most perfect specimens of ancient domestic architecture remaining in the neighbourhood of London, or perhaps in the whole kingdom. It is a strong wood and plaster building, consisting of three lofty stories projecting over each other in front, and forming bay windows, supported by brackets and caryatides of a grotesque form carved in wood. The centre projects several feet beyond the other part of the building, and forms a commodious porch, to which there is a descent of several steps. This is supported in front by two caryatides of carved oak, crowned with Ionic scrolls, standing one on each side the entrance. The floor of the front parlour is four feet below the surface of the highway, though a tradition prevails that the house originally was entered by an ascent of several steps. This, indeed, is not improbable, when the antiquity of the building is considered, and the vast accumulation of matter upon the road in the course of several centuries : add to this, that the new river, which passes under the highway in front of the house, has, in the foundation of its banks, and the turning an arch over it, occasioned a considerable rise in this place."

"This ancient fabric, like most of the old buildings in the parish of Islington, has panelled wainscots of oak, and stuccoed ceilings: the latter in the parlour is ornamented with dolphins, cherubs, acorns, &c., surrounded by a wreathed border of fruit and foliage. Near the centre of the ceiling is the medallion of a Roman head, crowned with bays; also a small shield, containing the initials 'I. M.,' surrounded by cherubim and glory. The chimney piece is supported by two figures carved in stone, hung with festoons, &c. The stone slab over the fire-place exhibits the story of Danaë and Actæon, in relief, with mutilated figures of Venus, Bacchus, and Plenty."

### Boar's Head, Great Eastcheap.

On the south side of this street, and near St. Michael's Lane, was the Boar's Head Tavern, celebrated as the place where the inimitable Shakspeare laid some of his best scenes of Henry IV. The original edifice was destroyed in the great fire, but it was rebuilt on the same site, with a stone sign let into the wall.

A few years ago the tavern was pulled down, and two houses built upon its site, but the original sign still exists in the front of one of the houses.

### Talbot Inn, Southwark.

On the east side of the High Street is the Tabard (corrupted to Talbot) inn. In which was the residence of the abbots of Hyde, near Winchester, whenever they came to the metropolis to attend their duty in parliament.

This inn was also the place of rendezvous for the pilgrims on their journeys to pay adoration to the shrine of St. Thomas-á-Becket, at Canterbury: Chaucer minutely describes their mode of behaviour at the inn, and the circumstances of their progress. After commencing his prologue with the time of the year and the state of the atmosphere when the 'yong Sunn hath in the Ram his halvè cours yrunn,' &c., the poet proceeds:

> Befell, that in that season, on that day,
> In Southwerk, at the Tabberd as I lay;
> Ready to wendin on my pilgrimage
> To Canterbury, with devote corage,
> At night wer come into that hostery,
> Wele nine and twenty in a company
> Of sundrie folk, by aventure yfall
> In felaship and pilgrimes wer they all;
> That toward Canterbury wouldin ride.
> The chambers and stablis werin wide,
> And well we werin expid at the best, &c.

He then introduces to view the various personages who composed the cavalcade, viz. the knight, the squire, the squire's yeoman, the prioress, the monk, a friar, a merchant, the clerk

BOAR'S HEAD, GREAT EAST CHEAP.          ANCIENT TABLET, NEAR HOLBORN BRIDGE.

TALBOT INN, BOROUGH.

of Oxenford, the serjeaunt-at-law, the frankelan (freeholder), haberdasher, &c., the coke, the shipman, the doctor of phisick, the wife of Bath, the parsonne, the plowman, the millare, the manciple (purveyor of viands), the reve (bailiff), the sompnour (apparitor), and the pardoner (seller of pardons)

> The state, aray, and number, and the cause
> Why that assemblid was thir companie
> In Southwerke, at this gentil hostelrie ;
> That hight the Tabbarde, fastè by the Bell.

## TEMPLE BAR.

### [*See Vignette to Title.*]

This is esteemed a very handsome gate, where formerly posts, rails, and a chain only, terminated the city bounds, as also at Holborn, Smithfield, and Whitechapel Bars. Afterwards a house of timber was erected across the street, with a narrow gateway and southern postern. The fire of London, however, having introduced a system of order and magnificence in the public buildings, Temple Bar offered an object for the exercise of Sir Christopher Wren's abilities. The centre is a broad gateway, sufficient for the passing of two carriages ; the sides are furnished with convenient posterns for foot passengers. The whole is constructed of Portland stone, with a rustic basement, surmounted by the Corinthian order. Over the gateway, on the east side, two niches contain the statues of Queen Elizabeth and James I., with the arms of England over the key-stone. On the west side are the statues of Charles I. and Charles II., in Roman habits. They are all the work of Bushnel. On the east side was an inscription, now nearly obliterated, to the following purport :

"Erected in the year 1670, Sir Samuel Starling, Mayor ; continued in the year 1671, Sir Richard Ford, Lord Mayor ; and finished in the year 1672, Sir George Waterman, Lord Mayor.

This gate, on account of its publicity, was made a place of exposure for the heads of traitors, who had forfeited their lives to the laws of their country. It has also long been the place at which the city magistracy receive the royal family, and other distinguished visitors, on solemn occasions : the Lord Mayor, as King's Lieutenant, delivers the sword of state to the sovereign when he enters the city, which his majesty returns. He is then preceded by the magistracy bare-headed, the Lord Mayor, by right of his office, riding on horseback, immediately before the king. Temple Bar, however, has been voted by the city to be removed, to open a more commodious communication with the city and liberty of Westminster, at the suggestion, and through the endeavours of William Picket, Esq., Alderman, and Lord Mayor in the year 1790. Whether this will ever be carried into effect is doubtful.

### St. Thomas's Hospital, Southwark.

Near the middle of the Borough High Street, on the east side, stands St. Thomas's Hospital, a very handsome stone building, and a noble and extensive charity for the reception of the necessitous sick and wounded.

With respect to the origin of this hospital, it is to be observed that the priory of St. Mary Overies being destroyed by fire in the year 1207, the canons erected an occasional edifice, at a small distance, to answer the same purpose, till their monastery could be rebuilt; which being accomplished, Peter de Rupibus, Bishop of Winchester, for the greater convenience of air and water, pulled it down in 1215, and removed it to a place where the prior of Bermondsey had two years before built an almonry, or almshouse, for the reception of indigent children and necessitous proselytes. The hospital was now dedicated to St. Thomas the Apostle, and endowed with land to the value of £343 a year: from which time it was held of the Abbot of Bermondsey, until the dissolution of the religious houses, when it fell into the hands of Henry VIII.

When the corporation of London purchased the manor of Southwark, in 1551, the hospital was immediately repaired and enlarged; and, in the November following, there were received into it 250 sick and helpless objects. The hospital still retained its original name of St. Thomas; and, in 1552, as hath been already mentioned, King Edward VI. granted a charter, by which the mayor and commonalty of London were incorporated governors of the same.

Though this hospital escaped the great fire in 1666, yet great part of its possessions were then destroyed; and two other fires, that afterwards happened in Southwark, reduced it to great distress. The building grew old and wanted repairs, and the funds on which it depended for support failed. However, in 1699, the governors opened a subscription for rebuilding it on a more extensive plan, which was executed at different times, and completed in the year 1742.

The hospital now consists of three quadrangles, or square courts. In the front, next the street, is a handsome pair of large iron gates, with a door of the same work on each side, for the convenience of foot passengers. These are fastened on the sides to stone piers, on each of which is a statue representing one of the patients. These gates open into a very neat square court, encompassed on three sides with a colonnade, surrounded with benches, next the wall, for the accommodation of people to sit and rest themselves. On the south side, under an empty niche, is the following inscription:

This building, on the south side of this court, containing three wards, was erected at the charge of THOMAS FREDERICK, of London, Esq., a worthy governor and liberal benefactor to this hospital, Anno 1708.

On the opposite side, under the same kind of niche, is this inscription:

This building, on the north side of this court, containing three wards, was erected at the charge of THOMAS GUY, Esq. citizen and stationer of London, a worthy governor and bountiful benefactor to this hospital, Anno 1707.

The centre of the principal front, facing the street, is of stone. On the top is a clock, under a small circular pediment, and beneath that, in a niche, the statue of king Edward VI. holding a guilt sceptre in his right hand, and the charter in his left. A little lower, in niches on each side, a man with a crutch, and a sick woman; and under them, in other niches, a man with a wooden leg, and a woman with her arm in a sling. Over the niches are the festoons, and between the last-mentioned figures, the king's arms in relievo: under which is this inscription:

King Edward the Sixth, of pious memory, in the year of our Lord 1552, founded and en-endowed this hospital of St. Thomas the apostle, together with the hospitals of Christ, and Bridwell, in London.

Underneath this is a spacious passage, down several steps, into the second court, which is more elegant than the former. This has also colonnades, except the front of the chapel, which is on the north side, and is adorned with lofty pilasters of the Corinthian order, placed on high pedestals. On the top is a pediment, as well as in the centre of the east and west sides, and above the piazzas, the fronts of the wards are ornamented with handsome Ionic pilasters.

In the centre of this court is a handsome brass statue of king Edward VI. by Mr. Schee-makers; behind which is placed, on a kind of small pedestal, his crown laid upon a cushion. The statue is enclosed with iron rails, and stands upon a lofty stone pedestal, on which is the following inscription, in capitals:

This statue
Of King Edward the Sixth,
A most excellent Prince,
Of exemplary Piety and Wisdom,
above his years;
The glory and ornament of his age,
and most munificent founder
Of this hospital,
Was erected at the expense
Of CHARLES JOYCE, Esquire,
in the year MDCCXXXVII.

On the opposite side of the pedestal is the same inscription in Latin.

In the centre of each side of this court is a spacious passage into the next, the structure above being supported by two rows of columns. The buildings in the third court are older than the others, and are entirely surrounded by a colonnade, above which they are adorned with a kind of long, slender, Ionic pilasters, with very small capitals. In the centre is a stone statue of Sir Robert Clayton, dressed in his robes as Lord Mayor, surrounded with iron rails; upon the west side of the pedestal is his arms in relievo, and on the south side, the following inscription :

To Sir Robert Clayton, Knt. born in Northamptonshire, citizen and Lord Mayor of London, president of this hospital. and vice president of the new workhouse, and a bountiful benefactor to it; a just magistrate and brave defender of the liberty and religion of his country. Who (besides many other instances of his charity to the poor) built the girl's ward in Christ's hospital, gave first, towards the rebuilding of this house, six hundred pounds, and left, by his last will, two thousand three hundred pounds to the poor of it. This statue was erected in his life-time, by the governors, An. Dom. MDCCI. as a monument of their esteem of so much worth, and to preserve his memory after death, was by them beautified, An. Dom. MDCCXIV.

Since the foundation of this extensive charity, an incredible number of distressed objects have received relief from it ; and though the estates originally belonging to the hospital were ruined, yet by the liberality and benevolence of the citizens and others, its revenues have not only been restored, but augmented, and its annual disbursements now amount to a very considerable sum.

It contains nineteen wards, and upwards of five hundred beds, which are constantly occupied, and the mode of admitting patients is the same as at St. Bartholomew's hospital; for which purpose, a committee of governors sits here every Thursday forenoon.

## GUY'S HOSPITAL, SOUTHWARK.

Behind St. Thomas's hospital, on the other side of St. Thomas's Street, stands another foundation of the same description, little inferior to it in extent, but more remarkable from the circumstance of its having been built and endowed by a single individual.

Mr. Thomas Guy, the founder, had, from a small beginning, by industry and frugality, amassed an immense fortune ; but more particularly by purchasing seamen's tickets, in the reign of Queen Anne, and by buying and selling South-sea stock, in the year 1720. He was never married, and had no relations ; therefore, towards the close of his life, considering how he should dispose of his wealth, he at length resolved to be the founder of the most extensive charity ever established by one man.

Mr. Guy was seventy-six years of age when he formed this resolution, and, having no time to lose, immediately purchased of the governors of St. Thomas's hospital, a lease of a piece of ground, nearly opposite to that hospital, for the term of nine hundred and ninety-nine years, at a ground-rent of thirty pounds a year. As this spot was covered with small houses, that were old and ill-tenanted, he gave proper notice to the inhabitants to quit them ; which being done he pulled down the buildings in the year 1721, and proceeding with the greatest expedition, he caused the foundation of the intended hospital to be laid the following spring ; and the building was pursued with such alacrity, that it was roofed in before the death of the founder, which happened on the 27th of December, in the year 1724.

ST. THOMAS' HOSPITAL, AND STATUE OF KING EDWARD VI.

GUY'S HOSPITAL, AND STATUE OF THOMAS GUY, THE FOUNDER.

The only motive which induced Mr. Guy to erect this hospital in so low and close a situation was his design of putting it under the management and direction of the governors of that of St. Thomas's. By the advice of his friends he altered his resolution; but it was too late to think of choosing another situation; for the building was at that time raised to the second story. However, he rendered the place as agreeable as possible, by its elevation above the neighbouring streets.

The whole expense of erecting and furnishing this hospital amounted to the sum of eighteen thousand seven hundred and ninety-two pounds sixteen shillings, great part of which Mr. Guy expended in his lifetime; and he left two hundred and ninety thousand four hundred and ninety-pounds to endow it; both together amounting to two hundred and thirty-eight thousand two hundred and ninety-two pounds sixteen shillings; a much larger sum than was ever left before in this kingdom, by one single person, to charitable purposes.

This building consists of two quadrangles, beside the two wings that extend from the front to the street. The wing on the west side had been lately added, and is built with such elegance and uniformity as to make the whole a very handsome and regular edifice.

The entrance into the building is by elegant and noble iron gates, supported by stone piers. These gates open into a square, in the centre of which is a brazen statue of the founder, by Mr. Scheemakers, dressed in a livery gown, and well executed. In the front of the pedestal is this inscription:

THOMAS GUY, SOLE FOUNDER OF THIS HOSPITAL IN HIS LIFETIME.
A. D. MDCCXXI.

On the west side of the pedestal is represented, in basso-relievo, the parable of the Good Samaritan; on the south side are Mr. Guy's arms; and on that side of the pedestal facing the east is our Saviour healing the impotent man.

The superstructure of this hospital has three floors beside the garrets, and the same construction runs through the whole building, which is so extensive as to contain twelve wards, in which are four hundred and thirty-five beds, exclusive of those that may be placed in the additional part; and the whole is advantageously disposed for the mutual accommodation of the sick, and those who attend them.

A short time after Mr. Guy's decease, his executors, pursuant to his last will, applied to parliament to get themselves, with fifty-one other gentlemen nominated by the testator, to be incorporated governors of the intented hospital; upon which all these gentlemen were constituted a body politic and corporate, by the name of the President and Governors of Guy's Hospital. By this act of incorporation they were to have perpetual succession, and a common seal, with the power of possessing the real and personal estates of the late Thomas Guy, Esq., for the purposes of the will, and to purchase, in perpetuity, or for any term of years, any other estate whatsoever, not exceeding twelve thousand pounds per annum.

As soon as this corporation was established by parliament, the Governors immediately set about completing the work, by finishing and furnishing the hospital, and taking in patients, the number of whom, at first, amounted to four hundred and two. The officers and servants belonging to this hospital are chosen by the Governors, who have ever since carried on this noble charity in such manner as to answer, in the strictest degree, the benevolent intentions of the founder.

The medical establishment and forms of admission are similar to those of St. Thomas's Hospital, but the day for receiving patients is Wednesday. There is a library and a collection of anatomical preparation belonging to this institution.

## BURLINGTON HOUSE, PICCADILLY.

*Piccadilly* is so called, from *Peccadilla Hall*, a sort of repository for ruffs, when there were no other houses where Sackville Street now stands. Piccadilly was completed, as far as Berkeley Street, in 1642. The first good house built here was *Burlington House*, the noble founder of which said, he placed it there " because he was certain no one would build beyond him !"

The front of this noble mansion is of stone; the circular colonnade is of the Doric order, and by this the wings are connected. This house was left to the Devonshire family, on the express condition that it should not be demolished. The heavy screen, which conceals this beautiful front from the street, has long been regretted as a nuisance.

## MELBOURN HOUSE, AND TREASURY OFFICES, WHITEHALL.

Adjoining the Horse Guards is *Melbourn House*, built by Sir Matthew Featherstonehaugh, and afterwards purchased by Lord Melbourn, who exchanged it with His Royal Highness the Duke of York, for York House, Piccadilly, who added the fronts and the dome-portico across the street. When the Duke removed to Portman Square, the house was restored to Lord Melbourn.

The *Offices of the Treasury* are contiguous; this is a handsome stone building, fronting the Parade in St. James's Park. The whole front is rustic, and consists of three stories; the lower Tuscan, and the second Doric, with good-sized arched windows. The upper part of this story is singularly adorned with the tryglyphs and metopes of the Doric frieze, though this range of ornament is supported neither by columns nor pilasters. A range of Ionic columns above this supports a pediment. Near the Treasury is the house usually appointed for the residence of the prime minister. A passage to the public street before Whitehall, under the Cockpit, is esteemed a part of the ancient palace. A little northward from this entrance was the beautiful gate belonging to this palace, built by order of Henry the Eighth, from a design of Hans Holbein, enclosing the Tilt Yard, &c.

*Whitehall*, originally built by Hubert de Burgh, Earl of Kent, in the reign of Henry the Third, was at his death, bequeathed by him to the Black Friars of London; from them coming to Walter De Grey, Archbishop of York, it became the town-residence of the

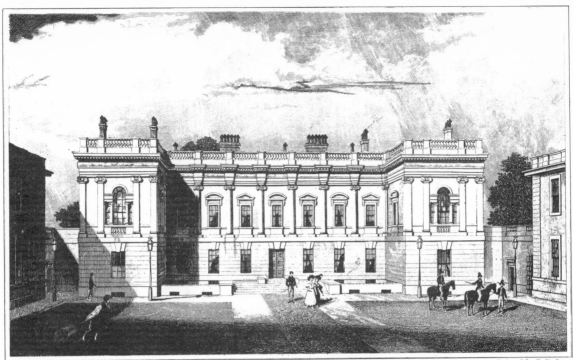

BURLINGTON HOUSE, PICCADILLY.

MELBOURNE HOUSE, AND PART OF THE OLD TREASURY, WHITEHALL.

archbishops of that see; till passing from the haughty Thomas Wolsey, the Cardinal, it came into the hands of the crown, and was formed into one of the royal palaces.

The old palace occupied a space along the northern bank of the river, a little below Westminster Bridge, and extended to St. James's Park, along the eastern end of which many of its various buildings lay, from the Cockpit to Spring Gardens. The ancient building, which contained upwards of 1000 apartments, was mostly consumed by a fire, which broke out in the year 1697.

### HOUSE OF CORRECTION, COLDBATH FIELDS.

On the north side of Coldbath Square, is the House of Correction for the County of Middlesex, which is formed principally in conformity to the judicious and humane suggestions of the late Mr. Howard.

This prison was erected in pursuance of an act of parliament passed in the twenty-sixth year of the reign of George III. "for enabling the justices of the peace for the county of Middlesex to raise money for building a House of Correction within the said county." But it is also used as a penitentiary house.

The spot on which this edifice is erected having been a swamp on the declivity of a hill, it was found necessary to lay the foundation so deep, and to pile it so securely, that it is supposed there are as many bricks laid under ground as appear in sight. The building, with few deviations from uniformity, is laid out and divided into separate and distinct cells, or single apartments, as well on the ground floor as on the upper stories, each cell being eight feet three inches long, and six feet three inches wide. To each cell are apertures, or windows for light and ventilation, each two feet six inches wide by two feet high; the one over the door, the other at the height of seven feet from the floor in the opposite direction: these apertures are closed or opened by means of wooden shutters, acting at the will of the person confined. The cells on the ground floor are built on arches, and are raised twenty-one inches from the pavement of the yards, those of the upper floors rest on the arches of those below; and, as the use of combustible matter is by this means excluded, they are all fire-proof.

The whole number of single cells is two hundred and eighteen, but sixteen of these which have no other light but from the apertures over the doors, are only used for the occasional confinement of refractory prisoners. In addition to these, in each of six of the yards belonging to the building, there are two apartments containing the space of two single cells, and intended for lodging two prisoners. Some larger apartments are formed by throwing together the space of several cells: these are used for various purposes connected with the institution, such as infirmary, work-rooms for the male convicts, a spinning-room for the female convicts, day-rooms with fire-places, used by the prisoners in winter; a laundry, store-rooms, &c.

There are eight large yards, to which the prisoners of different classes have occasional access, where they can be sheltered from the weather by pent-houses, which extend the whole length of them, there are also eight other airing grounds, to which the offenders of the least criminality have free access.    Water is brought into all these yards by pipes, for the use of the prisoners, either to drink or to wash themselves, which they are obliged to do every morning before they receive their breakfasts, and again in the evening before being locked up.

Communicating with the centre gallery there is a building of three stories, with two rooms in each story.    Three of these are let to such prisoners as choose to pay ten shillings and sixpence per week for their hire; the other three are occupied by the servants of the house, or as store-rooms.

At the entrance of the prison is a committee-room, and over it two lodging-rooms, occupied by servants belonging to the prison; and in the centre of the building is a neat and airy chapel, sufficiently spacious to contain the whole number of prisoners which can be accommodated in the cells.

The keeper's house is a distinct building on the east side of the entrance, and is an addition to the original plan, as are also commodious shops, suited to the several trades and manufactures, in which the prisoners are occasionally employed, particularly for carpenters, turners, sawyers, tailors, and shoemakers, with an extensive stage for drying oakum.

Extensive additions and improvements have however been recently made in various parts of the prison, and the whole of the building is surrounded by a high brick wall, strengthened on the outside with stone buttresses.


## The Old Bull and Mouth Inn, St. Martin's Le Grand.


Bull and Mouth Street takes its name from an inn of great antiquity, which has recently been pulled down and rebuilt, and formerly known by the sign of Boulogne Mouth, or Harbour, of which the present appellation is a corruption.    At the corner of this street, in Aldersgate Street, was the city mansion of the Earls of Northumberland.    In the seventh year of his reign, king Henry VI. gave this house, with the tenements thereunto belonging, to his queen Jane, and it then acquired the appellation of her wardrobe.

St. Martin's Le Grand, is a distinct liberty, subject to the dean and chapter of Westminster.    It was originally a college, founded in the year 700, by Wythred, king of Kent, but was rebuilt and endowed, about the year 1056, by a noble Saxon, named Ingelricus, and his brother Edwardus, for a dean and secular canons, or priests, and was dedicated to St. Martin: the epithet *le Grand*, was afterwards added on account of the great and extraordinary privileges, particularly the dangerous one of sanctuary, granted to it by different monarchs.

Drawn by Tho. H. Shepherd.                                   Engraved by W. Watkins

## HOUSE OF CORRECTION, COLDBATH FIELDS.

Drawn by Tho. H. Shepherd.                                   Engraved by W. Watkins

## THE OLD BULL & MOUTH INN, ST. MARTINS-LE-GRAND,

### NOW PULLED DOWN

## LONDON BRIDGE.

Pennant and other historians are not agreed as to the date of the foundation of the original edifice, which occupied the site of the present New Bridge. It is certain that, at the time of the Romans, there was merely a ferry to continue their "Watling Street," supposed to have been opposite to Dowgate Hill, which led in a straight line to Kent Street, Southwark. William of Malmsbury, however, states that, in 994, Sweyn, King of Denmark, in his attack on London, was so valiantly opposed by Ethelred II., and the citizens, that many of the Danish army were drowned in the river, because in their rage they took no notice of the *Bridge*; thus clearly admitting its existence at that date. Of the noble church, nearly adjoining the bridge on the Southwark side, tradition states, that a venerable ferryman died, and left all his gains to an only daughter, named Mary, who built the beautiful nunnery of St. Marie Overies, now St. Saviour's Church, and endowed it with the profits of the ferry. This convent falling into decay, was a second time endowed by a noble lady named Swithin, as a college for priests; and the clergy of that period, being men of public spirit, built the bridge and kept it in repair. It was at first rudely constructed of timber, and, according to Pennant, &c., in 1136, was burned down,—being rebuilt, it became so ruinous, that in 1163 it was taken down, and a stone bridge was begun by Peter, curate of St. Mary Colechurch, in 1176. This is the bridge now removed, in consequence of the completion of the new edifice adjoining, and intended to supersede it. The completion of the old bridge occupied 33 years, and on Peter's death, he was buried in a chapel which he had constructed in one of the centre piers. The stupendous work was founded on enormous piles, driven closely together, on the tops of which were laid long planks ten inches thick, strongly bolted; on these was placed the base of the pier, the lowermost stones being bedded in pitch. Around all this were placed the sterlings, designed for the preservation of the foundation piles, and which occasions a fall of five feet, on the retreat of each tide. The bridge was at one period crowded with houses, leaning over the river in a terrific manner, supported by props, as well as beams, which crossed in arches from the roofs. A very tragical event occurred four years after its completion. On the night of the 10th of July, 1213, a conflagration burst out on the south-west side: the bridge became thronged with people, all crowding from the city, when the fire communicating with St. Marie Overies, now called St. Saviour's Church, was by a strong southerly wind extended to the other end, and about 3000 persons are supposed to have lost their lives.

In 1282, at the breaking up of the frost, five arches of the bridge were carried away; and although immediately restored, yet in 1289, the bridge was so much decayed as to be dangerous for passengers, and a toll was levied in 1298, on goods and passengers to keep it in repair.

The bridge was so encumbered with houses, that the broadway between them did not exceed 12 feet in breadth; it nevertheless appears to have been the site of a market.

Tournaments were also held here, and on St. George's day 1395, there was a grand joust, at which Lord Wells undertook to maintain the renown of England against all comers.

There were originally three openings on each side of the street, whence a view might be had of the shipping. In one of these a drawbridge was contrived, useful either for purposes of defence, or for the admission of vessels to the upper part of the river. This was protected by a strong tower, which, being well manned and armed, occasioned the defeat of Falconbridge, with his Kentish mariners, in 1471, in his attempt to seize the city.

## The New Bridge.

The first pile of this New Bridge, was driven on the west side of the Old Bridge, March, 1824.

On the fifteenth of June, 1825, the stone was laid by the Lord Mayor of London (Mr. Alderman Garratt), in the presence of the late Duke of York. The ceremony was marked by great pomp and circumstance. The civic authorities, accompanied by his royal highness, having proceeded in procession to the principal coffer-dam of the bridge, Mr. Jones, sub-chairman of the committee, presented a silver trowel to the Lord Mayor, who then addressed the Duke of York and the company in a very appropriate speech. This was succeeded by the masonic ceremonies. A portion of fine mortar being placed around the cavity of the stone, by several of the assistants, and spread by the Lord Mayor with his splendid trowel, precisely at five o'clock the first stone was gradually lowered into its bed by a brazen block of four sheaves, and the power of a machine called a crab. When it was settled, it was secured by several masons, who cut four sockets close to it on the stone beneath, into which were fitted strong iron clamps, secured with plaster of Paris. The Lord Mayor then struck it with a mallet, and ascertained its accuracy by applying the level to its east, north, west, and south, surfaces. The work being thus perfected, the city sword and mace were disposed in saltire upon the stone; successive shouts burst from the numerous spectators; the bands played the national anthem of England; and, a flag being lowered as a signal, on the top of the dam, the guns of the Artillery Company, and the carronades on Calvert's brewery wharf fired a salute.

When the procession had left the dam, amidst the acclamations of the spectators and populace, many of the visitors went down to the floor to view the stone more closely, and to boast to posterity that they had stood upon it or walked over it.

The dimensions of the New Bridge are as follows :—Centre arch, span, 150 feet, rise, 32 feet, piers, 24 feet; arches next the centre, span, 140 feet, rise, 30 feet, piers, 22 feet, abutment arches, span, 130 feet, rise, 25 feet, abutment 74 feet. The full width, from bank to bank, 690 feet; length of bridge, including abutments, 950 feet; ditto, without abutments, 782 feet; width of the bridge, from outside to outside of the parapets, 55 feet; carriage way, 33 feet 4 inches.

The arches are constructed solely of granite, of the finest description and workmanship, from the quarries of Devonshire, Aberdeen, and Cornwall. The piers and abutments are

Drawn by Tho. H. Shepherd.

Engraved by R. Acon.

NEW LONDON BRIDGE.

Drawn by Tho. H. Shepherd.

Engraved by R. Acon.

VINTNER'S HALL, UPPER THAMES STREET.

also constructed externally of the same material; but are filled inside with the hardest Yorkshire and Derbyshire stone. The cornices and parapets are wholly of granite.

The stairs and the accompanying pedestals are also constructed of granite. We believe there are 77 steps, of which 30 are covered at high water. There are two landings, to break the abruptness of the ascent. The width of the stairs is proportioned to the bridge; while the beautiful pedestals of the summit, composed of granite blocks, weighing 25 tons, challenge the admiration of the spectators.

On the City side, the road-way, which extends to a fine open area, created by the demolition of the houses in front of the Monument, back to Crooked Lane, and thence to Eastcheap, is supported by eleven brick arches, with the exception of the elliptical arch over Thames Street. This latter arch is faced with granite, and the interior is constructed of Yorkshire stone. On each side of this arch are rustic gateways, leading to a succession of steps, which enable the passengers from Thames Street to reach the bridge without taking a circuitous route. At the Southwark side of the bridge the roadways are supported by twenty-two brick arches of a similar character to the City side, with the exception of a beautiful arch communicating with Tooley Street. This is faced with granite, but the interior is of brick, completed in the most masterly style of workmanship. The line of road on this side, for the present, terminates at the entrance to St. Thomas's Street; but it is intended ultimately that it should be carried forward to the wide opening in front of the Town Hall—a most desirable improvement. The side communicating with Tooley Street will, in like manner, open itself at the wide part near the entrance to Bridge Yard.

## OPENING OF THE NEW BRIDGE.

The bridge being so far completed as to admit of its being opened, the 1st of August, 1831, the anniversary of the accession of the House of Hanover to the throne of these realms, was appointed for the ceremony; and his Majesty, William IV., was graciously pleased to accept the invitation of the corporation of London to be present on the occasion, accompanied by his illustrious consort. His Majesty was pleased to command that the procession should be by water, with the double view of benefitting the men employed on the river, and of enabling the greatest possible number of his loyal subjects to witness the spectacle. As soon as his Majesty's intentions were known, preparations on the most extensive and magnificent scale were made; the arrangements on the river being entrusted to Sir Byam Martin, and the bridge and its approaches to the Bridge Committee. Vast numbers of Workmen were immediately employed in erecting an extensive triple awning along the London end of the bridge, which terminated in a magnificent pavilion for the reception of His Majesty, and various apartments for the use of the Queen and her attendants. The pavilion and awning were lined throughout with the colours of all nations, and upwards of 150 flags and banners floated from the top of the bridge. In the royal tent a table was laid for their Majesties, and the members of the Royal Family; and under the canopy two long tables were laid, capable of accommodating 1500 persons, for the use of the alderman and officers of the corporation, the common councilmen, and their ladies, &c.

To facilitate their Majesties' passage down the river, and to prevent confusion and inconvenience, two parallel lines of vessels were formed into a passage of about 150 feet wide, consisting of a double, and in many cases, a triple line of barges, steamers, yachts, and craft of every description, which extended from the upper water-gate of Somerset House next Waterloo Bridge, about halfway between Southwark Bridge and the new bridge, when the line became more open, and gradually spread to the stairs of the new bridge on each side, so as to afford ample space for the boats in the procession to land their inmates and retire. The termination of the lines at these points was formed by the eight city barges, with the navigation barge and shallops. These were new gilt and decorated with the gayest flags, and filled with gay company. Each barge had its appointed station; those of the Lord Mayor and Stationers' Company were rather in advance of the bridge; and all were provided with bands of music.

Several gun-brigs were brought up the river, from which and from the wharfs adjacent, salutes were fired throughout the day; flags and colours of all descriptions were brought into requisition; and even the vessels below bridge all appeared in their holiday decorations.

Until one o'clock in the day spaces were left in the line, midway between each of the bridges for the occasional passing of wherries, &c.

Boats were stationed at intervals within the line, in order to be ready to give assistance, in case of accidents; and officers belonging to the Thames police, with other authorized persons were placed in various situations to preserve the lines until their Majesties' return.

The appearance of the bridges contributed greatly to heighten the interest of the scene. The balustrades of Waterloo were crowded at an early hour, many persons having taken up their stations there as early as between five and six o'clock in the morning. On the whole length of the terrace of Somerset House, several tiers of seats were erected, which were occupied even at an early hour with a most respectable company, chiefly ladies. The windows behind, and the tops of the building in every place which could command a view, were also thronged with spectators. The balustrades of Blackfriars Bridge were also crowded with well dressed company.


### MERCHANT TAYLOR'S SCHOOL, SUFFOLK LANE.

This School was founded in 1561. The whole edifice was consumed by the great fire: the present spacious fabric is supported on the east side by stone pillars, forming a handsome cloister, containing apartments for the ushers. Adjoining is the chapel, and the library well furnished. Three hundred boys receive a classical education, one third of them gratis, and the rest for a very small stipend. It is esteemed an excellent seminary, and sends several scholars annually to St. John's, Oxford, in which there are forty-six fellowships belonging to it.

MERCHANT TAILORS' SCHOOL.

ST. MARY AT HILL.

ST. MICHAEL, CROOKED LANE.

ST. MARY SOMERSET, UPPER THAMES STREET.

## CHURCH OF ST. MARY AT HILL, LOWER THAMES STREET.

Opposite to Billingsgate is the street called St. Mary's Hill, on the west side of which is the parish church of St. Mary, called, from its situation, St. Mary at Hill, or on the Hill. The date of the foundation of this church is equally uncertain with that of most of the churches in this city. The first circumstances met with concerning it, are that Rose de Wrytel founded a chantry in the church of St. Mary at Hill, in the year 1330, and that Richard de Hackney presented Nigellus Dalleye to this living in the year 1337. Stow, on the authority of Fabian, who was living at the time, relates a singular occurrence at the rebuilding of this church in 1497. He says, "In the year 1497, in the moneth of Aprill, as labourers digged for the foundation of a wall, within the church of St. Marie-hill, neare unto Belingsgate, they found a coffin of rotten timber, and therein the corps of a woman, whole of skinne, and of bones, undisevered, and the joynts of her arms plyable, without breaking the skynne, upon whose sepulchre this was engraven: 'Here lieth the bodies of Richard Hackney, Fishmonger, and Alice his wife: the which Richard was sheriffe in the fifteenth of Edward II. (1323). Her bodie was kept above grounde three or four dayes without noysance, but then it waxed unsavorie, and so was againe buried.'"

Though this church was considerably injured by the fire in 1666, it did not require rebuilding, and was therefore repaired, after which the parish of St. Andrew Hubbard, the church of which was totally burnt, was united to it. It is a well-proportioned Gothic structure of stone, consisting of a plain body enlightened by large windows, with a cupola in the middle, and a square tower, crowned with a handsome turret, at the end. The dimensions are, length ninety-six feet, breadth sixty-feet, altitude, to the ceiling, twenty-six feet, to the centre of the cupola, thirty-eight feet, to the top of the turret, ninety-six feet.

It is a rectory, the advowson of which appears to have been always in lay hands; and, in 1638, was purchased by the parishioners, in whom it has ever since remained; but since the parish of St. Andrew Hubbard has been united to it, the Duke of Northumberland, who is patron of that parish, presents in turn.

Annually, on the Sunday after Midsummer-day, according to ancient custom, the fraternity of Fellowship-porters, of the city of London, repair to this church in the morning, where, during the reading of the Psalms, they reverently approach the altar, two and two, on the rails of which are placed two basons, and into these they put their respective offerings. They are generally followed by the congregation, and the money offered is distributed among the aged, poor, and infirm members of that fraternity.

The parish of St. Andrew Hubbard was a rectory, formerly called St. Andrew, Juxta Eastcheap, and was founded before 1389; in which year the Earl of Pembroke presented Robert Clayton to the rectory, in the room of Walter Palmer, deceased. On the death of the Earl of Pembroke, without issue, the patronage devolved to the Earls of Shrewsbury, in whose family it continued till 1460, when John, Earl of Shrewsbury, was killed, at the battle of Northampton, when it came to Edward IV. After this, it had divers patrons, till Algernon, Earl of Northumberland, presented Thomas Parker, who was burnt out in 1666.

### CHURCH OF ST. MICHAEL, CROOKED LANE.

Miles's, or rather St. Michael's Lane, was long distinguished by a Dissenting Meeting House. Crooked Lane runs from Miles's Lane to Fish Street Hill, and was remarkable for the manufacture of fishing-tackle, bird-cages, hand-mills, &c. At the south side of this avenue stood the parish church of St. Michael's, Crooked Lane, built by Sir Christopher Wren; but recently taken down in forming the approaches to the New London Bridge. Indeed, the whole of this neighbourhood is undergoing a total change for the above object, and will shortly retain little or no vestige of its former state. In this church William Walworth, who killed Wat Tyler, was buried, whose epitaph, in uncouth rhyme, is recorded by Weever, in his Funeral Monuments.

### CHURCH OF ALLHALLOWS THE GREAT, UPPER THAMES STREET.

This Church, which is dedicated to All Saints, was originally called Allhallows ad Fœnum, in the Ropery, from its vicinity to a hay-wharf, and its situation among rope-makers; and Allhallows the More, to distinguish it from another church, which stood a little to the east of it, and was called Allhallows the Less; but being both destroyed by the fire in 1666, the latter was not rebuilt, and the two parishes were united.

The church of Allhallows the Great was founded by the noble family of the Despencers, who presented to it in the year 1361; from whom it passed to the Earl of Warwick and Salisbury, and at last to the crown. In 1546, Henry VIII. gave this church to Thomas, Archbishop of Canterbury, in whose successors it has continued to the present time. It is a rectory, and one of the thirteen peculiars, in London, belonging to the see of Canterbury. The present edifice was finished in 1683. It was planned by Sir Christopher Wren, but not executed with the same accuracy that was designed. It is eighty-seven feet long, sixty feet broad, and thirty-three feet high, to the roof, built of stone, strong and solid. The walls are plain and massy, the ornaments few and simple, and the windows very large. The tower is plain, square, and divided into five stages, terminating square and plain, without spire, turret, or pinnacle. The cornice is supported by scrolls, and over these rises a balustrade of solid construction, suitable to the rest of the building.

Allhallows the Less, which was also called Allhallows on the Cellars, or Super Cella-rium, because it stood above vaults let out for cellars, was also a rectory, the advowson of which was in the Bishop of Winchester, until the college of St. Lawrence Pounteney was founded, when Sir John Pounteney purchased it, and rebuilt the church, which he appropriated to his college; by which means it became a donative, or curacy.

### CHURCH OF ST. BOTOLPH, BISHOPSGATE.

On the west side of Bishopsgate Street, just without the wall, and opposite to the north end of Houndsditch, stands the parish church of St. Botolph, Bishopsgate, which appears to

ALLHALLOWS CHURCH, UPPER THAMES STREET

ST. BOTOLPH'S, BISHOPSGATE.

T

Drawn by Tho. H. Shepherd.

Engraved by J. Hinchliff.

PANTHEON, OXFORD ST.

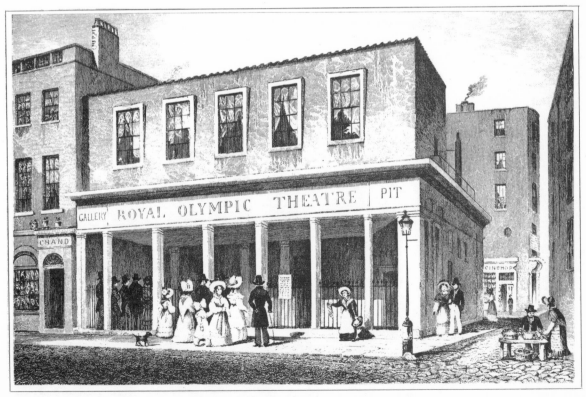

GALLERY ROYAL OLYMPIC THEATRE PIT

Drawn by Tho. H. Shepherd.

OLYMPIC THEATRE, WYCH ST.

be of very ancient foundation, dedicated to St. Botolph, an English Saxon Saint, who died about the year 680. But the first rector we have any account of was John of Northampton, who resigned the same on the 4th of June, 1323, at which time it was, and still remains, in the gift of the Bishop of London. The old church, which was built of brick and stone, escaped the fire of London, but became so ruinous, that the parishioners thought it necessary to apply to parliament to enable them to raise a new church: which was begun in 1725, and finished two years after.

The present structure is massy and spacious; the body is built with brick, and well enlightened, and the roof hid by a handsome balustrade. The steeple though heavy, has a magnificent appearance; but it has been justly remarked, that in the centre of the front under it, where every spectator would expect to find a principal entrance, he is shut out by a dead wall, and must enter the church by small side doors. Instead of a door, in the centre of the front is a large plain arched window, decorated at a distance with pilasters of the Doric order. Over this window is a festoon, and above that an angular pediment; on each side is a door, crowned with windows, and over these are others of the port-hole kind; above which rises a square tower, crowned with a dome, whose base is circular, and surrounded by a balustrade in the same form; by the side of which, on the corners of the tower, are placed urns with flames. From this part rises a series of coupled Corinthian pillars, supporting other urns like the former, and over them rises the orgive dome, crowned with a very large vase, with flames. The roof within-side is arched, except over the galleries, and two rows of Corinthian columns support both the galleries and arch, which extends over the body of the church, neatly adorned with fret-work.

## THE PANTHEON, OXFORD STREET.

On the south side of Oxford Street stands the Pantheon, erected in the year 1772, as a place of evening entertainment for the nobility and gentry; but which was principally used, of late years, for exhibitions, and, occasionally, for masquerades. It was a superb and beautiful structure, though concealed from public view, except the two entrances, the principal of which is in Oxford Street, and the other in Poland Street. After the destruction of the Opera House, by fire, the subscribers to that establishment removed the performances to this place; but, in the month of January, 1792, it shared the same fate, the interior of it being wholly consumed by the same destructive element. Having lost its licence it has now remained shut up for a considerable time, and was recently sold by public auction.

## OLYMPIC THEATRE, WYCH STREET.

The west end of Wych Street was formerly ornamented by Drury House, built by Sir William Drury, an able commander in the Irish wars, in the reign of Queen Elizabeth. In the next century it was possessed by the heroic Lord Craven, who rebuilt it. It was lately a large brick pile, concealed by other buildings, and a public house, the sign of the Queen of Bohemia's Head, for whom Lord Craven fought, and to whom, it is said, he was afterwards privately married.  When the house was taken down, a few years since, the ground was purchased by the late Mr. Philip Astley, of the Amphitheatre, Westminster Bridge, who built what he called The Olympic Pavilion, as a house of public exhibition in horse-manship and droll.  It is now in the hands of Madame Vestris, who holds it under a lease from Mr. Scott, the proprietor, and, who, by her able management, is turning it to a truly valuable account.

### CHURCH OF ST. LUKE, CHELSEA, AND SIR HANS SLOANE'S MONUMENT.

This church, dedicated to St. Luke, appears to have been ancient, by the old wall, now standing, on the north side, built of flint and rough stone, confusedly heaped together, as well as by the testimony of the most ancient inhabitants, who remember it before the rebuilding.

This rectory is within the diocese of London, and the archdeaconry of Middlesex.  The advowson anciently belonged to the Abbott and Convent of Westminster, till they ex-changed it, 17 July, 28 Henry VIII., together with their manors of Neyte and Hyde, with the King, for the priory of Hurley.  It continued in the crown till Queen Elizabeth, by letters patent, dated 3 July, second year of her reign, " demised to Ann, Duchess of Somer-set, the advowson of the parish church and rectory for her life, the reversion to the Queen." And after the death of the Duchess it was granted to the Earl of Nottingham and his Countess for three lives.  King Charles I. granted the advowson, with the manor, to James, Duke of Hamilton, and in the next reign Charles Cheyne, Esq., purchased the manor, to which the rectory has ever since been annexed.

The ancient parsonage house, with fourteen acres and twenty-two perches of land, stood where Mr. Priest's or Mr. Dowell's stands, west of the Duke of Beaufort's, then the Mar-quis of Winchester's, whence Mr. Priest's is called Parsonage Close to this day.  In lieu of which, upon an exchange, the present house and land about, it was given to the rectory for ever, by the consent of the Queen, the then patron, Dr. Edmund Grindall, Bishop of Lon-don, and Robert Richardson, Rector of Chelsea, who conveyed the old house and land to the Marquis by writing, bearing date May 3, 1566.

As far as an opinion can be formed from its present appearance, it seems to have been originally of small proportions.  In all probability the nave was not wider than the Law-rence chapel on the north-east, and More's chapel on the south-east, and the old belfry did not extend so far west by several feet; still it was sufficiently commodious for the scanty population of this parish, in those early ages when churches were first constructed, as well as for the celebration of the ceremonies of public worship; we find mention made of the north and south aisles, in the curious account of the celebration of the funeral of John Lord Braye. It is much to be regretted that no drawings exist of its pristine form and dimensions, to satisfy the laudable curiosity of the architectural antiquary; for, in the absence of such authentic memorials, conjectures, however plausible, can produce little or no beneficial result.  Nevertheless, it may be truly asserted that this church, in its present state, is exceeded by few in this county, either in a copious collection of monuments and epitaphs, or in a curious display of antique ornaments both architectural and heraldic.

Drawn by Tho. H. Shepherd.    Engraved by R. Acon.

CHELSEA OLD CHURCH, AND SIR HAN SLOANE'S MONUMENT.

Drawn by Tho. H. Shepherd.    Engraved by R. Acon.

CHRIST CHURCH, BLACKFRIARS.

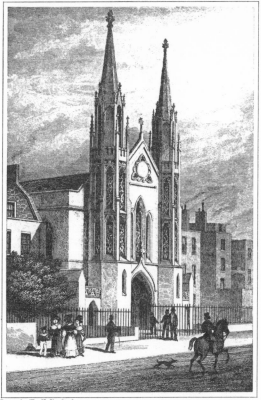

NEW CHURCH, SLOANE ST. CHELSEA.

NEW CHURCH, NORTH AUDLEY ST.

NEW CHURCH, SAFFRON HILL.

NEW CHURCH, LITTLE QUEEN ST. HOLBORN.

### CHRIST CHURCH, BLACKFRIARS.

On the west side of the road leading from Blackfriars' Bridge is situated *Christ's Church*, founded by Mr. John Marshall, of the Borough, Gent., in 1627, who endowed it with £60 per annum, towards the maintenance of a minister. In 1670 it was made a distinct parish from St. Saviour's, and a rectory. The present church was built in, or about, the year 1737, at the expense of the parish, and is a regular well-constructed building, with a square tower and turret. The patronage, at present, is in thirteen trustees.

### NEW CHURCH, NORTH AUDLEY STREET.

The west front of this building is the only part visible from the street, the sides being closely confined by the adjoining houses. The portico is of the Ionic order, and has two fluted columns, and two piers, ornamented with antæ in pairs. The entablature is composed of an architrave of three members, and a frieze with dental cornice. The cymatium, which is enriched with honeysuckles, and has lions' heads introduced on its facia, is surmounted by a lofty blocking course, terminated by a pedestal at each end.

The lantern or tower is in two portions—the first, a cubical pedestal—the second, an irregular octagon in plan, with an antæ at each angle of the superstructure; the intervals between are open, the larger spaces being filled up about a third of their height by a breastwork, and the remainder with iron work pierced in circles; the whole is surmounted by an entablature, the cornice of which is enriched with grecian tiles on its eaves, and covered with a pyramidal stone roof, having a pedestal supporting a ball and cross.

The first stone was laid September 7, 1825, and it was consecrated April 25, 1828. The edifice is dedicated to St. Mark, and is a chapel of ease to St. George's, Hanover Square. Mr. J. P. Gandy is the architect.

### NEW CHURCH, SLOANE STREET, CHELSEA.

This little church, which is in the Gothic style, stands on the east side of the street, and gives a relief to the monotonous line of houses which reach from Knightsbridge to Sloane Square, a distance of nearly half a mile. The front, which faces the street, is composed of a centre, having an excellent octagon turret on each side, lighted by long narrow windows to each angle, and divided into two compartments, with buttresses between, finished at top by crocketed pinnacles. Each turret is covered by an octangular spire terminated by a finial; the centre forms a pediment between the turrets, having a window divided into three. Over the centre in the pediment, is a circular blank or shield, as if intended for a clock : the great centre door has a considerable recess, forming a kind of porch. The wings project but little beyond the turrets on each side, they having a small door which communicates to the gallery. The cost of the building was under £6000. The foundations were began in May, 1828, and consecration took place May 8, 1830, being dedicated to the Holy Trinity. Mr. Savage, whose talents are so well known to the public, is the architect.

## New Church, Saffron Hill.

The situation of this church is very unfavourable, being built in a narrow lane, surrounded by a close neighbourhood, probably owing to the difficulty of procuring a more eligible plot of ground in the parish. The front faces the west, and is in three divisions. The centre contains a fine window, and is divided from the others by an octangular turret on each side, the upper divisions of which are pierced at each angle, and terminated by battlements; under the large window is the principal entrance, ascended by steps. The smaller divisions, contain a window in each, below which are doors communicating with the galleries. There is nothing particular in the external appearance of this building, save and except its neatness and durability. It is said to contain seats for 1800 persons, 800 of which are free. The foundations were begun in May, 1830, and the building was completed in 1832, being a chapel of ease to St. Andrew, Holborn. Mr. Barry is the architect.

## New Church, Little Queen Street, Holborn.

This excellent specimen of modern Gothic, deserves a better situation than that which it occupies, being much too confined to see it to advantage. The east front facing the street, and the only one that can be seen, is 76 feet wide, and 110 feet high to the top of the cross, and is of Bath stone. It has five divisions, separated by clustered buttresses, terminating in crocketed pinnacles; the central division contains the large chancel window; the two smaller divisions contain the principal entrances covered by porches, fifteen feet wide, and nine feet in projection, over which, are small windows, which give light to the staircases. The porches and windows are adorned with buttresses and pinnacles. The turret, over the centre, is connected to the others by flying buttresses on each side, above which it rises in three divisions, the whole terminating in a well-proportioned spire, with a ball and cross at the top. The foundations were began the latter end of June, 1829, and it was consecrated in February, 1831. This church is dedicated to the Holy Trinity. Mr. Francis Bedford, to whose talent it does credit, is the architect.

## New United Service Club-House.

This Institution is the same as noticed in another part of this work, and has been removed from the building formerly called the United Service Club-house, at the corner of Charles Street, Regent Street; now occupied by the junior club. It is an establishment for the accommodation and entertainment of the officers of the army and navy united, and is situated on the east side of Waterloo Place, at the corner of Pall Mall. The building presents three architectural elevations; each having a portico of eight columns, placed in pairs, and of the Roman Doric order, supporting an entablature; the frieze of which is ornamented with triglyphs, the same order being carried through the whole extent of the building. The entablature of the portico is crowned by a balustrade and piers, forming a balcony. The building consists of two stories; the ground story being rusticated, and having two windows on each side of the portico. The principal or upper story which contains an elegant suite of rooms, has seven lofty windows, with pediments in each elevation; over which, and

NEW UNITED SERVICE CLUB HOUSE.

EAST WING OF CARLTON HOUSE TERRACE.

Drawn by Tho. H. Shepherd.

Engraved by J. Tingle.

THE NEW ATHENÆUM, WATERLOO PLACE.

Drawn by Tho. H. Shepherd.

Engraved by J. Tingle.

ARTHUR'S CLUB HOUSE, ST. JAMES'S STREET.

running through the entire building, is an entablature with modillons under its cornice, the whole surmounted by a balustrade, separated at intervals by piers.

The south front is similar to the one described; but the north, or Pall Mall part, has a portico the whole height of the building, and is in two divisions; that of the ground floor being composed of eight fluted Roman Doric columns in pairs, having an entablature with triglyphs. This is surmounted by a balustrade, over which are eight Corinthian columns, arranged in the same order as those below, and crowned by an entablature and pediment. The building is from the designs of John Nash, Esq.

### EAST WING OF CARLTON HOUSE TERRACE.

Since the removal of the Palace of Carlton House, a grand space has been opened on the south side of Pall Mall, which affords at once a magnificent entrance to, and prospect of, St. James' Park; at east and west angles of which, nearest Pall Mall, are the United Service Club House and the Athenæum. On proceeding to the park from the former, we approach those splendid buildings, Carlton House Terrace. The principal façade faces the park, and consists of two portions, one to the east and the other to the west of this entrance; the former of which we shall now describe:—each division or wing of this terrace, forms of itself an entire building, and is composed of a centre or main body, and two wings; these consist of a beautiful and lofty colonnade, of the Corinthian order, the columns being fluted and elevated upon a plinth, supporting a well-proportioned entablature, which is carried without a break through the entire elevation. Above the cornice is the balustrade, separated over the columns by piers. In the intercolumniations are two divisions of windows, the lower tier having pediments, and other accessaries—the centre recedes from the wings and is in three divisions; the middle being crowned by a pediment, the tympanum of which is enriched; this recess is perforated with attic windows, and surmounted by a sub-cornice and blocking course. The wings are elevated above the main body of the building, and divided by antæ, arranged over the columns of the lower stories, and resting on the piers of the ba_ lustrade; between these are two series of attic windows, the lower decorated with cornice and trusses; the upper are oval, perforated in the centre of a square sunk pannel, with a similar one on each side; this is surmounted by a sub-cornice and blocking course. The terrace or basement on which this structure is raised, affords a spacious road in front, forming a delightful promenade; the outer extremity of this is inclosed by a handsome balustrade, supported from below by Grecian Doric columns of very low dimensions; the whole being bounded by the park, to which you may descend by three very spacious flights of steps. These splendid improvements were designed and executed by John Nash, Esq.

### THE NEW ATHENÆUM, WATERLOO PLACE.

This splendid establishment is nearly upon the same principle as the other club houses, as it respects private arrangements, and very similar to the United Service, in its external appearance. The east elevation, which is the one given in our view, has a rusticated basement with a portico, the ends of which are filled up and perforated with windows; the angles finished by a square pilaster and fluted column, of the Roman Doric order, the space between being divided by four columns in pairs, of the same order, and ascended by steps. The frieze is ornamented with triglyphs, and the cornice is surrounded by a balustrade, the space over the centre intercolumniations being filled up and crowned by a pedestal, supporting the statue of Minerva. Over the ground story, and on a line with the cornice of the portico, is a balcony running through the three elevations, and terminating at the angles by pedestals. The principle story contains seven lofty windows with French sashes, from whence there is access to the balcony, and which are ornamented with cornice and trusses; above this, and running through its entire building, is a beautiful frieze, charged with figures in basso-relievo, said to be copied from the Elgin frieze, deposited in the British museum. Over this is a cornice of very bold projections, the whole crowned by a balustrade. The north front, which faces Pall Mall, is adorned with a portico, similar to the one described; but the building is not so wide, having but five windows in width. The south corresponds with this, but is without a portico; there is also, adjoining, a delightful shrubbery enclosed by palisades. This building is from the designs of Decimus Burton, Esq., whose splendid specimens of architecture, contribute to adorn the metropolis.

### ARTHUR'S CLUB HOUSE, ST. JAMES' STREET.

This club house is situated on the same side of the street, and in a line with Crockford's, but differs materially in its architectural details. The basement story is rusticated and perforated by five openings; four of which are appropriated for windows, the other forming the principal entrance, and are at the left angle of the building. Although it is not wider than the window recess, yet is has a very lop-sided appearance, from not being in the centre. Over this story is a sort of sub-cornice and blocking, which supports six fluted columns of the Corinthian order, set at equal distances. The intercolumniations contain five windows, having a balustrade before each, reaching about one fourth of their height. They are crowned by pediments and simicircular heads alternately. The columns support an entablature; the cornice having dentils, and being of very bold projection. The whole is surmounted by a lofty blocking course and balustrades, intersected over the columns by acroteria. Mr. Hopper is the architect.

### VINTNER'S HALL, UPPER THAMES STREET. see p. 150

This building stands on the south side of Upper Thames Street, and on the west of the approach to the Southwark Bridge. It consists of three sides of a quadrangle, enclosing a square court, the north side of which is enclosed by handsome and lofty iron gates, hung on rusticated piers; the south portion of the quadrangle contains the hall; this side, like the other two, is divided by pilasters into three divisions, the intercolumniations containing windows of stained glass, which light the hall. Over this is an entablature carried through the entire building; each side of the quadrangle is surmounted by a pediment, the tympanum of the centre division being charged with a shield bearing the Company's arms (three tuns and a chevron).

# ALPHABETICAL LIST

OF THE

# ENGRAVINGS,

WITH A

## REFERENCE TO THE DESCRIPTION OF THE SUBJECTS.

## CHURCHES AND CHAPELS.